GALILEO'S REVENGE

GALILEO'S REVENGE

JUNK SCIENCE

IN THE COURTROOM

Peter W. Huber

BasicBooks
A Subsidiary of Perseus Books, L.L.C.

Library of Congress Cataloging-in-Publication Data
Huber, Peter W. (Peter William), 1952–
    Galileo's revenge : junk science in the courtroom / Peter
W. Huber.
        p.   cm.
    Includes bibliographical references and index.
    ISBN 0–465–02623–0 (cloth)
    ISBN 0–465–02624–9 (paper)
    1. Science and law.   2. Forensic sciences.   3. Evidence,
Expert.   4. Torts—United States.   I. Title.
K487.S3H82   1991
347'.067—dc20   91–70055
[342.767]   CIP

Designed by Ellen Levine

03 02 01 00 EBC 12 11 10 9

For Julia Christine

CONTENTS

PART III
The Rule of Fact

PREFACE TO THE PAPERBACK EDITION

There is a technique a good lawyer learns early on. The empty beer cans were scattered all over the front seat of your client's car, and he was barreling down the wrong side of the highway before he hit the lamppost. What do you do? You talk about the massive conspiracy to suppress air bags, about Lee Iacocca's salary, and about anything else you can think of—except your client's blood alcohol test.

Liability, my first book about the U.S. tort system, attracted a gratifying volume of comment along just those lines. I was accused of many errors and omissions—which was to be expected. Plaintiffs' lawyers prosper by maligning what other people do, and a lawyer rarely is happier than when denouncing some other lawyer's footnote. Predictably, many tort lawyers dismissed my larger argument—that America would be better off if its courts recognized more contracts and invented fewer torts—as dangerously unorthodox. Fortunately, many readers outside the legal profession disagreed, and sales of the book exceeded my best hopes.

Galileo's Revenge was, I thought, the perfect follow-up, a book about scientific cranks and iconoclasts who peddle their strange diagnostics and quack cures not at country fairs but in courtrooms across the land. I was amused to think that many tort lawyers would now have to concede that I might be an authority on iconoclasts, being one myself.

Galileo's Revenge has richly fulfilled my expectations. Judging from the reactions of nonlawyers, the book has touched a chord with many citizens who work in professions outside the courtroom. Meanwhile, critics from the tort bar are declaring once again that the book lies outside the mainstream of legal thought, and is not approved by the legal establishment. They are right, of course.

I continue to believe, however, that a nation marching to the drumbeat of its litigators is a nation marching into a swamp.

March 1993

INTRODUCTION

Ever wonder about Princess Di's recent affair with Elvis Presley? You can read all about it on the front page of the supermarket tabloid. Elsewhere on the page appear stories of bizarre accidents and fantastic misadventures. An impact with a car's steering wheel causes lung cancer. Breast cancer is triggered by a fall from a streetcar, a slip in a grocery store, an exploding hot-water heater, a blow from an umbrella handle, and a bump from a can of orange juice. Cancer is aggravated, if not actually caused, by lifting a forty-pound box of cheese. Everybody knows, of course, that such stories are fiction. Falls and bumps don't cause cancer.

Other stories tell how a spermicide used with most barrier contraceptives causes birth defects. We know it doesn't. The whooping cough vaccine causes permanent brain damage and death. That's not true either. The swine flu vaccine caused "serum sickness." It didn't. A certain model of luxury car accelerates at random, even as frantic drivers stand on the brakes. Not so. Incompetence by obstetricians is a leading cause of cerebral palsy. It isn't. The morning-sickness drug Bendectin caused an epidemic of birth defects. It didn't. Trace environmental pollutants cause "chemically induced AIDS." They don't.

How can anybody be absolutely, positively certain about these didn'ts, doesn'ts, and don'ts? No one can. But the science that refutes these claims is about as solid as science ever is.

And yet all of these bizarre and fantastic stories—Elvis and Di excepted—are drawn not from the tabloids but from legal reports. They are announced not in smudgy, badly typed cult newsletters but in calf-bound case reports; endorsed not by starry-robed astrologers but by black-robed judges; subscribed to not only by quacks one step ahead of the authorities but by the authorities themselves. They can be found on the dusty shelves of any major law library. The cancer-by-streetcar cases are decades old, but the others are recent.

When they learn of these legal frolics, most members of the mainstream scientific community are astounded, incredulous, and exasperated in about equal measure. Some now speak with open derision about tortogens, litogens, scientific bamboozlement, and the carcinogenic properties of insurance; others wonder why courts invite the inmates to run the asylum. The derision is understandable. Maverick scientists shunned by their reputable colleagues have been embraced by lawyers. Eccentric theories that no respectable government agency would ever fund are rewarded munificently by the courts. Batteries of meaningless, high-tech tests that would amount to medical malpractice or insurance fraud if administered in a clinic for treatment are administered in court with complete impunity by fringe experts hired for litigation. The pursuit of truth, the whole truth, and nothing but the truth has given way to reams of meaningless data, fearful speculation, and fantastic conjecture. Courts resound with elaborate, systematized, jargon-filled, serious-sounding deceptions that fully deserve the contemptuous label used by trial lawyers themselves: *junk science.* [1]

Junk science is the mirror image of real science, with much of the same form but none of the same substance. There is the astronomer, on the one hand, and the astrologist, on the other. The chemist is paired with the alchemist, the pharmacologist with the homeopathist. Take the serious sciences of allergy and immunology, brush away the detail and rigor, and you have the junk science of clinical ecology. The orthopedic surgeon is shadowed by the osteopath, the physical therapist by the chiropractor, the mathematician by the numerologist and the cabalist. Cautious and respectable surgeons are matched by some who cut and paste with gay abandon. Further out on the surgical fringe are outright charlatans, well documented in the credulous pulp press, who claim to operate with rusty knives but no anesthesia, who prey on cancer patients so desperate they will believe a palmed chicken liver is really a human tumor. Junk science cuts across chemistry and pharmacology, medicine and engineering. It is a hodgepodge of biased data, spurious inference, and logical legerdemain, patched together by researchers whose enthusiasm for discovery and diagnosis far outstrips their skill. It is a catalog of every conceivable kind of error: data dredging, wishful thinking, truculent dogmatism, and, now and again, outright fraud.

On the legal side, junk science is matched by what might be called liability science, a speculative theory that expects lawyers, judges, and juries to search for causes at the far fringes of science and beyond. The legal establishment has adjusted rules of evidence accordingly, so that almost any self-styled scientist, no matter how strange or iconoclastic his views, will be welcome to testify in court. The same scientific questions are litigated again and again, in one courtroom after the next, so that error is almost inevitable.

Junk science is impelled through our courts by a mix of opportunity and incentive. "Let-it-all-in" legal theory creates the opportunity. The incentive is money: the prospect that the Midas-like touch of a credulous jury will now and again transform scientific dust into gold. Ironically, the law's tolerance for pseudoscientific speculation has been rationalized in the name of science itself. The open-minded traditions of science demand that every claim be taken seriously, or at least that's what many judges have reasoned. A still riper irony is that in aspiring to correct scientific and medical error everywhere else, courts have become steadily more willing to tolerate quackery on the witness stand.

Experienced lawyers now recognize that anything is possible in this kind of system. The most fantastic verdict recorded so far was worthy of a tabloid: with the backing of expert testimony from several police department officials, a soothsayer who decided she had lost her psychic powers following a CAT scan persuaded a Philadelphia jury to award her $1 million in damages.[2] The trial judge threw out *that* verdict. But scientific frauds of similar character if lesser audacity are attempted almost daily in our courts, and many succeed. Most involve real, down-to-earth tragedies like birth defects, cancer, and car accidents. Many culminate in large awards. As the now dimly remembered cancer-by-streetcar cases illustrate, junk science is not an altogether new phenomenon in the courtroom. But its recent and rapid rise is unprecedented in the history of American jurisprudence. Junk science verdicts, once rare, are now common. Never before have so many lawyers grown so wealthy peddling such ambitious reports of the science of things that aren't so.

Yet among all the many refractory problems of our modern liability system, junk science is the most insidious and the least noted. Some say that legal standards have grown too strict; others sharply reply that they have not changed at all, or have changed only for the better. A lonely few—mavericks themselves, no doubt—have argued that notions of consent and contract should replace much of modern tort law; most others dismiss such ideas out of hand. Some complain that awards are too high, that legal fees are excessive, that punitive verdicts are unpredictable, that litigation drags on too long; others vehemently disagree on every count. Nobody much disputes, however, the idea that responsibility for accidents should depend on facts about who or what caused what to whom. If the operator of a streetcar is to be blamed for cancer, serious science should be on hand to certify the connection. But often it isn't. The rule of law has drifted away from the rule of fact.

What is to be done? Lawyers have long debated how best to attack the dangerous incompetence of some doctors, drug companies, and car manufacturers. Today an even more urgent question is what to do about accidents in court: how to stop legions of case-hardened lawyers from attacking false causes, on behalf of false victims, on the basis of what nobody but a lawyer and his pocket expert call science. Of course we want a legal system that can deter malpractice in the clinic or on the assembly line. At least equally grave is the problem of malpractice on the witness stand. As we shall see, it too can be lethal.

No one would suggest that junk science should generally be banned or its practitioners silenced. Freedom of speech includes the freedom to say silly and false things, even things that mislead, miseducate, or endanger. But our cherished freedom to say what we like on the front page of the *National Enquirer* need not imply the freedom to say similar things from a witness box in the solemnity of a courtroom. "By giving us the opinions of the uneducated," Oscar Wilde once observed, "modern journalism keeps us in touch with the ignorance of the community."[3] But judges have a quite different function. It may be funny to see whimsical science in the astrology column next to the comics. It is considerably less funny when something masquerading as science is taken seriously in court, less funny still when millions of dollars change hands on the strength of arrant scientific nonsense, and not funny at all when such awards lead to the disappearance of valuable and perhaps even life-saving products and services. If it is wrong to condemn the visionary whose science conflicts with established religion, it is also wrong to worship the crank whose superstition conflicts with established science.

"It is hard to tell which exhibits the greatest departure from the normal," the distinguished physicist David Hering remarked almost seventy years ago. Is it "the eager chaser after the will-o'-the-wisp, who is so wholly possessed by his idea that it becomes an obsession?" Or is it "the admirers and victims themselves who, astute enough in general, are peculiarly susceptible to some particular form of deception . . . even in some instances pleased at being humbugged?"[4] We will never determine who is more strange, the sellers of junk science or its buyers. But in the pages that follow we shall be meeting them all: the eager chasers, the susceptible admirers, and the numerous victims. We shall find them converging in numbers in the modern American courtroom. And we shall encounter many otherwise astute people who are pleased at being humbugged.

They have reason to be pleased. Scientific humbuggery in court has become an immensely profitable business.

PART I

THE LAWYER
AND THE SCIENTIST
TRADE PLACES

CHAPTER 1

Liability Science

Better Living Through Litigation

Who is so dense as to maintain . . . that all their witchcraft and injuries are phantastic and imaginary, when the contrary is evident to the senses of everybody? —Heinrich Institor and Jakob Sprenger
Malleus Maleficarum (1486)

W. C. Clark tells the story in his classic 1981 essay, "Witches, Floods, and Wonder Drugs."[1] Contemporary accounts "record wheat inexplicably rotting the fields, sheep dying of unknown causes, vineyards smitten with unseasonable frost, human disease and impotence on the rise." Fifteenth-century authorities set out to protect the public. The afflictions were real enough, but remedies were a puzzle. Finally, Heinrich Institor and Jakob Sprenger figured out what was going on. They explained it all in their *Malleus Maleficarum* ("The Hammer of the Witches"), which hit the bookstores in Germany in 1486.[2] The book was destined to become the medieval environmentalist's *Silent Spring*. Its encyclopedic scope, rich evidence, and persuasive argument convinced much of the informed public that witches did in fact exist and were causing great harm. The pope himself, Innocent VIII, officially endorsed Institor and Sprenger's findings.

Under the aegis of the Inquisition, a legal process supervised by the ecclesiastical courts, witch-related litigation became "the growth industry of the day, offering exciting work, rapid advancement, and wide recognition to its professional and technical workers."[3] And no wonder: if the critics were right, the witches were taking a dreadful toll, and exterminating them would be immeasurably valuable. A prudent society of course errs on the side of safety.

Although the women of darkness fared badly in court, they did not seem to be easily deterred from pursuing their antisocial activities. Far from abating, the witch problem seemed to grow as the witch hunters proliferated. The first major witch-hunt occurred in Switzerland in 1427, even before *Malleus* was published. After *Malleus*, prosecutions surged; witch-hunting peaked between 1580 and 1660, when witch trials spread throughout western Europe. More than three thousand witches were executed in southwestern Germany alone. In the English colonies forty people were executed for witchcraft in the late 1600s, half of them in the famous Salem trials of 1692. Between the Renaissance and the Reformation, half a million witches were burned at the stake, for crimes committed only in other people's dreams.

BEYOND RIGHT AND DUTY

While the ecclesiastical authorities engaged in the exciting business of hunting witches, common-law judges were painstakingly assembling a different body of law, one addressing more prosaic civil wrongs—assaults, negligence, routine faults and trespasses that can be quite as harmful as witches, though far less mysterious. Over the course of several centuries, these judges slowly developed a catalog of detailed liability rules to cover barroom brawls, smoke, floods, biting dogs and runaway horses, accidents on the public highway and on private land—almost every conceivable kind of misadventure or misconduct.

The rules took aim at various kinds of hurtful behavior, but they recognized that litigation itself can be manipulated and misused, that a false claim is itself an injustice and well worth avoiding if possible. They were therefore shaped to be clear and predictable, to facilitate planning outside the courtroom, and to discourage speculation, negligence, and malice within.

No grand theory animated common-law liability, and judges didn't talk much about the broader social implications of the rules they applied. If you took a swing at someone in a bar, you would have to pay if the punch landed or if the intended victim ducked in anticipation, but not if he never saw it coming and your fist missed. Why? Because it is your legal duty to abjure both assault and battery, and it is your fellow tippler's right to be secure from the same; but a battery occurs only if the punch actually connects, and an assault requires apprehension by the victim. *Duties, rights,* and the detailed rules and limits that defined and surrounded them, were established not by deductive logic but by custom and long experience; the legal vocabulary reflected nothing more than that. Duties and rights changed only at the glacial pace of the common law.

So the law evolved over the course of several centuries, by slow accretion in hundreds of different courtrooms. It was indeed "common" law—not the law laid down by princes and philosophers, but the law of common observance and tradition, law developed by practice and long usage. It was law robust enough to cross to America with the settlers, and to take firm root in American legal soil. There it continued to grow quietly and inconspicuously until well into the twentieth century.

In the late 1960s and 1970s, an aspiring new generation of legal academics decided that the whole process could be rationalized. The new school had an ambitious mission, summarized lucidly in an elegant book, *The Costs of Accidents,* written by Yale law professor Guido Calabresi.[4] Accidents are costly, reasoned the newcomers. Liability's principal purpose should be to control their costs efficiently. The common law should be, above all, a far-reaching instrument of social control. And the most efficient way to control the costs of accidents is to charge each one to the person who might have prevented it most cheaply. Or, in the new jargon that quickly swept through the legal literature, to charge each accident to its "cheapest cost avoider."

This was a remarkably ambitious plan. Common-law judges

had never before maintained that their primary mission was social engineering. History, tradition, and experience had counted far more than theory and logic. The old rules had struck a balance between deterring wrongs outside the courtroom and deterring speculative, error-prone litigation within. Respect for custom, consensus, and tradition had provided great stability and predictability. For the new school, however, the inherited wisdom of legal ages was of small relevance, especially since technology was changing quickly. No matter how familiar and predictable they may be, rights and duties are useful, it was now argued, only if justified in terms of some much broader public policy.

Suddenly everything looked simpler and clearer. Epidemiology, engineering, accidentology, or some other branch of conventional science would trace out for the jurist all the antecedent causes of a calamity, from the crushed sports car at the intersection, to the accommodating bartender who had poured drinks for the driver, to the great-aunt who had lent the car, to General Motors which had designed it, to the municipality that had planted the hedge near the traffic light, to the psychiatrist who had counseled the driver on alcoholism. Economics would reveal where the disaster might have been most cheaply controlled: by the driver, the bartender, the entruster of the car, the designer of the vehicle's brakes, the trimmer of the hedge, the psychiatric counselor, or perhaps the distiller of the spirits. The old, formalist rules would have cut through a crowd like this in short order, shunning speculation about remote causes on the assumption that such speculation would more likely cause accidents in court than prevent them elsewhere. But with the new rules, the law could range far afield and pursue the most distant suspected malefactions. Economics would tell what was cheapest. Science would tell what might beneficially have been avoided. The cheapest cost avoider would be located, somewhere or other, and the bills for the accident redirected accordingly. The whole theory seemed to offer clarity and rigor. It felt like a new science. Liability science.

Science or otherwise, it was certainly a liberating way of looking at things. The myriad rules, refinements, limits, and stopping points developed by the ancients had hardly been scientific, after all. The Calabresian would have to determine, in the specific case at hand, who was best positioned to reduce the social costs of accidents at intersections. And in the next trial, which might instead involve cancer or cerebral palsy, a whole new scientific inquiry would be in order.

This was, in short, a prescription for bringing innumerable new scientific controversies into court. Many venerable defenses based on contract, consent, assumption of risk, informed choice, social custom, and reasonable care had cut off liability long before blacksmiths, laboratory technicians, or nuclear physicists were required on the witness stand. But these first-line defenses seemed out of place in the new liability science. As courts crept toward absolute liability for harm caused, more cases began to turn entirely on the science of cause and effect. Many judges protested that they were ill equipped to deal with difficult scientific questions, and didn't wish to. But they steadily reoriented the law toward science anyway. The legal lips murmured no, no, to seductions scientific, but the eyes and the arms said yes.

TOWARD THE FAR SIDE

The common law had recognized its first expert witnesses in fourteenth-century England. They were called by the court itself, to testify on such things as shipping or accounting. Over the next few centuries, expert witnesses gradually came to be treated much like other witnesses, though the experts were given more freedom to render opinions.[5] Experts hired by the disputing parties slowly replaced court-appointed experts in nineteenth-century America, a transition that did not occur without protest. In one 1884 decision, for example, the New York Court of Appeals suggested that "twelve jurors of common sense and common experience" would do better on their own than with the help of hired experts, "whose opinions cannot fail generally to be warped by a desire to promote the cause in which they are enlisted."[6] Nevertheless, parties gradually began to hire and present their own expert witnesses with some regularity.

Courts did, however, continue to insist on a carefully limited role for such experts. Indeed, the rules of evidence embodied the same cautious respect for tradition as did the liability rules themselves. Experts were not given a free hand to speculate; their function was to convey the consensus views of their profession. Courts were willing enough to pass judgment on the alleged malpractice of an obstetrician or engineer, but they recognized that a swearing contest between self-styled experts would not yield an answer. If expert witnesses were unconstrained by professional tradition and consensus, malpractice was as likely to be promoted on the witness stand as deterred at the defense table. Once again, a balance had to be struck between the need to police incompetence outside the courtroom and the risk of rewarding incompetence within.

In 1923, a federal appellate court issued a landmark ruling in *Frye v. United States* aimed at accommodating these competing concerns.[7] Thereafter, federal courts, widely copied by the states, were bound by the *Frye* rule, which allowed experts into court only if their testimony was founded on theories, methods, and procedures "generally accepted" as valid among other scientists in the same field. In deferring to the scientific community, the rule conceded the courts' own limits. *Frye* marked a reasonable compromise between a populist rejection of all expertise and what was to follow, the equally populist view that experts are everywhere and there's no choosing among them.

Like all verbal standards the *Frye* rule could be bent, and it sometimes was. Charlatans of many stripes establish societies, attend national conventions, set up certification boards, and otherwise go through the motions of serious science. Are they then (as they themselves vehemently insist) a "relevant scientific community" qualified to testify that trace ambient pollutants cause narcolepsy? Such questions arose frequently enough, even in the time of *Frye,* and were not always answered intelligently. But *Frye* did at least serve a hortative purpose, stiffening the judge's spine and steeling his nerves when a brash scientific iconoclast presented himself at the courthouse. *Frye* held out the hope that, with the help of determined judges, the legal consensus would in time converge with the scientific one.

Frye held sway until the 1970s, when it collided with the high ambition of the Calabresians. They had come of age in a time of technological pessimism. Popular wisdom had it that great new epidemics of cancer and birth defects were sweeping the nation, that crops were (or soon would be) rotting in the fields, that sheep were dying of unknown causes, that vineyards were being smitten with summer frost and winter heat, that human disease and impotence were on the rise. The broomsticks flew through the air once again, even more pernicious and wicked than they had been half a millennium earlier. Unfortunately for the lawyers, however, established mainstream scientists seemed to view the world with much less alarm. And *Frye* seemed to give mainstream science the final word in declaring just why (or if) crops were rotting in the fields.

This was especially galling because the legal community's pessimism about technology was matched (paradoxically enough) by its optimism about liability science. Science might go awry everywhere else, but courts got things right. The chemists, the engineers, the doctors, and the druggists had demonstrated that they sometimes lost control; the lawyers, however, applying their brand of science, could restore it. It seemed utterly perverse to many in the legal community that the consensus views of the very professions causing all the problems might stand in the way of legal solutions. Viewed from any angle, *Frye* clearly threatened to cut short the great Calabresian search for cheap, wide-ranging control.

Lawyers couldn't change what mainstream science maintained, but they could decide whether mainstream science mattered. That is exactly what they did. Some courts candidly stopped screening experts altogether. Others simply created majorities by gerrymander, defining "scientific communities" narrowly and uncritically. One way or another, judges gave up on the possibility of drawing firm lines between serious science and junk. When the Federal Rules of Evidence were first codified in 1975, they made no mention of *Frye* whatsoever. Expert testimony would be allowed, thenceforth, "[i]f scientific, technical, or other specialized knowledge will assist the trier of fact to understand the evidence or to determine a fact."[8] Mainstream scientific consensus didn't matter any more. Social engineering in the courtroom would find its support wherever convenient; any iconoclast whose views might prove "helpful" to the jury would be welcome in court.

Before long, many judges came around to the view that in matters testimonial "new" probably meant "improved" and "one of a kind" probably meant "one of the best." Today's junk science may be tomorrow's orthodoxy. "There always has to be a first," one jurist earnestly explained in 1990. The expert with the maverick theory may just be "too qualified and advanced in his thinking, based upon his extraordinary expertise." If rules like *Frye* had been applied in other fields "Christopher Columbus could never have been qualified as an expert to render an opinion on circumnavigation and the Wright Brothers would never have been able to testify as experts and give opinions relating to flight, because their views never gained 'general acceptance in the scientific community.' "[9] For this jurist, as for many others, it scarcely seemed to matter that Columbus was in fact mightily confused about circumnavigation (ask any "Indian"), or that the Wright brothers' achievement was in fact immediately and widely accepted as a great achievement.

Columbus and the Wright brothers have nevertheless served their purpose: standards for expert witnesses have all but disappeared. Today, virtually any doctor armed with a medical degree is qualified to testify. Sometimes he will be expected to assert that his opinion has a "reasonable basis," that it does not originate in chicken entrails or phases of the moon, but this is not much of a standard. He need not be a recognized authority or specialist. He need not reconcile his opinions with public-health statistics of epidemiology. He need not establish that his diagnostic methods or logical leaps enjoy "general acceptance" among other doctors. Quite the contrary: he may insist that he alone among doctors understands the importance or origins of certain symptoms. He may claim, in short, to be a new Galileo, a lonely, misunderstood genius who can see wonders that others neither discern nor understand. The standards are almost equally loose for other, nonmedical experts.

The academics (as academics are prone to do) have continued

to debate *Frye*'s demise long after the debate has ceased to be of any practical importance. Some insist that *Frye* still lives; others that it is dead and buried; others that, dead or alive, *Frye* no longer makes any practical difference. But with *Frye* certifiably absent from the rules of evidence, the academics might as well be debating the survival of Elvis Presley in the indubitably silent halls of Graceland. Whether or not *Frye* still lives, the conviction is gone, the music has died. Most courts have slouched toward what federal judge Patrick Higginbotham dubs the let-it-all-in approach to expert testimony.[10] By the 1980s, countless courts had opened their doors wide to claims based on methods or theories not generally accepted as reliable by any scientific discipline. As Yale Law School's Donald Elliott observes, "[t]he law extends equal dignity to the opinions of charlatans and Nobel Prize winners."[11]

There are many more charlatans than Nobelists, they come cheaper, and their views are often much more readily adapted to litigious ends. And so, diligent lawyers have set off in pursuit of scientific mystics, speculators, cranks, and iconoclasts, and rushed to the waiting arms of far-siders straight out of a Gary Larson cartoon.

GALILEO'S REVENGE

One would not normally associate declining quality with increasing demand for a service. In court, however, what is bad for one side is almost invariably good for the other. The worse things are, in other words, the better they are; it's all a matter of where you're sitting. Viewed from the right side aisle, bad expert testimony looks excellent.

Why would you, the diligent lawyer, settle for a scientist who will say that PCBs may in some circumstances affect health, though how and at what concentrations is most unclear, if you can find one who will swear that they are one of the most lethal substances known to man, that they subvert the immune system, and they undoubtedly were to blame for this plaintiff's migraine headaches? Why settle for one who will say that 60-cycle electromagnetic fields probably don't injure human health, though one must concede certain small pieces of disquieting evidence to the contrary, if you can find one who will take the Federal Express pledge, and absolutely, positively promise that the fields do no harm, nohow? The middle of the road, in law even more so than in politics, belongs to the yellow stripes and the dead armadillos. So, as you labor to assemble your case, the strength of the scientific support for an expert's position is quite secondary. It is the strength of the expert's support for *your* position that comes first.

No doubt you will consider the jury's perspective too. You naturally want an expert who also has impressive experience, along with just the right graduate degrees, timbre of voice, sartorial habits, and such. But testimony taking the form of on-the-one-hand-this and on-the-other-that is useless, no matter how credible, while vehement support for your side of things, no matter how dubious the science behind, may always be of some help. After all, there's always some chance the jury will make a split-the-difference call, especially if the scientific testimony is sharply divided. So while you will undoubtedly consider some modest trade-off between the expert's actual fealty to your cause and his apparent fealty to science, when the chips are down your cause must come first. "I would go into a lawsuit with an objective uncommitted independent expert," says an ex-president of the American Bar Association, "about as willingly as I would occupy a foxhole with a couple of noncombatant soldiers.[12] "If I got myself an impartial witness, I'd think I was wasting my money," says Melvin Belli, self-crowned "King of Torts."[13]

The witness approached by a man like Belli will understand the economics of the relationship quickly enough. A witness may not work directly for a contingent fee, but the expert is a contingent player anyway, and he knows it. His continued employment today, and reemployment tomorrow, depends critically on the strength of the support he can supply. His lawyer's ability to pay even the promised fee may depend on victory, especially if the meter has been running for years and the lawyer is overextended financially. The entrepreneurial expert, in short, is a repeat player, or aspires to be, and such players repeat only if they win. In its synopsis of major new victories, *ATLA Law Reporter*, a journal for the edification of plaintiffs' lawyers, lists the name of the winning expert side by side with the name of the winning lawyer.

In this kind of legal environment, the trial lawyer serves as a sort of Darwinian avenger, like a breeder of prize pigs or exotic dogs. The scientific community is large and heterogeneous to begin with. The lawyer's livelihood depends on selecting witnesses who win—*cases*, that is, not Nobel Prizes. The survivors in this process of unnatural selection evolve toward extremes: they develop exorbitant plumage and distinctive songs. They are groomed in law and medical schools, which offer classes on how to deliver testimony. They learn "the importance of speaking in terms that jurors can understand, such as making analogies to sporting events." They are sought out for their appearance, charm, and charisma. They attend seminars "where scruffy academics and disheveled doctors learn how to speak, act, and handle themselves on the stand."[14]

They are hardly ever called scientists, at least not by those in the know. Other labels abound, and most are not flattering.[15] The "hired gun" is the most overworked, though one of the less pejorative. A prominent design engineer refers to "willow in the wind" consultants, who "blow in whatever direction the client wants them to blow at the expense of everybody else involved."[16] Some call the entrepreneurial experts "saxophones," because the lawyer calls the tune and the expert plays it.[17] But overwhelmingly, the metaphor of scatological choice is sex. "You get a professor who earns $60,000 a year and give him the opportunity to make a couple of hundred thousand dollars in his spare time and he will jump at the chance," says Dennis Roberts, a criminal and personal injury lawyer from Oakland. "They are like a bunch of hookers in June."[18]

So here he is, Mr. Professional Witness, U.S.A. He works alone, or in partnership with a handful of others. He advertises. His clients gradually learn that they can't risk going without him, for the opposition surely will surely hire his mirror-image clone from the other referral agency. He is "neat but not dapper; respectable but not pompous; mature but not senile."[19] He is cautious about putting things in writing,[20] far more comfortable when working strictly with his mouth. He sees himself as a team player, who helps with trial preparation, assists in the examination of opposing witnesses, advises on new areas of inquiry. He works consistently for one side (insurance companies) or the other (plaintiffs' lawyers). He has honed strong, adversarial instincts, he loves "going before a group of people where some are trying to build me up and some are trying to destroy me."[21] He can earn hundreds of dollars an hour, hundreds of thousands a year. For all practical purposes, he is working on a contingency fee, though the contingent nature of his employment and compensation will always be angrily denied. Where have we seen this character before? In his employer's office. He is the spit and image of a trial lawyer.

THE ENDLESS SEARCH

The new, let-it-all-in standards of evidence are perfectly matched to the new go-after-everyone possibilities of liability science. The old legal school preferred inaction to the risk of doing positive harm through litigation; the new is hugely ambitious, far more willing to press forward in the face of uncertainty. The old school trusted in rules because they had evolved and endured, because they reflected consensus and experience. The new school places its faith in the omniscient science-and-economics analyst. While its practitioners are sure that science is highly fallible when left to scientists, they are confident that it is perfectible when overseen by lawyers.

The new optimism runs so high that the creators of this new jurisprudence have quite neglected to specify any stopping rules. Science will always hold out a hope of finding some more distant cause just over the horizon. Economics will always hold out a hope that controlling the more distant cause will be cheaper. The new legal search, it turns out, can therefore be ended only when lawyers run out of time, patience, or money. Controlling misadventure outside the courtroom is so surpassingly important, so urgently needed, that no one is going to spend much time worrying about the excesses of the controllers themselves.

Social control is indeed critical; in fact, it redefines the very meaning of cause. "[S]o far as legal language is concerned," Calabresi wrote, "the 'cause' of a disease would depend on how, at any given time, it could be most easily controlled."[22] Thus, in the nineteenth century, tuberculosis was caused by "the absence of sun and the presence of bad living conditions." Then, as science evolved, by the Koch bacillus. Today, "one can, in a meaningful way, speak of genetic predisposition as a 'cause' of tuberculosis." The judge as engineer is to be promoted far above the judge as forensic scientist. It is the "prospect of genetic engineering"—*not* the science of genetics—that makes it legally "meaningful" to treat genes as a cause of tuberculosis.[23] If we merely understand the role of genes but can't control them, why then genes don't cause anything at all, at least nothing of any legal consequence. The judge's business is to get out and burn someone. Not witches, of course: cheapest cost avoiders.

Sometimes—quite often, many of the new school are inclined to think—the cheapest point of control will be at quite some distance from the scene of the accident. After all, if we are seriously to consider genes as a "legal cause" of tuberculosis, we must look back a lifetime plus, and who knows how great a distance in space. And then, the genes in question may have been corrupted by something still earlier: a drug used in pregnancy, perhaps, or chemical exposure at the mother's workplace, or maybe radiation during the father's military service. The farther we ramble in our hunt for cheap cost avoiders, the greater the temptation to don the Calabresian robes.

And rambling far is essential. The search for the cheapest possible control must inevitably lead out to the edges of scientific knowledge. No one can be quite certain why the kingdom was lost, and who might most cheaply have avoided the disaster, until the question of missing nails in every single horse's shoe has been examined in depth. Esoteric afflictions like cancer and birth defects, and mundane ones like accidents with cars or

Cuisinarts, can always be tracked back and back, into the mists of space and time. Liability science requires no less.

Even when causes are utterly obvious, the economics half of liability science will still demand a far-flung search. The good Calabresian will litigate endlessly over the crashworthiness of cars, though the injuries could have been completely prevented by seat belts and sobriety; regrettably there seems to be no cheap way to get people to buckle up and quench their thirst on lemonade. He will blame workplace stress and a host of other peripheral factors for cardiac problems that would have been prevented by better diet; regrettably there seems to be no cheap way to get people to eat sensibly. He will support victims of venereal disease in their suits against contraceptive manufacturers; regrettably there is no cheap way to compel safe sex. He will back the heavy smoker in blaming an employer for lung disease; regrettably it's more difficult to quit smoking than to clean up a factory. If casting out beams seems to be just too expensive, he will be content to spend almost any amount of time and effort casting out the cheap motes. With control as his paramount mission, he will control what he can.

A far-ranging search for causes to control is needed—indeed, it is needed all the more—when known causes are in short supply. Mainstream science often offers little more than speculation about the true causes of cerebral palsy and other birth defects, most nontobacco cancers, and many chronic diseases. What then? What do we do when, much like fifteenth-century clerics, we are unable to understand the crop blight? Whatever we do (many an overeager Calabresian quickly concludes), we must do *something*. Perhaps the scientist who claims ignorance is just too cautious. The rules must therefore be changed, so that the oxymoronic scientist—the one too cautious to sound a specific alarm quite yet—will not stand in the way of the oxymoronic lawyer—the one whose extreme caution impels him to rush into action at once. The law must go after causes. Laggard science refuses to finger any cause in particular. The law will pursue cause anyway. Which one? Why, the one that feels right, not to the good scientist who won't commit but to the rest of us. And who, if not the good scientist, will tell us what to burn? Why, a scientist who is a shade less particular about the details.

Thus, a profession whose declared mission is control, first and last, *will* control, one way or another, even if it comes (as it has in times past) to burning witches. Starting the fires is what's important. Extinguishing them isn't.

ALONSO SALAZAR Y FRIAS

Come to think of it, what did finally quench the Inquisition's fires? We shall return to this vital question at the end of this book, but let us consider it very briefly here at the outset. In 1610, 124 years after the publication of *Malleus* and after a century of enthusiastic burning, the exceptional Inquisitor Alonso Salazar y Frias took a first, serious look at who was being burned for what in the town of Logrono in Navarre, Spain. He found what today seems obvious: the accusations had been false, confessions had been induced by torture, and—notwithstanding *Malleus* and the solemn findings of countless trials—there was no credible evidence of any witchcraft at all.

Salazar y Frias did not (and in the context of his times undoubtedly could not) summarily declare that witches didn't exist. What he could do, and firmly did, was to change the rules of evidence. Thereafter, accusations would be considered only when supported by independent evidence. The Spanish Inquisition would no longer use torture. "In modern terms," Clark observes, Salazar y Frias "had introduced rules of evidence which recognized the perverse and essentially meaningless forms which unstructured 'facts' could take."[24]

This was not the end, but it was the beginning of the end. The number of witches brought to trial dropped sharply. The first major witch-hunt had occurred in Switzerland in 1427. Europe's last legal execution of a witch occurred, again in Switzerland, in 1782.

CHAPTER 2

The Science of Things That Aren't So

Junk Science and Its Origins

"I see nobody on the road," said Alice.

"I only wish I had such eyes," the king remarked in a fretful tone. "To be able to see Nobody! And at that distance too! Why, it's as much as I can do to see real people in this light!" —Lewis Carroll
Through the Looking Glass (1872)[1]

It was 1903, a propitious time for new rays. Just eight years earlier, W. K. Röntgen had discovered X rays. Others soon announced the discovery of alpha rays, beta rays, and gamma rays. Then finally there appeared the most remarkable rays of all, N rays, named after France's University of Nancy, where they were discovered.

Their discoverer, René Blondlot, was a distinguished French physicist and a member of the French Academy of Sciences. He first detected N rays by observing their ability to brighten an electric spark through which they were beamed. Blondlot's observations were soon confirmed by more than twenty French physicists, physiologists, and psychologists, including Jean Becquerel, son of Henri Becquerel, the discoverer of radioactivity. Many scientists personally observed the N rays in Blondlot's laboratory. Some insisted that they, not Blondlot, had discovered them first.

A rush of scientific papers documented the properties of the new rays. They could be bent by an aluminum prism. Wood, paper, and thin sheets of iron, tin, silver, and gold efficiently transmitted them; water and rock salt blocked them. They could be stored in such things as a brick, though ten bricks irradiated with N rays produced no stronger effects than one. Heat increased their strength. One of Blondlot's colleagues on the Nancy faculty announced in 1904 that N rays could be used effectively to explore the human body, just like X rays. The younger Becquerel would eventually report that he could stop pieces of metal from emitting N rays by "anesthetizing" them with chloroform. Alarmingly, N rays were found emanating profusely from the Welsbach mantle, a type of gas burner widely used at the time for home lighting. In the year and a half following Blondlot's announcement, publications on N rays proliferated rapidly. In 1904, the French journal *Comptes rendus* published only three papers on X rays but fifty-four on N rays.

Almost none were published thereafter. As Irving Klotz would note eight decades later in *Scientific American,* "[s]cience, like any other area of human endeavor, has had its grand illusions." N rays were "completely imaginary." They are remembered today "only for the insights they provide into the psychosociology of science."[2]

THE CHESHIRE FACT

"There is something fascinating about science," Mark Twain once observed. "One gets such wholesale return on conjecture out of such trifling investment of fact." Sometimes the factual investment is even less than trifling. There is in science something known as the "Cheshire fact." It is the datum solemnly recorded, earnestly explained, vehemently defended, and then never seen again. The annals of science are filled with mistakes of this kind. In a famous 1953 lecture, the Nobel chemist Irving Langmuir called this kind of research "pathological science": "the science of things that aren't so."[3]

There are many things that aren't so, and the records of pathological science are correspondingly voluminous. Langmuir mentioned a few of the better-known episodes. Blondlot's N rays, to start with. Then the Davis-Barnes effect, which involved experimental observations on the combination of alpha particles and electrons. The claimed effects seemed to match Bohr calculations of electron energies with great accuracy, and were confirmed in several laboratories. But neither Davis nor Barnes nor any of the rest were observing anything real at all. Equally unreal were the mitogenetic rays emitted by onion roots, said to bring about a sort of extrasensory perception among growing cells. Then there was the Allison effect, which allowed the identification of now long-forgotten new elements (Alabamine, Virginium) and a slew of nonexistent isotopes. The effect is remembered today as "Allison wonderland."

Such errors have been recorded many times before and since. Years after Langmuir's lecture there would be polywater, discovered in 1969 by Soviet scientists, confirmed by various researchers from around the globe—a dread compound that (some U.S. scientists warned) might turn the world's oceans into gel if accidentally released. The world of nonscience has likewise documented extrasensory perception, telekinesis, parapsychology, and flying saucers. Many believed, for a while at least. Many tested. Many published. There were eyewitness accounts and photographs, data bases, statistical correlations, and regression analyses. Yet in the end, it became clear that all of these seemingly serious observers were "counting hallucinations."[4]

There are patterns in everything, even in hallucinations and dreams. Even pathological science exhibits a certain indubitable order. For example, it usually takes a form that seems avant-garde but not utterly spacey. The scientist on this kind of frolic, Martin Gardner observes, usually "rid[es] into ignorance . . . on the coattails of reputable investigators."[5] He is always to be found in the vicinity of the latest epidemic, the trailblazing diagnostic procedure, the trendiest new therapy or technology. Thus, an 1881 treatise blamed "neurasthenia" on "steam power" and "the mental activity of women" among other alarming hazards new to that era.[6] Blondlot's discovery of N rays, which don't exist, came close on the heels of Röntgen's discovery of X rays, which do. The development of serious chemotherapy in the treatment of cancer was soon followed by the development of Krebiozen, Laetrile, and AIDS therapies based on cucumber extracts.

The influences and effects of pathological science phenomena are often independent of intensity or, better still, almost inversely related to intensity, so that the strongest effects come from the most diffuse excitations. Why should this be? Because increasing intensity provides the easiest, most definite sanity check in real science. With N rays, mitogenetic rays, and the rest, as Langmuir observed, the stimulus "had to be low intensity. We know why it had to be of low intensity: so that you could fool yourself so easily. Otherwise it wouldn't work."[7]

For similar reasons, pathological science often depends on experiments at the threshold of detectability, or at the lowest margins of statistical significance. The claims frequently emerge from a body of data that is selectively incomplete; wishful researchers unconsciously discard enough "bad" data to make the remaining "good" points look important. That the measurements are at the very threshold of sensitivity is an advantage, not an obstacle: data that don't fit the theory are explained away; those that fit are lovingly retained. Professional statisticians call this "data dredging."[8]

Dredging is easiest in loose and formless mud. Thus, pathological science does best when recording swings in mood, disruption of brain-wave patterns, and things of that sort, for it is with such imprecise, mercurial, subjectively calibrated variables that bias can most easily creep into the results. In responding to his critics, Blondlot emphasized how extremely difficult it was to detect the effects that N rays had on sparks. "It was essential," Klotz recounts, "to avoid all straining of vision, whether deliberate or the result of accommodation to low levels of illumination, and to avoid any conscious fixing on the luminous source whose variations in brightness it was sought to ascertain. One had to, so to speak, see the source without looking at it, and even to glance in a slightly different direction."[9]

Selective amnesia can work further wonders in making order

out of random data. You dream that your aunt in Australia was in an airplane crash, only to wake up and discover that she is safe at home in Wagga Wagga, Wollongong. The nightmare is immediately forgotten, until the day comes when the plane really does crash. Selective amnesia, a pick-and-choose economy with the truth, has a remarkable power to make the dreams that do occasionally come true seem important. In a similar manner, great catalogs of data that don't track the hoped-for results can be explained away before they are ever recorded in the laboratory notebook. Once again, error of this kind is easiest when the observation is at the threshold of detectability. "There is a habit with most people," Langmuir explained, "that when measurements of low significance are taken they find means of rejecting data."[10]

Autosuggestion often comes into play as well. Even the most reputable scientists can talk themselves into seeing things that just aren't there. Scintillations on a phosphorescent screen in a darkened room, for example, as Blondlot's documentary evidence of N rays perfectly illustrates. He offered photographs of sparks with and without enhancement by N rays; in the pairs of images he produced, the one spark was indeed much brighter than the other. But the photographs had been prepared in ways so ripe for experimenter bias as to make accurate work impossible. Each photograph had been made by exposing both sides of a photographic plate; the experimenter had to slide the plate from one side (where the spark was screened from the N-ray source) to the other (unscreened) at five-second intervals. An unconsciously biased experimenter, however, could easily give the N-ray side a tiny bit longer exposure. That, apparently, is precisely what happened.

Pathological science often needs to assert claims of great accuracy as well, to convert random noise into an apparently meaningful pattern. Observed effects rise and fall as the intensity of the field (or the alpha rays, or the ambient traces of dioxin, or whatever) are steadily increased. The skeptic concludes: there is no effect here at all. Oh no, says the believer. *Oh no.* There are "windows" of sensitivity and response here. Resonances. The effects are highly sensitive to the precise frequency of the electric field, or dosage, or what have you. To the well-calibrated eye, there is order here. The wide variations in response just reveal exquisite sensitivity to the stimulus.

However gathered, bad data serve as a springboard for spurious inferences. Temporal errors are the most familiar. To the uncritical mind, a sequence of events can be powerfully suggestive. Intuitively unlikely sequences (serious trauma to the chest followed by breast cancer, say) are in fact quite common. But the cause/effect correlations they suggest are spurious far more often than they are real. The classic illustration is the linear relationship between pig iron production in the United States and the birthrate in Great Britain. By pure chance, quite a few children in a nation of 240 million will be vaccinated on a Monday and fall sick by that Friday even if the vaccine is completely harmless. "Recall bias" (the aunt-in-Australia problem) compounds the likelihood of error. The mother of a child with a birth defect is far more likely to remember later on that she once used a spermicide or morning-sickness drug than is the mother of a healthy baby, and is then very likely to confuse temporal coincidence with cause and effect.

Fantastic theories follow naturally. Small wonder: a theory to explain what is really random noise, in the experiment or in the observer's brain, must have many adjustable knobs and buttons. On one occasion, for example, Blondlot attributed a failed experiment to "insufficient regulation of the spark,"[11] but he might equally well have chosen the precise orientation of the earth's magnetic field in Nancy, or the heady aroma of quiche Lorraine wafting through the laboratory from nearby kitchens, which (as every Frenchman knows) are the finest in the world. It is a general characteristic of pathological science that the number of adjustable parameters will have to increase in proportion to the amount of data gathered. Simple theories immediately offer predictions that can be independently verified in new experiments far removed from the original ones. But with nonscience, nothing is going to work as promised under different conditions. So the theories must be so complicated that no concrete prediction is possible. They invariably are.

Criticisms are met with ad hoc excuses. No matter how sincerely they believe in their results, scientists who tilt at windmills like N rays must make it all up as they go. In Blondlot's laboratory, for example, the process of rationalization soared to stratospheric heights. As the objections to N rays grew, so did the number of reasons why others had failed to observe them. Blondlot published an elaborate list. As described by Klotz:

The observer was required to play an absolutely passive part, on pain of perceiving nothing useful. Silence had to be kept as much as possible. Any smoke, particularly tobacco smoke, had to be avoided, as it was likely to perturb or even entirely mask the effect of the N rays. The observer had to accustom himself to looking at a luminous detector in the way a painter, particularly an impressionist painter, would look at a landscape. To gain such abilities would require practice and would surely not be easy. Some people, in fact, might never be able to gain them.[12]

Such lightfooted evasion of critics is not uncommon in pathological science. The experiment doesn't work when an outside observer is there? The sample today happens to be contaminated. The experiment does work even though some key piece has been surreptitiously removed? Well, some other extraneous factor must have temporarily corrupted these results. As Langmuir observed, "[t]hey always had an answer—always."[13]

The last, most irrefutable answer is invariably that the solitary believer just sees, senses, and understands better; the crowds of skeptics are reactionary, dull, or myopic. One of the most convenient discoveries by the N-ray investigators was that the rays sharpened the senses. Augustin Charpentier, whom Klotz describes as "a respected professor of medical physics,"[14] reached this conclusion first; by the end of 1904 Blondlot and his colleagues had reached it as well, possibly quite independently. Best of all, N rays improved the eyesight. The wonderful thing about *that* was that N-ray pioneers, having spent more time observing N rays than anyone else, would certainly remain the best at detecting them. When others began to doubt, Blondlot and his supporters answered in just this way, calling into question "the sensitivity of the observer rather than the validity of the phenomena." By 1905, Klotz notes, some of the N-ray faith-ful "maintained that only the Latin races possessed the sensitivi-ties (intellectual as well as sensory) necessary to detect manifes-tations of the rays."[15]

THE FAITH HEALERS

Not every investigator who falls hard for pathological science is weak-minded, sloppy, or inclined to fraud. Some are seduced simply because they are irrepressible rebels, compulsively driven to dispute orthodox views, whatever they may be. Dozens of cranks and mavericks have spent lifetimes heaping ridicule and scorn on the likes of Newton or Einstein. For others, the flight to bad science is all part of a misdirected search for cleans-ing and absolution. Fear of things scientific or high-tech some-times seems to substitute for fear of the satanic. As the historian Paul Johnson observes, "The religious impulse—with all the excesses of zealotry and intolerance it can produce—remains powerful, but expresses itself in secular substitutes."[16]

Still others embrace bad science for reassurance. Cancer and birth defects, horrible calamities, are doubly horrible because they seem to strike randomly. So, as humans have done since time immemorial, we invent fictions to impose order. Capricious deities once sufficed; today, we are more inclined to coat our superstitions in a veneer of pseudoscience, so that ignorant fear can be organized into a sort of system. Anthropologists report a similar phenomenon: venereal disease, the paradigm of repul-sive afflictions almost entirely within the ambit of individual control, is almost universally blamed on foreigners. "[B]y plac-ing blame on 'other groups' or on 'deviant behavior'—we try to avoid the randomness of disease and dying, to escape from our inherent sense of vulnerability, to exorcise mortality inherent in the human condition."[17]

The most insidious thing about bad science is that it can afflict even some of the more intelligent, methodical, and honest mem-bers of the scientific community. The reason is that it appeals to a broad element in human nature, not just to vices but to some virtues as well. The opportunities for bad science are everywhere. And the temptations to pursue it are often strong.

One, as Langmuir has noted, is the researchers' "quite normal scientific desire to make discoveries and to understand things."[18] Blondlot was, by all accounts, a sincere and enthusiastic physicist. So enthusiastic, however, that he made fundamental mistakes that he could never bring himself to acknowledge. The child too eager to report on something interesting observed on the walk home from school will transform a horse and cart on Mulberry Street into a circus parade. And so it has been with many a scientist: no one has a keener eye than one who is too eager to see.

But it is in the healing business that the temptations of junk science are the strongest and the controls against it the weakest. There is more incentive, to start with: sick people are desperate for help, and would-be healers can be equally desperate to help them. Humans, moreover, are far more complex than, say, the elementary particles of physics, so it's correspondingly harder to keep track of everything. And then the human mind, with its infinite capacity for complication and convolution, comes into play. If autosuggestion is a problem even for a physicist counting scintillations on a screen, it is a far greater problem for a patient reporting aches and pains, or for a physician sincerely hoping to alleviate them.

The coattail effect is much in evidence in the quack-cure industry. Radical new technologies seem to have an almost irresistible allure for the quack therapist, who is usually paired one for one with a fringe scientist in search of a horrifying new terror. The advent of electricity brought electric belts from the McIntosh Galvanic and Faradic Battery Company of Chicago, because "Disease Yields Under Electrical Treatment."[19] Electricity, however, also shattered the peace of mind of James Thurber's grandmother, who (as Thurber described in a delightful 1933 essay) "lived the latter years of her life in the horrible suspicion that electricity was dripping invisibly all over the house."[20] Over the years, magically curative (or dangerously pernicious) properties have been detected in such things as magnetic fields, X rays, microwaves, ultra-dilute solutions of various toxins, and, of course, snake oil from the venomous snake. The techno-terrified invariably detect a grave new threat, but the techno-utopians always discern a new miracle cure.

With allowances for the differences between particle physics and medicine, quack-cure movements track Langmuir's more general taxonomy of pathological science. According to a 1986 federal study, quack-cure practitioners commonly "rely heavily on testimonials and anecdotes as evidence that their remedy is safe and effective. . . . [They] don the mantle of science while at the same time traducing the reputable scientists of their day. . . . [They] cite examples of physicians and scientists of the past who were forced to fight the rigid dogma of their day. . . . They do not use regular channels of communications, such as journals, for reporting scientific information, but rely instead on the mass media and word of mouth."[21] Their facts are always thin, their theories grand but silly, their methods can be mastered only by true believers, and they dismiss mainstream science as reactionary and obtuse. Criticisms are met with anger and ad hoc excuses. Support waxes and wanes, moved not by science but by the fickle winds of public fad and fantasy.

It has always been thus. For centuries, druggists sold useless ointments to cure syphilis—and the customers were always satisfied. If the chancre didn't disappear in a week or two, the helpful apothecary would offer a second dose for this unusually stubborn case. It always did go away sooner or later. The ointment business thrived. Certainly the patients believed in the therapies, at least for a time, and no doubt many of the ointment sellers did too. Everyone concerned sincerely wanted to do good. They concocted their remedies in the best of faith, and could even collect accounts of seemingly successful treatment. But the syphilis patients still died.

Sometimes they died faster. Despite earnest good intentions all around, quack-cure artists often manage to do considerable harm. Some simply divert patients from effective cures that might otherwise be used. Others cultivate in their patients a sense of dependence, victimization, and hypochondria, which of course helps secure further sales. Still others sell outright poisons. The Curies' discovery of radium, for example, kicked off the Mild Radium Therapy movement among American socialites, and precipitated a lucrative trade in radium-based belts, hearing aids, toothpaste, face cream, and hair tonic. Most lucrative of all was Radiothor, a glow-in-the-dark mineral water of the day, which promised a cure for more than 150 maladies. The Federal Trade Commission, ever vigilant, cracked down on competing potions that *lacked* advertised levels of radioactivity. The steel mogul, socialite, and amateur golf champion Eben MacBurney Byers faithfully drank Radiothor every day for four and a half years. By 1931 his whole upper jaw and most of his lower jaw had to be removed; all the remaining bone tissue of his body was disintegrating. Holes were forming in his skull. He died miserably in 1932.[22]

THE IRRELEVANT PRISM

What *did* finally happen to N rays? They were killed by an American scientist, R. W. Wood. A professor of physics at Johns Hopkins University, Wood was an expert in optics and spectroscopy. He was also, as Klotz describes, "an inveterate perpetrator of pranks and hoaxes" and a "relentless pursuer of frauds such as spiritualistic mediums."[23] He had tried to reproduce Blondlot's experiments but failed completely. In 1904, Wood visited Blondlot's laboratory and shortly thereafter published a report of his visit in the journal *Nature*.

Blondlot had been pleased to demonstrate the phenomenon to Wood through a variety of experiments. The first had purported to show that a human hand interposed to block an N-ray beam would decrease the brightness of an electric spark otherwise amplified by the rays. Blondlot and his colleagues could see the effect clearly, but Wood "was unable to detect the slightest change." "This was explained," Wood reported, "as due to a lack of sensitiveness of my eyes." Wood proposed repeating the experiment with Wood moving his hand and others observing the spark, and invited the observers to "announce the exact moments at which I introduced my hand into the path of the rays, by observing the screen. In no case was a correct answer given."[24]

Wood was then shown a series of photographic plates, which

clearly showed less-bright sparks recorded when a water-soaked piece of cardboard had been used to block the N rays. Wood proposed a blinded test, in which the experimenter would not know whether a sealed screen contained water, but this test somehow could not be performed right away.

Finally, and most devastatingly, came the experiment showing N rays being bent ("deviated" in physicist's jargon) by an aluminum prism. The N-ray scintillations were being observed on a phosphorescent screen in a darkened room. As Blondlot enthusiastically described the prismatic effects, Wood surreptitiously removed the prism. Blondlot's enthusiasm, however, was undiminished. The removal of the supposedly critical prism, Wood reported in his *Nature* article, just didn't change the effects at all.

Blondlot was furious, and dismissed Wood's test as contemptible trickery. "Several eminent physicists, who have been good enough to visit my laboratory, have witnessed [the photographic detection experiments]," Blondlot wrote indignantly after Wood's visit. "Of . . . forty experiments, one was unsuccessful. . . . I believe this failure, unique, be it noted, to be due to insufficient regulation of the spark, which undoubtedly was not sensitive."[25] But the damage had been done. Many still believed in N rays, indeed believed very earnestly. Wood, however, had shown that the world behaved no differently with or without the N-ray prism. The prism, in short, was irrelevant. Its important and finely calibrated effects existed only in the minds of certain zealous faithful.

Do similar things happen today? Do some among us, utterly earnest (no doubt) in their desire to do good, still peddle Radiothor, not in bottles but perhaps in briefs? Do our lawyers cherish some magical prisms of their own, and extol their wonderful effects in the face of all evidence to the contrary? It is much harder to recognize our own fads and fallacies than those of our grandparents. This much, however, is known for sure: when René Blondlot died in Nancy in 1930, N rays died with him. They have never been seen since.

PART II

LAW AND
PSEUDOSCIENCE

CHAPTER 3

The Midas Touch

How Money Causes Disease

Unfortunate indeed is the man who works for a firm covered by insurance, for even his slightest injury may result in cancer.
—R. Crane
"The Relationship of a Single Act of Trauma to Subsequent Malignancy" (1959)

Anita Menarde's misfortune began, apparently, on the morning of May 16, 1949, when she was injured slightly while alighting from a Philadelphia streetcar. She sued, of course. For breast cancer.

The facts did seem powerfully suggestive. Immediately after her fall, Menarde was treated at a local hospital for scrapes and bruises to her left ankle, right knee, and both hands. Dr. Koebert, her family doctor, saw her in the early evening. Upon disrobing that night Menarde noticed a discoloration on her right side and breast. She called Koebert again the next day about the bruised breast; he examined it, found no lumps, and prescribed hot compresses. He examined her periodically for the next two months; the breast seemed perfectly normal. At the end of July, however, Menarde detected a lump in her breast "at the exact

spot" of the earlier bruise. Dr. Beck, a cancer specialist, diagnosed cancer and performed a mastectomy.

During the trial, Koebert provided key support:

Q: Could there possibly have been something else which contributed to this cancer?
A: I do not think we are able to say.
Q: Can we say that this particular bruising or injury, to the exclu-
sion of everything else, caused this cancer?
A: I believe other conditions which had happened, and according
to the highlights of the case as I examined her originally, and
in that it arose in that immediate area, I believe that this cancer
was caused directly by the injury.
Q: Is it not possible that something else contributed to it?
A: Within the knowledge of man, I think not. . . .
Q: Would you say that it is impossible that there was any other
thing that could have caused this cancer other than the blow?
A: In this case I would say not. . . .
Q: Doctor, is there even the slightest idea of speculation in your
mind as to the judgment you have come to in concluding that
this accident caused this cancer in this girl's body?
A: I believe that this accident was the direct cause of this woman's
cancer.
Q: And is that judgment based on any speculation whatsoever in
this case?
A: Not in this case, no.[1]

Dr. Beck acknowledged differences of opinion "among outstanding authorities" as to whether simple trauma could cause
cancer. But in the end, he too agreed that in Menarde's case, at
least, there was a connection. The jury awarded her $50,000,
a considerable sum at the time, which the trial judge cut to
$25,000. A unanimous Pennsylvania Supreme Court affirmed.

CARCINOGENIC MONEY

As we have seen, junk science springs from many different im-
pulses. Some proponents are just too eager to make profound

new discoveries. Others embrace junk science for peace of mind, because it seems to explain all sorts of otherwise terrifying mysteries. It is a devastating blow to learn that you have cancer, or that your child has a birth defect. Many victims of tragic misfortune desperately need to explain the disaster as a product of something other than random hard luck. Blaming something or other, no matter how far off base scientifically, brings meaning to otherwise senseless suffering, and the meaning seems to supply some measure of comfort.

Still more comfort may be at hand when the returns on off-base science are paid in cash. We were once more candid about such things than we are today. A critic of quack medicine ads published in 1836 in the *New York Herald* received the following straightforward reply from the paper's owner, James Gordon Bennett: "Send us more advertisements than Dr. Brandreth does—give us higher prices. We'll cut Dr. Brandreth dead. . . . Business is business—money is money. We permit no blockhead to interfere with our business."[2]

Money is money in the legal business too. Before Calabresi, before liability science, and long before *Frye* surrendered to the far-siders, litigation was what it remains to this day: a demand for payment. Money is what brings claimants to court. Money pays their lawyers. Money attracts their expert witnesses. Money can, in fact, create experts where none existed before. It can fund scientific chairs for the study of almost anything, real or imaginary.

By the time Anita Menarde arrived in court, her medical theory was almost three centuries old. In 1676, an eminent English surgeon, Richard Wiseman, had reported two interesting cases of cancer.[3] Both patients, he observed, "thought [the cancer] came from an accidental bruise."[4] Wiseman thought so too; he proceeded to identify bruises, "error in diet," and "ill handling" as among the causes of cancer. In time, many doctors came to believe that simple trauma could trigger a malignant tumor.

By the mid-nineteenth century, however, the theory was in decline. Most physicians were beginning to understand that chronic irritation or abrasion, heat, and chemicals can cause cancer, but that simple trauma does not. In the normal course of things, the traumatic cancer theory would gradually have been relegated to the museum of scientific curiosities.

Then, quite abruptly, many doctors became believers once again. The rapid shift in medical attitudes began in Germany in 1884, and swept across the American continent in the first decades of this century. Individual doctors began to report frequently of connections between trauma and cancer.[5] Eager statisticians then set to work. Literature dating back to 1875 had suggested that one in eight tumors might be caused by previous trauma.[6] By 1897, another estimate blamed trauma for half of all bone cancers. As late as 1932, one researcher would attribute two out of five brain tumors to either physical trauma or purely psychological upset; the latter connection must surely have intrigued more than a few neurotics and hypochondriacs.[7]

Had there been a breakthrough in laboratory work, or an eye-opening epidemiological study? No. What had changed was the law. Germany had introduced the world's first worker's compensation program in 1884. In the remainder of the nineteenth century, two thousand new books and papers on traumatic cancer were published in Germany alone.[8] By the early 1920s, all but eight American states had enacted worker's compensation laws too, and the traumatic cancer epidemic had reached American shores. The one new fact on the medical scene was that attributing cancer to trauma helped pay bills all around. As one exasperated observer would note in 1959, the carcinogenic properties of trauma "increase in potency each year and in direct proportion to the broadening of insurance coverage."[9]

METASTASIS IN COURT

At first the prospects in court for traumatic cancer claims did not look promising. One early case, for example, was filed by Levy D. Jewell, who had been hit on the arm while loading freight onto a train and subsequently developed cancer. A jury awarded him $960. The New Hampshire Supreme Court, however, was deeply skeptical when the case reached it in 1874. "[I]t would be a reproach upon the administration of the law if such mere speculative possibilities, unsustained by proof, were permitted to become the basis of awarding heavy damages of this sort," wrote one Justice. "Few things are more difficult, and require more close observation, than the just determination of the causes of disease, or the effects of injuries to the person," agreed the Chief Justice.[10] The award was overturned, though ultimately on other grounds. Other courts started out equally firm. As late as 1921, for example, the Iowa Supreme Court would overturn an award to a man who claimed his stomach cancer was caused by breaking his leg when he fell into an elevator pit. The expert testimony, the court declared, is "wholly in the realm of conjecture, speculation, and surmise."[11]

But as worker's compensation laws proliferated, many other judges joined the ranks of the conjecturists and speculators. One 1917 case involved Candelario Villa, who fell on the job and injured his left clavicle. Villa testified that he immediately saw the bump that eventually was diagnosed as cancerous.[12] Villa's doctor noticed it a few days later. All the doctors who testified agreed, however, that cancer would take longer than that to develop. A worker's compensation award was upheld anyway.

Proof of similar character would suffice for most U.S. courts for the next half century. A blow to a miner's face with a piece of coal caused his cancer some weeks later, agreed the Colorado Supreme Court in 1922.[13] A violent assault on a policeman during an arrest caused his abdominal cancer six weeks later, the Minnesota Supreme Court was persuaded in 1923.[14] Another worker's five-foot fall from an elevator triggered cancer of the rib, concluded the Virginia Supreme Court in 1927.[15] Two severe blows to a man's testicles caused malignant cancer seven days later, a Texas appellate court found in 1941.[16] A woman hit with a large can of orange juice developed breast cancer as a result, the Rhode Island Supreme Court allowed in 1949.[17] Another worker's bone cancer developed from a twist to the leg caused by heavy lifting, the New Mexico Supreme Court found in 1958.[18]

In time, traumatic cancer claims spilled over to ordinary tort cases, wholly outside the realm of worker's compensation laws. This, as we saw at the beginning of the chapter, is how Anita

Menarde came to collect for breast cancer caused by a streetcar. Others would win similar claims. In 1963, Jack Murdock was thrown violently against his fastened seat belt when his car was hit from behind. "[A] possibility exists," a doctor later testified, that "trauma induced by pressure from a seat belt might have led to an inflammatory condition in the testicles," which might "conceivably" have triggered cancer in Murdock's left testicle. A Georgia court of appeals agreed.[19] A year later, another cancer victim, Marie P. Daly, bruised her breast and broke her leg in a fall at the Duffy Brothers store in Rosemount, Minnesota. When she developed breast cancer fourteen months later, one physician discerned a connection, six did not, and the jury awarded $40,000.[20] The same year, a rear-end collision threw Jerome Baker against the steering wheel of his car. His chest was bruised; two months later he died of lung cancer. A jury verdict for the plaintiff was upheld by the Pennsylvania Supreme Court.[21]

What was most remarkable in the heyday of such lawsuits was just how many different kinds of things could be bumped, banged, or collided with to cause cancer: not only streetcars and orange-juice cans, but metal bobbins,[22] slippery floors in grocery stores, hot-water heaters,[23] umbrella handles,[24] car dashboards,[25] and a forty-pound box of cheese, to list just a few. Since the thigh bone connects to the hip bone and all that, blows were sometimes nearer to, sometimes farther from, the site where cancer eventually developed. Lifting the heavy cheese put "such a strain upon the muscles which were connected, or nearly so, with the diseased tissues, i.e., the cancer,"[26] that the lifting undoubtedly hastened the cancer's progression. Abdominal pressure from a seat belt might have inflamed the testicles, which "might conceivably squeeze the tumor cells into circulation and into adjacent areas."[27] In a 1954 ruling, the Ohio Supreme Court approved compensation to a worker who claimed to have been struck on the left side of his chest by a heavy piece of equipment on the last day of his employment.[28] Cancer was later found in his *right* lung. The worker's widow, however, located an expert who believed in the "contra-coup" theory, whereby the cancerous effects of chest trauma cross the body in just this way.

Here and there some judges did demur. Four dissenting Georgia judges, for example, consigned the evidence on testicular-cancer-by-seat-belt to "the scrap heap of conjecture," pointing out that the plaintiff claiming a traumatic cause of his cancer had also been involved in three other car accidents, and had even shot himself in the leg with a .22-caliber pistol. Two dissenting Pennsylvania Justices were equally skeptical of the "far-fetched . . . contradictions" and "conjectures" in the lung-cancer-by-car-accident case.[29] So were two dissenting New Mexico Justices in a bone-cancer-by-heavy-lifting ruling: "If the judgment in this case can be upheld . . . there is not an ailment in the whole category of disease known to the medical profession that may not become the basis of a workmen's compensation award."[30] Occasionally such views even coalesced into a majority. In 1948, the Washington Supreme Court rejected a jury finding that fractured bones in a foot worsened into arthritis of the spine, causing cancer of the intestine ten years later, even though one doctor had testified that there "probably could" be a connection.[31] But until well into the 1960s, such opinions remained the exception. Most appellate decisions sided with claimants.

RATIONALIZATIONS

How could so many judges get the science so wrong in so many different cases spanning so many years? Some, no doubt, really did believe in traumatic causes of cancer. Many more saw only a Depression-era worker or widow who really could use the money. *In dubio pro laeso* (when in doubt, favor the injured).

Still, someone must supply at least a shadow of a *dubio,* and this is where the junk science in court really flowered. The traumatic cancer cases presented a catalog of bad observation, worse logic, wishful thinking, and epidemic judicial credulity.

The credulity was the easy part. Judges were often able to blame others for the science, and many gratefully did. By state law, worker's compensation boards usually made the initial call on the validity of the claim. Sympathetic judges could then simply suspend disbelief and humbly defer to the expertise, such as it was, of the compensation board. The board, of course, could do the same thing, by humbly deferring to the family doctor. And the family doctor surely understood that the one bit of good he could do for his unfortunate patient was to testify with an unusually open mind, even if the testimony had to be cocooned in mights, maybes, and possibles. And so, everyone deferred to everyone else, except the first G.P., who deferred to no one. After the bowing and scraping, the insurer paid.

The less courts required of medical witnesses, the less witnesses supplied. In one case, a first doctor allowed that the blow "might" have caused the cancer, although probably not; a second, that cancer "may result from a blow," the inference being "possible, but not reasonably probable"; and a third, that the blow "might be a contributing cause," though this was not "a reasonable probability."[32] For the Minnesota Supreme Court, these views sufficed to support an award. Over time, expert witnesses came to recognize how little was required of them, and grew all the more willing to testify. Even a great scientist can concede that fairies might possibly once have appeared in England, and may perhaps have been photographed by some young friends of Sir Arthur Conan Doyle, though of course it's not very probable.

Appellate courts grew increasingly adept at accommodating this sort of thing. In late 1941, for example, nineteen-year-old Charles Ellis was working for the Virginia State Highway Commission. Although he did not report the incident at the time, he later remembered that a falling rock dislodged by rain had struck him one day on the leg. Soon after, doctors discovered bone cancer. "[I]t is a well established and recognized fact in the medical profession," one doctor testified, "that trauma, especially occurring to young people, is the sole cause of many malignancies developing shortly thereafter and that the result which followed in the instant case is a common one." But a pathologist was quite certain that bone cancers of this type are not caused by rocks, and he persuaded the compensation board to deny damages. The Virginia Supreme Court overturned the board's ruling and ordered payment. The young worker, the court emphasized, had been "attended by two experienced and competent physicians" who were "thoroughly familiar with all of the conditions" of both the trauma and the cancer. The defense's experts had given only a "theoretical opinion." "The positive opinions of the two attending physicians" must outweigh "the general view of the medical authorities."[33]

Playing the experts off each other in this way enabled many a judge to lament "the usual conflict of medical opinion,"[34] then endorse the check. In 1958, for example, James Bentley would win damages for cancer of the jaw because (by his own unverified account) he had earlier cut his lip on a cardboard carton.[35] One testifying doctor was sure the cut had caused cancer on the lip that spread to the jaw. A pathologist was certain that cuts don't cause cancer. A third doctor, who had actually treated Bentley, would testify only that the cancer had originated on the lip: "[I]t is possible that the trauma might play a part or be a factor. I am not saying it produced it. I am saying that it may be a factor in the production of this lesion." This span of opinions satisfied the Michigan Supreme Court, which stated: "The record is replete with medical assertions of lack of positive knowledge about the cause of cancer." The court followed this with a curious non sequitur: "And yet, with all this uncertainty, the patient was diagnosed and treated. The appeal board had the task assigned by statute to make [a] finding of fact. . . . We cannot say that its decision is unsupported by competent evidence." Under a "not unsupported" standard, of course, traumatic cancer was going to endure forever. Sympathetic family doctors or imaginative medical mavericks could always be located, somewhere or other, to not-unsupport traumatic cancer claims.[36]

Picking and choosing among witnesses and compensation boards was easy enough. But most appellate courts recognized their obligation to do somewhat more. Accordingly, they marched through a textbook demonstration of junk science observation and reasoning in action.

In order to consider trauma as the cause of cancer, the court needed first to establish that there was no cancer beforehand. That was easy enough: just ask friends, family, or lawyers. Beforehand, the claimant was "a perfectly healthy, strong man who has never lost any time from work or complained of any illness,"[37] or perhaps a "well nourished boy, nineteen years of age," though he did have a chronic limp before the rock hit his knee.[38] In one early case, a court agreed that a man had died from cancer caused by a fall from a streetcar twenty months earlier, even though an autopsy showed that the victim had been suffering from tuberculosis, Bright's disease, acute and chronic cystitis, acute and chronic prostatitis with abscess formation, and chronic selenitis.[39]

Some courts were equally nonchalant about the trauma itself. No matter that the employee didn't report the blow until after the cancer was diagnosed. No matter that the whiplash, or the impact against the steering wheel, seemed inconsequential at the time. Trauma and cancer are, of course, connected, the Virginia Supreme Court reasoned in 1927, but "the degree of injury plays no important part."[40] "[T]he connection between trauma and the subsequent development of sarcoma," the Minnesota Supreme Court observed indulgently in 1931, "may be many times overlooked due to the triviality of the injury. Just a mere bump the patient doesn't remember."[41]

With the health-trauma-cancer sequence established to the court's satisfaction, the rest was easy. There *was* no rest: the sequence was everything. "[I]t should be recognized that inferences, if rational and natural, which follow from a sequence of proved events may be sufficient to establish causal connection without any supporting medical testimony."[42] This quote comes from the Minnesota Supreme Court in 1964, but virtually identical language appears in dozens of other rulings. The Rhode Island Supreme Court overturned a lower court ruling and determined that a light, glancing blow to the nipple of Laura Valente's breast caused the breast cancer discovered some weeks later.[43] Where "injury appears in a bodily member reasonably soon after an accident, at the very place where the force was applied," the court reasoned, there arises "a natural inference that the injury, whatever may be the medical name, was the result of the employment." And what of statistical evidence establishing that such sequences are just meaningless coincidence? "Facts prevail over possibilities or probabilities," wrote one court dismissively.[44]

Thus, some courts defer responsibility for upholding the bad science to others; other courts set out and endorse the bad data and spurious inferences themselves; still others find ways to explain why science shouldn't really be dispositive at all, to locate some reason that *cause* doesn't mean quite the same thing in law as in science.[45] "Causation is not necessarily and exclusively a medical conclusion,"[46] one court explained. "[T]he doctor is thinking in terms of a single, precise cause for a particular condition," reasoned another, but the law "recognizes more than one cause for a particular injurious result."[47]

This sort of thing can always be reinforced by an appeal to common sense and the intuition of the layman. "When there is such a divergence of competent medical opinion, we, as laymen, must necessarily look to the facts for a way out of a seeming dilemma," explained one court.[48] And for another, "The lay mind, under such circumstances, can reach no other conclusion than that . . . the sarcoma was either caused by the injury or was aggravated by it."[49] The evidence "would be quite convincing to the mind of the layman," reasoned yet another, and that, apparently, was good enough.[50]

In extreme cases, the court just rejected science altogether. The trauma-cancer link should not be determined "by nice philosophical reasoning, nor by the reluctance and hesitancy of the scientist to accept as satisfactory a conclusion not demonstrated to be necessarily a fact to a scientific certainty," declared one Rhode Island trial court.[51] "An inference, if rational and natural, based on proven facts, will stand even though not supported by expert medical opinion," announced Rhode Island's Supreme Court in another case in 1950.[52] Of course we can't wait for "medical evidence establishing indisputable causal connection," reasoned the New Mexico Supreme Court in 1958. "Medical men are justifiably reluctant to make a definite statement" because "they have no actual knowledge at the present time on which such a statement could in all good conscience be made." In court, however, the cancer connection was deemed "inferable despite the lack of medical evidence."[53]

Science really *is* remarkably ignorant about cancer, and that in itself sometimes became reason enough to uphold the award. "The whole subject is shrouded more or less in mystery," observed the Supreme Court of Colorado in 1922.[54] Either trauma causes cancer or cancer remains "a medical mystery," explained the Supreme Court of Minnesota in 1925,[55] and if it's all a mystery, who's to say that the claimant *shouldn't* be paid? "It appears that none of [the six doctors who testified] knows the cause of the petitioner's cancer," explained the Tennessee Supreme Court in 1970, so naturally it upheld the award.[56] Thus, judges invoked ignorance of the facts as their main excuse.

MEDICAL SCIENCE

While family practitioners speculated, compensation boards deferred, judges rationalized, and juries voted, the mainstream scientific community was off nailing down the facts. Prominent among the investigators was the American pathologist James Ewing. Ewing began publishing authoritative papers on traumatic cancer in the mid-1920s, drawing on both his own research and numerous other studies.[57] Accepting the possibility that trauma might, in rare instances, cause cancer, he recognized that it was being blamed far too often.

By 1935, Ewing had assembled his own work and consensus views of other medical scientists in a major treatise. He presented five postulates that would have to be met before traumatic cancer could even be considered a possibility. First, you have to be sure there really was a trauma; vague patient recollections cannot suffice. It would require "time, patience, and ingenuity to establish the facts." Unless such an inquiry is "competently made, the report of the case is, for scientific purposes, worthless." Second, you must establish convincingly that the cancer didn't precede the trauma. Since most people are *not* medically examined shortly before a car accident or fall in a grocery store, and since early-stage cancer is difficult to detect in any event, most reports of cancer discovered sometime after trauma are meaningless. Third, the tumor must originate at the exact site of the earlier trauma; the same general vicinity is not good enough. Fourth, the interval of time between the trauma and the appearance of the cancer must be biologically reasonable: for example, cancers from chronic irritation never develop in less than five years, and incubation periods of ten to twenty years are more typical. Fifth, the cancer must be diagnosed positively; a biopsy must be performed.[58]

Ewing's postulates were already familiar to doctors in the field when he formalized them in 1935. Of course you can't find cause and effect unless you are careful about recording cause (postulate 1) and effect (postulate 5). Of course you have to check that the effects weren't there before the cause (postulate 2). And of course the links must make some kind of biological and physical sense (postulates 3 and 4). Ewing's purpose was horticultural—to weed out junk case reports that were stifling scientifically useful vegetation.

As the grubbing and uprooting proceeded, the flowers of serious science soon bloomed once again. Football players do not have higher rates of cancer than the crowds in the stands. Systematic studies of World War I veterans found no cancer correlation with wartime injury. Broken bones are extremely common, but bone cancer is rare and statistically unrelated to prior fracture. Patients who undergo surgery do not develop skin or tissue cancer near the incision more often than elsewhere, or more often than anyone else. Controlled studies show no positive correlation between head trauma and brain tumors; to the contrary, some correlations seem to run the other way, though researchers have prudently refrained from announcing that head trauma cures brain cancer. Crushing, hammering, and smashing various parts of laboratory animals, from rooster testicles on out, produced nothing but the expected mutilation. A 1974 literature review in the *Mayo Clinic Proceedings* firmly concluded that "no experimental evidence ever has shown that trauma—single, uncomplicated trauma—produces cancer."[59]

REMISSION

Single, uncomplicated trauma had, however, produced cancer verdicts in steady numbers. Appellate decisions upholding traumatic cancer awards rose steadily from the 1920s into the 1950s, about three in four allowing compensation. Only in the 1950s and thereafter did Ewing finally begin to register reliably in legal circles; traumatic cancer litigation finally dropped off the charts in the 1970s, more than thirty years after Ewing's seminal work. The once sacrosanct expertise of the compensation tribunal began to be desecrated with some regularity.[60] And judges grew increasingly willing to set aside the testimony of maverick witnesses and to reject post hoc reasoning.

New York's top court firmly overturned a $45,000 jury award in 1952, in yet another case of a woman claiming breast cancer as a result of a car accident.[61] The Ohio Supreme Court rejected a similar claim in 1954.[62] New York courts solidified their support of Ewing a few years later, by rejecting a claim for cancer allegedly caused by the metal flap of a paper towel holder striking the bridge of a woman's nose.[63] Other courts gradually fell in line. Traumatic cancer, the Texas high court announced in 1966, is "a question of science determinable only from the testimony of expert medical professionals," not to be inferred simply from a sequence of events.[64] The Montana Supreme Court issued a similar opinion the same year, in a case involving cancer of the vertebrae attributed to a blow from farming machinery: "Not every supposition or theory of a witness concerning *what might be* has the force of evidence, even though he be licensed to practice medicine. . . . Everything in this troubled world is 'possible' and this is particularly true in the scientific world."[65] In 1967, a New York appellate court rejected a jury's finding that a soda machine operator had developed cancer because of a slip and fall on the sticky floor of the Fourteenth Street subway station in New York.[66] In 1969, after a jury had been persuaded that whiplash from a rear-end collision caused metastasis of a throat cancer, the South Carolina Supreme Court declared that "[t]he narration of the sequence of events" could simply not suffice.[67]

For a while, well-advised litigants kept their claims alive by a change of emphasis. Trauma didn't "cause" cancer after all, the new line ran, but it did aggravate or accelerate the cancer.[68] The Minnesota Supreme Court approved a worker's compensation award that linked the progress of a malignant breast tumor to a blow from a drill on the nipple of a man's right breast.[69] The Supreme Court of Tennessee agreed that injury to the back and the left foot accelerated metastasis of a cancer of uncertain origin.[70] The Louisiana Supreme Court accepted cancer acceleration from a bruise to the leg,[71] ignoring the views of the one cancer specialist in the case, who concluded that the trauma had probably helped *save* the victim's life by bringing attention to already developing disease.

When even "aggravation" wore thin, some courts took final refuge in a vocabulary so empty that it no longer admitted to scientific contradiction at all. Johnny Hammond was a beneficiary of this kind of lego-babble after his cancerous arm was bruised by the steering wheel when his truck struck a pothole. All the medical witnesses agreed that potholes do not cause bone cancer. So did the trial court. And a court of appeals. But in 1979, four of seven Justices on the Louisiana Supreme Court ruled otherwise. "[M]edical testimony must be weighed in the light of other credible evidence of a nonmedical character, such as a sequence of symptoms or events," the court declared. "The employee's disability is compensable if a preexisting disease or condition is activated or precipitated into disabling manifestations as a result of a work accident."[72]

Another cancer-by-pothole award went to a New York bus driver in 1985. An X ray revealed that the wrist he broke in the accident had been weakened by cancer; fortunately the cancer, once revealed, could be promptly treated. At whose expense? The employer's, of course. "It is sufficient," the New York high court declared, "if the employment acts upon that disease or condition in such a manner as to cause a disability which did not previously exist. . . . The growth in claimant's wrist was asymptomatic and not disabling prior to the accident. Indeed, claimant did not know that it existed."[73]

Thus the word *cause* quietly slinks out of the legal vocabulary, to be replaced with *activated, precipitated into disabling manifestation, aroused into disabling reality,* and other lawyerly evasions. Or else *cause* finds itself paired with legal vacuities (like *disability*) rather than medically meaningful terms (like *cancer*). Once serious, the claims are now trivial; once specific, they are now surpassingly vague; once factual (though baseless), they are now so afactual as to be entirely beyond scientific refutation. Cause and effect are gently verbalized out of existence. As the great, irascible physicist Wolfgang Pauli once remarked about a report he had read: "That paper isn't even good enough to be wrong!"

TRAUMATIC DETERMINISM

No one would have been less surprised by this last chapter of the trauma-cancer chronicles than Ewing himself. Simple trauma does not, in fact, cause cancer. Cancer does sometimes cause trauma. Cancer does not cause a bus to hit a pothole, of course, but it can make bones, breasts, and other body parts unusually susceptible to accident. "The presence of an unsuspected tumor tends to bring about the occurrence of injuries at the tumor bearing area and to intensify the subjective symptoms and local effects of the injuries," Ewing had observed.[74] The bulk of a tumor might make a blow more painful. The bone cancer might make one's leg more susceptible to breaking. And occasionally cancer will indeed cause trauma. A man is found unconscious at the bottom of the stairs. He later suffers recurrent headaches and vertigo. When the brain tumor is finally discovered, it is all too easy to say it was caused by the fall. But in fact, it was the tumor that caused the first dizzy spell, which caused the fall.

Ewing called this kind of event "traumatic determinism." The suggestive sequence of events in fact implies just the opposite of what the layman commonly infers. As the South Carolina Supreme Court would recognize in 1980, in a case involving cancer and a door hinge striking the arm, "[y]ou really don't know how many times a day you hit your thumb until you have a sore thumb, and then it seems like you are hitting it every five minutes. . . . [Y]ou are not aware of it until you have something that calls your attention to it."[75]

For just this reason, trauma is often the best possible accident that could befall the cancer victim. The one thing a broken bone, sprained back, or bruised chest undoubtedly does cause with some frequency is a visit to the doctor. "Traumas reveal more malignant tumors than they cause," Ewing noted in 1935.[76] As another researcher would point out ten years later, "[t]he injury certainly does not create sarcoma, but it may bring it into the foreground."[77]

And what does serious science have to say about the "aggravation" theory? To this day one school of thought maintains that in certain rare instances, trauma may aid the spread or accelerate the development of an already existing cancerous mass, most particularly when "trauma ruptures the capsule of the encapsulated tumor."[78] The presumption is against aggravation, however. And a mirror-image theory posits that trauma sometimes *retards* growth of preexisting tumors, the thought being that trauma may decrease blood flow to the cancerous area. Both theories remain speculative, because cancer is an exceptionally variable disease and doctors possess no fine scale to clock its progression, accelerated or otherwise.

Without doubt, trauma's single most important cancer-related effect is to accelerate discovery and thus treatment. By the grand, cost-shifting logic that the Calabresians embrace, it is the trauma victim who usually owes the traumatizer, for having supplied the beneficial bump that led to discovery of the disease. This idea is silly, of course, but perhaps less silly than any of the countless other twists of science and logic by which insurers are regularly ordered to send checks in the other direction.

THE COURTROOM CURE

After years of floundering in the junk science morass of traumatic cancer, judges slowly abandoned sequence-of-events logic, turned away from the sympathetic speculations of family doctors, and struggled on to the higher and firmer ground of epidemiology and medical science. Eventually, the change of heart among appellate judges was communicated back down to trial judges and worker's compensation boards, and traumatic cancer went into almost complete remission.

What became apparent, in the end, was that the disease had for years been nourished by judges themselves. Mainstream scientists had been saying so all along. "The cancerigenic potentialities of mechanical trauma would probably have long since ceased to stimulate any significant amount of scientific interest," wrote one weary commentator in 1954, "were it not for the fact that so many claims for compensation are filed each year."[79] Traumatic cancer would have been "relegated to limbo" far sooner, concluded the Mayo Clinic review twenty years later, but for "lawyers constantly keeping the question alive."[80]

It is fair to say that the final cure for traumatic cancer was discovered where the disease had first originated: in court. A prescient article published in the *New York Journal of Medicine* in 1962 suggested that traumatic cancer could be cured only by substitution: lawyers would have to be given some other cause of cancer to pursue. "[I]f the truth is that single injury cannot cause a malignant tumor, we see little hope in the present imperfect state of science and society of ever establishing such a fact to the satisfaction of everyone," the article concluded. "It may be that the relationship of trauma to cancer will be explained not by experiments designed to study this specific problem, but rather by an overwhelming clarification of the etiologies of malignant conditions."[81]

This was a great insight. For nonscientists, no strictly negative proofs were ever going to suffice. Some other explanation for cancer would have to grip the legal imagination before traumatic cancer claims would be abandoned. Perhaps the new explanation would be a better one, an "overwhelming clarification" of the real causes of cancer. Or perhaps, as we shall see, something less solid would suffice.

CHAPTER 4

Sudden Acceleration
Runaway Panic in the Mass Media

ED BRADLEY: [A]n automobile malfunctions, causing several deaths, hundreds of injuries and thousands in property damage. . . . What we're talking about is the sudden rocketing of a car out of control after the driver switches gears from park into either drive or reverse. . . . [T]he car . . . is the Audi 5000, years 1978 to 1986. . . .

Six-year-old Joshua Bradosky liked to open the garage door when he drove home with his mother. The Reverend and Mrs. Bradosky told us what happened after she let the little boy out of the car to open the garage.

KRISTI BRADOSKY: I got back into the car and put my foot on the brake to put it in drive, and the car surged forward, and I saw that I was going to hit him. So, I put my foot on the brake, but it didn't stop the car. (Crying.) It pushed him through the garage. And we had a panel partition, and it went through the partition. He went through it. (Crying)

BRADLEY: You put your foot on the brake?

BRADOSKY: Mm-hmm. ——"60 Minutes" (1986)

It was surefire fare for "60 Minutes." A mother is distraught with grief. Her six-year-old child lies dead. And what has killed him? A defective Audi 5000. Audi has claimed its car is an "engineering marvel." But "60 Minutes" has uncovered its "darker side." It seems that the car has a deadly propensity to take off at full speed even as the terrified driver jams the brake pedal to the floor.

"Consumer groups" of shadowy provenance but unmistak-

able belligerence have already sprung up to trumpet their out-
rage. One of them, the Audi Victims Network (AVN), was
founded by Alice Weinstein, who appears prominently on the
show. She demands answers: "Why are people landing on diving boards? Why are they leaping over marina walls? Why are
they going down elevator shafts? Why are they driving through
people's houses and landing on their beds? Each day, the stories
become more and more bizarre."

Bizarre, yes. Perhaps the most bizarre aspect involves the
Audi's brakes. Investigation after the accidents typically finds
the brakes to be in perfect working order. And in the Audi, as
in any car, the brakes will easily overcome an engine even at full
throttle; press the brakes hard, and the car will come to a stop
whatever the engine may be doing. So during the Audi accidents
the brakes must somehow have failed. And, yes, the drivers are
all certain they had a foot on the brake, as they assure "60
Minutes": "The foot was on the brake so hard, Mr. Bradley, that
I had a shin splint. The entire foot was black and blue from
pressing so hard on the brake."[1]

THE CHEERLEADERS

Television didn't create the Audi story, any more than Hollywood created *Gone With the Wind.* Television just made the
movie, and projected it one Sunday evening into 30 million
living rooms. In February 1986, Kristi Bradosky's car had
surged forward and could not be stopped. "60 Minutes" showed
it all: the tragedy-stricken parents, the crash site, and the sheep-
ish Audi spokesman who kept insisting that the car was not to
blame.

But some players, perhaps thinking themselves less photo-
genic, stay off-camera. Just outside camera range, it turns out,
are some lawyers. In fact, a lot of lawyers. The Bradoskys had
already hired one. So had Alice Weinstein. So had many others.
The suspicious mind might even be inclined to think that "60
Minutes" was a plant, an opening shot in the litigator's struggle
for public sympathy, tactical advantage, and psychological edge.

Massive publicity would certainly prove essential in the litigation campaign against Audi that was to follow. Not because complaints of sudden acceleration are in fact so bizarre, but because they are so common. Similar charges, it would later emerge, had been made at one time or another against almost every car on the highway. So how did Audi become the star on "60 Minutes"? No doubt the same way Ed Bradley did: through a combination of blind luck and hard work. In Audi's case the luck was bad, and the hard work was done by others. Led by Alice Weinstein, the "Audi victims" organized, hired lawyers, and built up a relentless campaign of pressure and publicity.

None of the campaigners seemed to have the slightest idea about what really caused the Audi's sudden acceleration, but the Weinstein crew offered many suspects. The Audis, like other new cars, had come packed with sophisticated electronics to maintain idle, to regulate emissions, and to operate cruise controls. Never before had car engines been built around such sophisticated computers. Nor had computers ever been so widely deployed before in the bumpy, hostile surroundings of the open road. So from the beginning, the car's electronics were numbered among the lead suspects. There were other clues, but of uncertain significance. Most sudden-acceleration incidents occur in driveways or parking lots. More than half the time, the car has just been shifted into reverse. And after the accident, the brakes are always found to be functioning just fine. Always.

When it came to blame, however, the *who* would prove much easier than the *what*. In April 1986, shortly before the "60 Minutes" story aired, the Bradoskys filed suit against Audi, demanding $12 million in compensatory and $18 million in punitive damages.[2] Among other litigants were Diane Rose, who had smashed her 1981 Audi 5000 into a stone planter; Germaine Gibbs, whose apartment had been stormed by an Audi driven by Harold Horowitz; Alice Weinstein, who had crashed her Audi into a tree and broken her nose; Frances Martin, who said she had shifted her Audi into park and put her foot on the brake when the car rocketed forward and slammed into an embankment; and Marie Ruston, who had been waiting in a drive-through bank line when a runaway Audi propelled another car into hers.

The AVN soon linked up with other outspoken pressure orga-
nizations. The most prominent and skillful in the publicize-or-
perish campaign would be Clarence Ditlow's Center for Auto
Safety (CAS), an advocacy group founded by Ralph Nader in
1980 and funded at least in part by selling information packages
to plaintiffs' lawyers. Few of CAS's fourteen employees have any
engineering expertise. Ditlow himself makes do with an under-
graduate degree in chemical engineering from Lehigh University.[3]

The CAS quickly decided that the Audi's problem was both
real and grave. "[T]he increasing use of electronics and computers" was probably to blame. The cars would rocket out of control because of an "electronic glitch" in the computer that determines the air-fuel mix, or maybe "defects in the accelerator and
shift linkage," or perhaps "a voltage surge or drop in the car's
computer."[4] In time, the CAS would grow more cautious, insisting only that the defect was utterly mysterious. "Someone can
be poisoned," Ditlow declared, "but we don't have to know what
the poison is."[5]

By February 1986, the National Highway Traffic Safety Administration (NHTSA) had been harried into including the
1984–85 Audi 5000 and four other cars on its sudden-acceleration docket. A month later, the CAS rushed in, teaming up with
another Nader spinoff, the New York Public Interest Research
Group (NYPIRG), the New York attorney general, and Alice
Weinstein's newly formed AVN.[6] The coalition demanded that
NHTSA recall more than 200,000 Audi 5000 cars.[7] In April
1986, the CAS called for further investigation from NHTSA[8]
and, shortly thereafter, action by the Illinois attorney general.[9]
In early November, the CAS wrote another hectoring letter to
NHTSA, insisting that the agency should immediately subpoena
all of Audi's sudden-acceleration records. Two weeks later, the
CAS called on Transportation Secretary Elizabeth Dole to order
Audi to repurchase 227,000 cars.[10] Four days after that, "60
Minutes" aired the Bradosky segment.

FEEDBACK

Plaintiffs' lawyers could hardly have produced a better story on "60 Minutes" if they had written the script themselves. The news magazine happily tracked Ditlow's line, heightening the drama by mixing the diabolical with the inexplicable.

To whom did "60 Minutes" turn for information? Well, there was a Dr. Paul Ast, who (like the CAS) believed the Audi's computer-controlled idle stabilizer to be the culprit. Audi hadn't found the problem itself, suggested Ast, because "[i]t's a very elusive thing. It'll cause a transient malfunction in the computer, and it may not happen for the next 10 years." And then there was William Rosenbluth, who, Bradley reported, "took a car that had already been involved in two sudden-acceleration incidents and, without his foot on the gas pedal, showed it could do this." Do what? Take off like a rocket, that's what, and 30 million viewers saw it with their own eyes. "Rosenbluth says that unusually high transmission pressure could build up on certain model Audis causing the throttle to open up," Bradley explained. "Again, watch the pedal go down by itself."[11] What the viewers couldn't watch was where the "unusually high transmission pressure" had come from. It had come from a bottle. Rosenbluth had drilled a hole in the Audi transmission and pumped in air at high pressure.[12]

Media coverage of the Audi 5000 story built slowly through the summer and fall of 1986, when the first lawsuits were filed. But the "60 Minutes" story propelled the publicity to stratospheric new heights. In April 1988, *Business Week,* not usually thought of as a tool of hysterical consumer activists, ran a somber story about "cars that seem to develop minds of their own," this "most baffling cause of auto accidents," this "terrifying phenomenon" and its "thousands of victims."[13]

The mounting publicity triggered further regulatory action. On December 23, 1986, barely a month after the CBS story, NHTSA asked Audi to recall some cars to address the complaints, generating still more publicity and attracting still more lawyers. The claims against Audi would experience a sudden acceleration of their own. By mid-1988, lawyers had filed about a hundred lawsuits.[14] The numbers were still rising in 1989,[15] by which time the dollar value of outstanding claims against Audi reportedly totaled an astronomical $5 billion.[16] Such totals mean nothing, of course; plaintiffs' lawyers routinely put ridiculous figures on the papers they file. Alice Weinstein, she of the broken nose, filed four identical suits against Audi and its dealers, demanding $9 million in damages in just one of them, and extortionate punitive damages in another.

L'affaire Audi had now become viciously circular: the publicity attracted suits, the suits generated publicity, and the more people heard about sudden acceleration, the more they came to believe in it. As soon as you're *told* that your car is possessed by engineering demons, you're likely to understand in a flash just what it was that caused the stupid accident you were in last week. Last week you thought it might have been your own dumb fault, but now the matter is suddenly clearer. As NHTSA would later observe, Audi complaints peaked in 1986, in exact synchrony with the swelling publicity.[17] An official from the Canadian transportation department would similarly note a surge of sudden-acceleration complaints against Hondas and Audis in Ottawa and Toronto right after television reports on the cars aired in those two cities.[18]

Four months after the "60 Minutes" report, the publicity itself became the basis for yet another suit. On March 3, 1987, an enterprising Chicago lawyer, Robert Lisco, filed a class action suit on behalf of 350,000 Audi owners, named and unnamed. No, they hadn't all crashed through walls, run into planters, or collided with trees. The wreckage, Lisco contended, was to the value of their vehicles. The Audi's resale value had been destroyed by the bad publicity, and the bad publicity was all Audi's fault. Potential buyers of secondhand Audis could read all about it in Lisco's own inflammatory press release, distributed over the PR Newswire.[19]

THE HAPLESS DEFENSE

Almost unnoticed in all the swirling publicity was Audi's pathetic defense. "Audi says it happens when a driver steps on the gas pedal when he means to step on the brake," reported a skeptical Ed Bradley on "60 Minutes." But "if the accidents are the fault of the drivers," he asked, "why do people only make that mistake in the Audi 5000?" Curiously, Bradley himself had noted the answer just a few minutes earlier in his own show: "there've been reports of all makes of cars doing this." Indeed there have.[20] On November 3, 1986, just a few weeks before the CBS story aired, NHTSA closed a sudden-acceleration probe of 1984–86 Honda Accords. A month later, NHTSA reopened a similar investigation of 2.3 million GM J-cars. Six months later, in June 1987, NHTSA was looking at sudden acceleration in 3.2 million mid- and full-size Fords; two months after that, in 816,000 Buick Le Sabres, Oldsmobile Delta 88s, and Pontiac Bonnevilles; then in the Mercedes Benz 300E—in fact, its investigations at that time implicated nearly 10 million cars. The Canadian Department of Transportation closed its sudden-acceleration review of GM cars in November 1986, but initiated another of Honda Accords two months later. In July 1987, Prime Minister Nakasone promised Japanese citizens that their Department of Transportation, which had already received 178 sudden-acceleration complaints, would investigate Nissan, Toyota, Honda, Mitsubishi, and Mazda cars. NHTSA's investigation would eventually encompass *all* 1984–88 automatics.

It took Ed Bradley about five seconds to cover and dismiss all these other reports. Audi owners, he emphasized, are "mostly affluent, well-educated and sophisticated drivers." One accident victim was a police officer "trained to drive under emergency conditions." "[M]aybe you ought to have a special course to teach these articulate, well-educated people who buy the Audis the difference between the gas and the brake," Bradley sneered to a miserable Audi spokesman.

Nonetheless, Audi still had the temerity to insist that nothing whatsoever was wrong with its car. After investigating all critical engine components, electronic idle, cruise control, transmission, and other elements, along with the mysteriously failing brakes, it just couldn't find a thing. When "60 Minutes" had finished, the viewer was left with only one question: Are the people at Audi incompetent liars, or are they just incompetent fools?

In early 1987, Audi responded to NHTSA's request by recalling 250,000 1978–86 Audis.[21] The company installed a shift-lock device on the transmissions, which prevents them from moving out of park until the driver's foot is firmly on the brake. Accelerator and brake pedals were also moved farther apart. CAS derided what it called Audi's "fat foot theory," and scoffed at the suggestion that Audi drivers "are more inept than most."[22] Clarence Ditlow denounced Audi's recall. "If NHTSA allows Audi to do this, it's putting a seal of approval on a phony repair that will lead to the deaths of more Americans."[23] A few months later, NYPIRG published its own scientific rebuttal, neatly titled "Shifting the Blame."[24] Well, not quite "scientific." The report consists of a survey of 594 members of the Audi Victims Network, fewer than half of whom actually responded, together with NYPIRG's interpretation of 86 Audi accident files.[25] According to NYPIRG, 81 percent of these rocketing Audis experienced "total brake failure." In a phone survey of 35 Audi drivers, NYPIRG claimed to have found 33 who had experienced sudden acceleration in their vehicles.[26] NYPIRG also asked respondents (just for the record, of course) whether they were suing Audi, and whether they knew any members of Congress or the media "who would be interested in this issue."[27]

Apparently some did. After the "60 Minutes" segment aired, Congresswoman Barbara Boxer (D.-Cal.) circulated a "Dear Colleague" letter to House members, asking the Transportation Secretary to initiate a recall. Sixteen dear colleagues signed the NYPIRG report, which was then sent on to Transportation Secretary Dole along with further exhortations to recall the car. Meanwhile, *Road and Track* magazine dismissed the NYPIRG report as "statistical rubbish."[28]

THE BLUE KNIGHTS

And what do twelve stout citizens and true have to say about the Audi? It rather depends on which particular twelve. Far away from the courtroom, scientists were conducting careful, patient studies of the problem. But the courtroom proceedings took a different tack, more along the lines of how the kindergarten student determines the sex of a frog. "I wonder if it's a boy frog or a girl frog," muses one student. "I know how we can tell!" pipes up another. "All right, how?" asks the teacher, resigned to the worst. Beams the child: "We can *vote.*"

The first important victory for sudden-acceleration theory came, ironically, when William Rosenbluth was summoned by a *defendant.* At an outing of the "The Blue Knights" motorcycle club in Alaska, Wende Gatts climbed into her 1983 Audi 5000 and prepared to follow Darlene Norris's motorcycle out of the parking lot. After running Norris over (causing an estimated $300,000 in injuries and damage) and then "careening around the parking lot out of control," Gatts hit a mound of dirt and came to rest against a wood pile. Norris sued Gatts; Gatts replied that she wasn't to blame because her car accelerated uncontrollably and the brakes failed. A witness could not recall seeing the car's brake lights come on, however, and immediately after the accident the brakes were found to be working fine. William Rosenbluth was not deterred. Summoned by the defense, he pointed to complaints that had been filed against Audi with NHTSA, showed a videotape simulating a doctored Audi out of control, and opined that the throttle in Gatts's car had jammed at exactly the same instant that the car's brakes had temporarily failed. The jury apparently accepted every detail. Norris, the innocent motorcyclist who had been mowed down, was left to take care of her own expenses, and ordered to pay both Gatts's attorney fees ($46,500) and Rosenbluth's expert witness fees ($17,931). The Alaska Supreme Court affirmed.[29]

Rosenbluth's first clear-cut test sitting on the *plaintiff's* side of the courtroom came soon after, in the Bradosky trial of June 1988. The proceedings would be described as "a course in automotive design with heavy emphasis on electronic cruise-control components."[30] William Rosenbluth was again the star witness. Eleven other Audi owners testified for the Bradoskys, claiming that they too had been victims of sudden acceleration. But Audi, it turned out, had a stronger defense than one might have guessed from the television movie. To start with, a distraught Kristi Bradosky had told the police shortly after the accident that her foot had slipped off the car's brake onto the accelerator.[31] Audi demonstrated working models of the car's cruise control and related components. Tire marks on the floor of the Bradoskys' garage had been photographed and analyzed. The jurors trooped down to the courthouse garage, where Audi demonstrated that the car's brakes can easily overpower the engine and keep the vehicle from moving, no matter how fast the engine may be running.[32] After only about an hour of deliberation, the jury found for Audi on all counts.

The Audi Victims Network was stunned. "I don't know how the jury could come out with that decision based on the facts," exclaimed a spokeswoman. "How they could say that Audi has absolutely no guilt in this is incredible."[33]

NHTSA'S FINDINGS

There would be more Audi litigation to come—much more. As we shall see, a handful of other cases have already been decided, and many others are still pending. It's all marvelous theater. But is it sudden acceleration?

Far behind the legal lines, NHTSA engineers and their contractors meticulously examine 400 Audi complaints, 300 accident records, 175 injuries, and 4 deaths. In August 1986, after Audi had recalled cars to install the new shift-lock device, NHTSA decided to open a formal investigation. Three years later, after dozens of engineering amateurs, speculators, and witnesses put forward a shopping list of explanations ranging from the somewhat plausible to the utterly ridiculous, the NHTSA engineers would find nothing.

The Audi's idle stabilizer valve? "[A] 100 percent open stabilizer valve will only produce approximately 20 horsepower (one fifth of full throttle power) and that amount of power is not sufficient to produce the powerful acceleration which [has] occurred during most 'Sudden Acceleration' incidents." Nor is sufficient power controlled by any part of the engine that adjusts the air/fuel ratio, including the fuel meter and fuel injection computer. That ratio can affect engine power by no more than 5 percent, which is "not sufficient to cause 'Sudden Acceleration.'" How about ignition timing? The largest possible swing changes engine power by only 3 percent of open throttle, the equivalent of moving the accelerator pedal about a tenth of an inch. The transmission system? "The transmission by itself cannot accelerate a car because it only transmits whatever power is produced by the engine." Transmission fluid pressure is therefore "extremely unlikely to have caused 'Sudden Acceleration' incidents," at least, presumably, in cases where an expert witness with a tank of compressed gas was not seen running from the site of a mishap. Throttle linkage jammed by impacts or stones? Possible, but easy to detect after an accident—and never in fact detected. Throttle push rod crimp failures? Wiring harness snagged on the steering column? Gear selector/kickdown linkage interaction? Again, such defects are easily discovered after an accident and were never found.

Much attention is focused on the cruise control. A Swedish study has simulated a cruise control malfunction, but no U.S. car has ever exhibited similar damage to its system. Moreover, even if such a defect were present, a driver could still close the throttle by stepping on the brake pedal, which would immediately disconnect the cruise control. And the cruise control receives its electrical power from a switch that simply cannot be activated when the car is in reverse, as was the case in more than half of the reported sudden-acceleration incidents. Miscellaneous electrical problems? Yes, electric and radio fields might conceivably have interfered with the car's electronic devices, including the cruise control, but again, stepping on the brakes would instantly disconnect the cruise control; the deactivation is mechanically, not electronically, controlled. Moreover, tests with very high radio and electromagnetic signals never succeeded in opening the throttle. And most sudden-acceleration accidents occur in driveways near private homes, far from "radio or television transmitters, airport radars, or other powerful sources" of radio frequency interference. There is, finally, the simple, inescapable point that brakes are much stronger than accelerators. Whatever the electrical system, idle control, cruise control, engine, or transmission may be doing, if your foot is jammed on the brake and the brakes have not failed, the car just won't move.

So what *is* going on? People sometimes get their foot on the wrong pedal, that's what. "If a driver unknowingly steps on the accelerator pedal and continues to push on the same pedal because he or she believes it is the brake pedal," the car will accelerate and the brakes will seem to have failed. "[I]t is reasonable to expect that drivers would be more likely to step on the wrong pedal the first time after entering the car, or when their body is twisted out of normal position to look to the rear for backing up," which explains why most incidents occur in cars backing up from rest. In a number of cases NHTSA engineers found direct evidence that drivers had been stepping on the wrong pedal. They discovered one projecting part of the gas pedal broken off after some accidents, and they found electrical switches underneath the accelerators crushed by the desperate pressure of the driver's own foot. When Audi had recalled its cars and installed automatic shift locks, which force drivers to step on the brake when shifting out of park, there was "a substantial reduction" in incident reports.[34]

The CAS dismissed the entire NHTSA report as incompetent nonsense. CAS claimed to have received a hundred sudden-acceleration complaints for Audis *with* shift locks. As Clarence Ditlow would steadfastly maintain, "It is clear that sudden acceleration continues in those cars."[35] "Not only are the Audis flawed, but so is the government's investigation," another Ditlow commando declared. "The government has absolutely no proof that the accidents are caused by driver error and they are not aggressive enough to find the real defect."[36]

Governmental timidity apparently extended beyond U.S. borders. In December 1988, Transport Canada had released its sudden-acceleration study, which concluded: "The present study, and all others known to Transport Canada, confirm that sudden acceleration . . . occurs as a result of driver error."[37] The

Japanese Ministry of Transportation released its final report in April 1989. After analyzing 1,108 sudden-acceleration incidents and performing experiments on fifteen different cars, the ministry came to exactly the same conclusion: no defect in the car causes both high engine power and loss of brake effectiveness.

Sudden acceleration, in short, was a problem of lawyers, not of cars.

THE HEADLINES THAT WEREN'T

Ed Bradley had been utterly refuted. Sudden acceleration was exactly what Audi had said all along: a foot on the accelerator. Three independent government investigations had all confirmed what Bradley, Ditlow, Weinstein, miscellaneous members of Congress, and others had all stridently denied. Sometimes drivers place a foot on the wrong pedal. "CASE CLOSED," trumpeted Audi's full-page newspaper ads after NHTSA released its report.[38]

A marvel of the U.S. legal system, however, is that pseudo-scientific cases are never closed. As the comedienne Gilda Radner used to say, it's always something. "The case is not closed," declared Robert Lisco, the lawyer who had filed the class action against Audi. "Those guys must be smoking something."[39] Lisco then rushed to court and attacked Audi's ads as an unauthorized attempt to dissuade Audi owners from joining Lisco's class.[40] What class? None had yet been formally certified in court. "[W]ho would I send the notices out to?" inquired Cook County Circuit Judge Thomas R. Rackowski. But some prospective clients were confused by the advertising, complained Lisco. "I am sure there are a lot of class members that would be confused by next to anything," snapped the judge. In any event, Judge Rackowski concluded, "I don't think [the ad is] misleading."[41]

Ditlow, more royalist than the king, would continue to insist that sudden acceleration was a diabolical (though as yet unexplained) engineering mystery. Most plaintiffs' lawyers had more sense. Indeed, they had understood from the beginning that being persistent mattered more than being consistent. In litigation you win some, you lose some, the profit's in the volume, and the key is to keep on plugging.

In March 1988, well before NHTSA's report, lawyers had already tried the case of Germaine Gibbs and her three children, whose home was unexpectedly visited by Harold Horowitz in his '79 Audi. The car had penetrated the apartment building's wall, showering bricks everywhere. Horowitz admitted that he had put his foot at least partly on the wrong pedal. So James Hely, the Gibbses' lawyer, argued that "[t]he pedals are arranged close enough that the accelerator often is applied when a driver attempts to brake."[42] A big score was unlikely because no one was badly hurt, but it happened to be Hely's lucky day: the jury agreed that Audi had put its pedals where Horowitz's foot wanted to land. The jury found only $14,000 in actual injury to the Gibbses, but settled on a round $100,000 in punitive damages.[43]

And thus, from the P.R. mists of the convoluted theories of pressure buildup in the transmission, idle stabilizers gone haywire, cruise controllers with malignant minds of their own, out of this Stephen King miasma of the incredible and the insubstantial, and notwithstanding all the people who vehemently swore they had a foot firmly on the brake, the trial bar arrived at a new, winning theory for what was *really* wrong with the Audi: its pedals were in the wrong place.

William Rosenbluth had also been scheduled to testify for Diane Rose, the California woman seriously injured when she ran her Audi into a planter. But after Rosenbluth's repudiation in the *Bradosky* trial, Rose's lawyer quickly decided not to rely on his theories. Indeed, he dropped the sudden-acceleration theory altogether. *Gibbs* had already established that clumsy-foot cases were winnable. An expert was located to testify that the Audi pedals were defectively designed, as a result of which Rose must have pressed the wrong one. Rose didn't remember a thing, and no one had seen the crash. But what else could explain the accident? Well, come to think of it, quite a few things. Audi's view of the accident was that Rose had accidentally drifted into a catch basin on the right side of the road, then swung too sharply across the street as she pulled out of it. The Los Angeles jury, however, didn't see it that way. On July 11, 1988, it awarded Rose just under $3 million, and her husband another $700,000 for loss of her companionship and such.[44] The verdict "comes one step closer to holding Audi ultimately responsible for the sudden-acceleration phenomenon," declared Jeff Schroeder of the CAS.[45] It hardly mattered that the theory now winning in court was pretty much what used to be Audi's defense—what CAS had derided earlier as the "fat foot" theory.

When the NHTSA report finally appeared in 1989, it left the lawyers just enough room to keep on plugging. Unwilling to have any impact on litigation whatsoever, and in contrast to its blunter counterpart in Canada, NHTSA shied away from calling anything "driver error." "[T]he term 'pedal misapplications' is more appropriate," NHTSA stated, "because the design and performance of the vehicle, and not only the driver, can be a significant factor contributing towards the wrong pedal being applied." This is not to say that Audi's pedals were positioned worse than anyone else's. To the contrary, NHTSA allowed that the Audi pedal design might even be *safer*. The pedal placement question, profoundly subjective in any event, simply wasn't (and perhaps couldn't be) resolved. At least not by NHTSA. *Car and Driver* described NHTSA's "pedal misapplication" as a "candy-coat[ed]" euphemism that provides "exactly the sort of opening that incompetent drivers will exploit to keep the controversy alive until somebody finally pays them to shut up."[46]

The cheerleaders rejoiced again—not at *Car and Driver*, of course, but at the opportunity left open by NHTSA. A lawyer for AVN promptly announced that the NHTSA report had strengthened his clients' cases: "It establishes there are design and manufacturing defects in the Audi 5000 and that there are a number of different problems that led to unintended acceleration."[47]

Meanwhile, the Audi lawyers plodded along defending their beleaguered client. Marie Ruston, the woman injured by a runaway Audi in a drive-through bank line, had her claim tried early in 1988. The jury exonerated the driver (who had failed to respond to the Audi recall that would have installed a transmission shift interlock), attributing the accident to Audi's "faulty transmission." Judge Matthew Coppola threw out the verdict and ordered a new trial. The case was then settled.[48] In June 1990, one of Alice Weinstein's four lawsuits was thrown out of federal court because of her persistent refusal to obey court orders.[49] Another trial judge threw out her state claims and entered a $20,000 judgment *against* Weinstein on the defendants' counterclaim for frivolous litigation. But that, according to Weinstein, "had absolutely nothing to do with the problems of the car or merits of the case."[50] As of early 1991, that award was still under appeal. In two other cases put to juries, negligent drivers attempted to shift the blame to their Audis; both juries agreed that the cars were not at fault.[51] Frances Martin, who had driven her Audi into a hospital parking lot embankment, now ran into other problems. It was her boss's car, and her boss had sold it. No expert had ever even examined it. No car? No expert? No case, the trial judge ruled.

An indifferent record for plaintiffs, one might think, but lawyers tend to be irrepressible optimists in these matters. By mid-1988, on the basis of *Rose, Bradosky, Gibbs,* and *Ruston,* the *National Law Journal* was reporting the record as one of "mixed signals" on unintended acceleration. The CAS proclaimed the results "3 to 1 for plaintiffs." "The word on the street," CAS exulted, "is that now Audi is settling a very substantial number [of cases] as confidentially as possible."[52] Lawyers were urged to file still more claims.

And still pending was Robert Lisco's huge, 350,000-member class action. Seeing the relentless publicity drag down its business, Audi offered to settle the suit by giving owners of its cars credits ranging from $300 to $2,000 toward the purchase of a new Audi. The lead plaintiffs' lawyers (who stood to collect a large fee in any settlement) urged acceptance of the offer, now conceding that they had been quite unable to find any defect in the car.[53] Indeed, the proposed settlement agreement was to declare *expressly* that the Audi was *not* defective.[54] A poll of Audi owners indicated they would accept the deal, and the trial judge gave preliminary approval. The CAS, AVN, and NY-PIRG objected hysterically.[55] The case was transferred to another judge, who overturned the settlement.[56] Audi then opted to go to trial. As of this writing the suit is still unresolved. Elsewhere, at least 144 other sudden-acceleration lawsuits are still pending.[57]

By 1989, however, media coverage had at last begun to swing in Audi's favor. "If ESPN ever tired of tractor pulls," suggested a piece in the *Chicago Tribune*, "the cable sports channel could substitute a nightly Sudden Acceleration Derby with randomly picked citizens, a fleet of Audi 5000s and stands filled with personal injury attorneys."[58] P. J. O'Rourke, in "The Sudden Acceleration Media Hack and Liability Lawyers Bottom-Feeder Tournament," sympathetically described sudden acceleration as a "mysterious phenomenon in which a short, silly, middle-aged woman with a lawyer gets into an Audi 5000 and—all of a sudden, for no apparent reason—goes through the back wall of her garage and onto the CBS '60 Minutes' television program."[59] *Car and Driver* begged to differ with NHTSA's suggestion that even the "most attentive" driver might put his foot on the wrong pedal, now and again.

Only a nitwit (or a government agency) would make such a statement. . . . Some of the unintended-acceleration incidents go on for more than a hundred feet before the wreckage is complete and total. These are not the most attentive drivers. These are dimly aware humans who normally operate in borderline control of their cars. . . . [L]et's not compound the problem by allowing that they might be the most attentive drivers. By definition, they aren't.[60]

And what did "60 Minutes" have to say about all this? Did it retract, recant, and apologize to Audi? Did it run a segment on how veteran media types are sometimes spoon-fed and bamboozled by glib plaintiffs' lawyers? Not exactly. After airing the briefest imaginable follow-up comment on the NHTSA report, it then reran the original, devastating clips.

UNSAFE AT ANY SPEED

What exactly did sudden acceleration—of the kind supplied by "60 Minutes" and plaintiffs' lawyers—achieve? Audi, followed by many other manufacturers, introduced an idiot-proof transmission shift lock, which by NHTSA's assessment did save a detectable number of inexpert drivers from fat-foot accidents. This was progress, even if it was denounced as useless and irrelevant by CAS and the sudden-acceleration faithful.

As for pedals, no one to this day knows just what pedal design is safest. The brake and accelerator pedals in the Audi 5000, like those in some other European cars, were slightly closer together than those in many American designs. This arrangement allows all drivers, good and bad, to move their feet faster between the pedals in a high-speed emergency. Perhaps the arrangement also makes it easier for the bad driver to mix up the pedals when starting from rest. As NHTSA concluded, "[c]ontrol pedal location and feel is a complex issue and considerations unrelated to 'Sudden Acceleration' are also involved." Changing the brake pedal's position might "increase the number and severity of other accidents by increasing brake reaction time," or might "affect the performance of the braking system and the ability of drivers to accurately control the brakes to avoid skidding on slippery surfaces." What is known is that only a tiny fraction of drivers make fat-foot mistakes, whereas virtually all drivers "will require the best braking performance possible during several occasions in the life of the vehicle."[61]

What is also known is that the Audi 5000 had one of the lowest fatality rates of any car on the market, according to the Insurance Institute for Highway Safety.[62] NHTSA's Fatal Accident Reporting System statistics likewise place the 1978–85 Audi 5000 among cars having the very lowest fatality rates on the road.[63] NHTSA's New Car Assessment Program subjected the 1989 Audi 100, the Audi 5000's direct successor, to the agency's standard crash tests; it performed better than any other car then sold in the United States.[64]

So at the end of the Audi story, only a few numbers remain utterly beyond dispute. Audi lost a few cases and paid millions in damages and settlements. Its sales plummeted, from a peak of 73,000 cars in 1985 to 23,000 in 1988.[65] Where did the 50,000 lost buyers choose to shop instead? Wherever it was, they very likely ended up in less safe cars.

CHAPTER 5

Gadgets and Knives
Cashing In on Magical Cures

In lingering labours when the head of the child hath been in the pelvis, so that the bones ride over one another, and the shape is preternaturally lengthened, the brain is frequently so much compressed that violent convulsions ensue before or soon after delivery to the danger, and oft-times the destruction of the child. —W. Smellie
Treatise On The Theory And Practice Of Midwifery (1774)

Alena D. weighed in at two pounds, nine ounces, when she was born in a breech delivery, ten weeks premature, on June 14, 1978. By her sixth birthday she weighed only thirty-one pounds. She could not walk, crawl, or even raise her head for more than a few seconds without help. Every joint in her body had to be massaged daily to prevent stiffening. She seemed destined to remain incontinent and wheelchair-bound for life. Alena suffered the devastating effects of severe cerebral palsy.

Her parents sued the Medical College of Pennsylvania and three doctors who had assisted in the complicated delivery. A breech birth and improper oxygen levels, the lawyers contended, had caused her injuries. They demanded $5 million in compensation.[1] The doctors answered that they had done everything in their power to help the child. The trial, before a Delaware County jury, lasted a month. When the jury retired to deliberate, the defendants offered Alena's parents $2.2 million in settlement. The offer was refused. Hours later the jury returned a verdict for the defense; Alena would get nothing at all.

Births like Alena's, though profoundly upsetting and never expected, are also, paradoxically, a routine part of the human condition: at least four thousand children are born with cerebral palsy every year.[2] What causes the affliction? Is it acquired at birth, or is that just when it is first revealed? These questions have long been the subject of scientific speculation. Two centuries ago Smellie, a leading English physician of his day, attributed afflictions like cerebral palsy to the violence of labor.[3] In 1861, William John Little, an orthopedic surgeon, likewise concluded that cerebral palsy was caused primarily by trauma and other stresses during labor and delivery.[4] Others would later maintain that "adverse events during labor and delivery, particularly asphyxia and difficult birth" were the main cause.[5]

For over a century many physicians agreed that delivery was "an especially treacherous time for the fetus."[6] In 1951, two eminent physicians suggested that complications in delivery could lead to a range of brain injuries, the most serious of them causing a child to be stillborn, the somewhat less serious resulting in such things as cerebral palsy.[7] Trauma could cause birth defects like cerebral palsy, just as it could cause cancer. It seemed plausible enough.

IN PURSUIT

For personal-injury lawyers, tragedy always means opportunity. A lifetime of institutional care is shockingly expensive; if there is talk of legal damages, negotiations are likely to begin at $1 million and go up from there. Everyone on the scene, in both clinic and court, will naturally be overwhelmed with sympathy for the child and family. Modern medical science compounds the problem by reason of its very successes: obstetricians have become so skilled at saving babies that their failures are all the harder to accept.

Beginning in the 1970s and accelerating through the 1980s, plaintiffs' lawyers took after cerebral palsy in hot pursuit. They relied on two distinct branches of the birth-trauma theory. Some, adopting the eighteenth-century theory, emphasized physical trauma during delivery. The baby must have been delivered too violently, the violence had stressed the child's skull, and everyone knows that head injuries can cause brain injury. Others emphasized asphyxia. The baby must have been delivered too slowly, the delay had caused suffocation, and everyone knows that lack of oxygen can harm the brain.

The details, of course, varied from case to case. One mother successfully attributed her son's cerebral palsy to trauma caused by her fall at work shortly before his birth.[8] Forceps, when they were still widely used, proved to be an especially popular target, as did drugs like Pitocin, which is used to stimulate labor. One claimant recovered $7.5 million on the theory that Pitocin caused unusually strong contractions, which were said to have injured the infant's brain.[9] Asphyxia claims generally involved diametrically opposite charges, emphasizing not the abrupt violence of the birth but rather its unaccountable slowness. The infant's umbilical cord became compressed. Or the placenta was detached or deteriorating. Or anesthetics administered to relieve the mother's pain had prolonged labor. One way or another, the birth was either too quick (and concomitantly violent) or too leisurely (and therefore suffocating).

The courtroom timing standards for delivering babies became exquisitely fine. One doctor was blamed for failing to induce labor, as was a second, but a third was blamed for inducing premature labor, as was a fourth. One doctor was faulted for using labor-stimulating Pitocin when it supposedly wasn't needed; another for failing to perform a cesarean when Pitocin was used; and yet another for administering Pitocin early in labor but then administering an anesthetic, which tends to counteract Pitocin's effect.[10] Why, after all, would a doctor waste time relieving someone in pain when there is a baby to deliver?

While few obstetricians cheered the lawyers on, many were inclined to agree that cerebral palsy might well be something they could beat, given enough information and skill at the time of delivery. Many—perhaps the best ones most especially—craved better understanding of how medicine itself might sometimes be the cause of great harm. What doctors needed, or so some sincerely believed, was a better way to detect signs of trouble during delivery before trouble turned into disaster.

In 1972, the electronic fetal monitor arrived on the medical scene. Electronic fetal monitoring (EFM) uses a sensor inside or outside the uterus to trace out the infant's heartbeat and the mother's contractions throughout labor, recording both on a long paper chart. Many doctors welcomed EFM with high optimism, as "a medical breakthrough that could reduce the incidence of cerebral palsy, stillbirth and infant death."[11] "[H]opeful that closer surveillance of labor would lower the number of handicapped infants," obstetricians hailed EFM and extolled its virtues in respected medical journals.[12] By reading the heart monitors, doctors would be able tell when an infant was in "distress." When it was, they would perform cesarean sections, thus preventing trauma or suffocation. One way or another, doctors would intervene promptly. Two pieces of fairly simple technology, a monitor and a scalpel, would finally put an end to the tragedy of cerebral palsy.

Optimism ran so high that EFM became widely used before anyone set about methodically testing its efficacy.[13] By the end of 1972, more than one thousand EFM systems were in use in the United States. Five years later, over 70 percent of physicians believed that births should be electronically monitored. By 1986, 75 percent in fact were. There appeared "numerous reports indicating that electronically monitored fetuses did much better than those undergoing [manual monitoring] during birth."[14] These reports, however, were entirely anecdotal, a grab bag of impression, hunch, and hope.

If EFM raised the hopes of doctors in the delivery room, it most assuredly raised the hopes of lawyers in the courtroom. Before EFM, obstetricians had monitored fetal distress with a stethoscope. In court a year or two after a child had been delivered, all the speculation in the world from the plaintiff's expert witness might be countered by the defending doctor's simple, confident recollection that there had been no evident fetal distress, and therefore no cause either to slow or to accelerate delivery. EFM changed everything: it supplied a paper chart for the record. After-the-fact speculation could now focus on something much more concrete than the obstetrician's own, undoubtedly self-serving recollections. Another doctor could now deliver the baby a second time, in court. More successfully, of course.

In increasing numbers, juries began to be persuaded that cerebral palsy might well have been averted if only the obstetrician had properly used or understood the EFM trace.[15] The rural hospital (for example) didn't even own a $10,000 fetal monitor; that must explain the child's cerebral palsy. Or perhaps the problem was a monitor that was misused or malfunctioning. Had EFM been properly conducted, and the results correctly interpreted, a competent obstetrician would of course have hustled the mother into the delivery room and grabbed a knife.[16] There is no disputing that a good surgeon with a sharp knife can do in a matter of minutes what the most athletic woman's abdominal and uterine muscles normally require hours to complete. If a cesarean was performed, it should have been performed sooner.[17] The stories hadn't much changed, but the reams of new paper could now make them seem much more immediate and plausible.

On one significant count, however, the doctors' early enthusiasm for EFM diverged sharply from the lawyers'. EFM, it soon became apparent, was imprecise. "Fetal distress" is itself a fuzzy term, if only because some quite variable degree of distress is normal when undergoing the first and most traumatic of all partings in the human experience. Nature seems to have deliberately designed the hydraulics to be stressful, partly to allow the infant as long a time as possible in the shelter of the womb, partly to help clear the infant's lungs when time finally runs out. In any event, obstetricians often disagreed on just what EFM recordings meant.[18] For obvious reasons, this unsettled the doctors. For reasons equally obvious, it delighted the lawyers.

It turned out that the lawyers, and the doctors they were able to hire, had much less trouble reading EFM charts than did doctors generally. "It's unbelievable—it's so clear-cut," exclaimed one "ecstatic" lawyer when he first got hold of Alissa G.'s medical records.[19] Ten days after her due date, Alissa's mother had gone in for a first EFM trace. Labor began the next day, prompting a second trip to the hospital, a second EFM trace, and a second return home to wait for further dilation. On the third visit, Alissa was born, apparently without complication, but with cerebral palsy. The lawyer, in contrast to the several doctors who had attended Alissa's mother before and during delivery, immediately discerned "[s]ome irregularity" in the first EFM trace and plain signs of "distress" in the second. Best of all, the first trace had been recorded by a doctor inexperienced in using the monitor. Delayed labor (the plaintiffs would claim) had allowed disintegration of the placenta, causing oxygen deprivation. Competently interpreted EFM would have led to induced labor or a cesarean, and Alissa would be a normal child today. The insurance companies settled for $2.5 million.[20]

Such formulas could be rolled out a thousand times. "Fetal distress" was staring the attending physician in the face, yet she missed it all. The doctors and nurses "failed to interpret fetal monitor readings showing the fetus in distress"; or failed "to accurately analyze and act upon warning signs indicated by the fetal heart tone monitor"; or overlooked significant distress for an hour and a half during labor; or failed "to properly read a fetal heart monitor during the six hours of labor"; or "failed to notice a fetal heart monitor . . . showed the unborn infant was not getting an adequate oxygen supply."[21] The doctor on the witness stand understands the critically fine variables at work far better than did the doctor who actually delivered the baby. Just a wee bit faster with the knife, or easier on the forceps, or lighter (or heavier) on the Pitocin or the labor-slowing anesthetic, and things would undoubtedly have worked out better. The beauty of selling techno-magic elixirs in court is that no one even has to produce the bottle for close examination. An earlier cesarean would have done the trick. How much earlier? Well, earlier. EFM would have revealed fetal distress. And just what is distress? Well, a good doctor like me knows it when she sees it.

Today, this line of attack has become one of the most spectacularly lucrative enterprises known to lawyers, quite possibly the single largest revenue raiser in all of medical malpractice. About four million babies are born healthy every year. Ignore them. Some four thousand babies a year are born with cerebral palsy. Ignore most of them too. But four hundred (say) of those had a complicated delivery. These are the cases most likely to arrive in court. And there, the facts are reviewed chronologically, so that the jury sees the undisputed trauma first, the disputed negligence second, the undisputed cerebral palsy third. It is a perfect setup for misinterpreting sequence as cause. Litigated a mere forty times with a one-in-two success rate, that setup can yield a small law firm $50 million or so, on an upfront investment for expert witness fees and administrative costs of maybe $5 million at most.

The promise of such profit inevitably attracts some shady characters. One former New York lawyer confessed in grand jury proceedings that he had earned $1.5 million selling about one hundred cerebral palsy cases to other New York firms between 1979 and 1982. How had he come to own them in the first place? He bought them from staff employees at cerebral palsy rehabilitation centers, who at $2,000 a shot turned over confidential files of patients who were then solicited to bring malpractice suits. Twenty-one New York law firms were named as buyers of the information.[22] Another part of this brokering service involved prepping compliant expert witnesses, who were normally paid $5,000 a case. This story may be atypically sordid, but the general method is standard. First, a victim is located, then the lawyer and a well-paid expert root about for a cause plausible enough to pitch to a jury.

In every lawsuit the stakes are huge and the outcome highly unpredictable. Alena D.'s distraught parents turned down $2 million that was there for the taking. The insurance company almost gave away what was theirs to keep. An expert once suggested that the classification of "low-risk" pregnancies is best made "by exclusion, three months after birth."[23] He might more accurately have said three *years* later, just minutes after the jury returns to the courtroom. Few smart players on either side of the aisle dare to wait quite so long, which is why many cerebral palsy cases are settled on the eve of trial. Defendants fear runaway sympathy. Plaintiffs fear plodding science. No one knows which will carry the day's jury, and often the uncertainty is simply more than either side can stand.

The trial, for the defendant who dares wait for it, proceeds like a techno-thriller. There is a rich veneer of pseudoscientific detail over trauma and oxygen levels, monitors, labor-enhancing drugs, and labor-slowing anesthetics. The gadgets and props all heighten the tension that something very high-tech is about to go horribly wrong. The detail can be gripping. *Let me take you back to the delivery room, ladies and gentlemen. The mother is exhausted. EFM reveals an infant in distress. And yet the doctor doesn't act. Look! A child's brain is disintegrating before your eyes! Do something!* A good lawyer can direct this kind of production like a Hitchcock horror flick, with all the agonizing suspense of a murderer, knife in hand, creeping up on the unsuspecting young woman in the shower. The only difference is that in cerebral palsy cases the trick is to get the audience to scream for more knife rather than less. Many audiences do indeed scream. But the scientific story is about as real as celluloid.

LOCATING A CAUSE

"The anomaly of the birth process, rather than being the causal etiologic factor, may itself be the consequence of the real prenatal etiology."[24] Sigmund Freud, a neurologist in his first career, wrote those words about cerebral palsy in 1897. Almost a century later, they still accurately summarize the best medical guess we have.

Most cerebral palsy babies, it in fact appears, are doomed long before an obstetrician comes near them. More than half who display at least one sign of asphyxia at birth also exhibit some more important risk factor, like congenital malformation, low birth weight, or microcephaly—problems completely beyond the control of obstetrical science today. We know this from (among numerous other scientifically solid sources) a major epidemiological study by the National Institutes of Health, published in the *New England Journal of Medicine* in July 1986.[25] That study, the largest ever of its kind, surveyed some

54,000 pregnancies at twelve hospitals between 1959 and 1966. The results of a study this size are about as solid and certain as medical science can supply.

So, is the baby who has been pummeled about the head with forceps, or expelled from the womb with undue force, more likely to be afflicted with cerebral palsy? Generations of doctors have subscribed to the theory. Generations of doctors have been wrong. Forceps, rough delivery, trauma of any kind at birth, just don't cause cerebral palsy in any significant degree. Breech delivery, which commonly involves a pretty violent exit if a cesarean is not performed, hardly correlates with cerebral palsy at all. (Breech *positioning is* associated with fetal problems, but is not a matter under the obstetrician's control.)

What about oxygen? Yes, it is possible for asphyxia to cause cerebral palsy, but only if the asphyxia is exceptionally severe and prolonged. Newborn mammals have an astonishing resilience to oxygen deprivation; a newborn's fetal hemoglobin allows it to survive much more severe oxygen shortages than it will be able to tolerate even a few weeks after birth. In fact, only oxygen deprivation at virtually lethal levels will produce severe brain damage in a newborn;[26] most newborn infants subjected even to severe, prolonged asphyxia recover and suffer little or no neurological damage.[27] So asphyxia does not explain any significant fraction of cerebral palsy infants. Neither does the duration of labor, low placental weight, or a low fetal heart rate—the one thing EFM may help flag.

What, then, *are* the important causes of cerebral palsy? No one knows. Prematurity does not correlate significantly with it. Nor even does drug use by mothers, or family history. Genetic makeup may be a factor. Chronic fetal distress—not during delivery but sustained throughout pregnancy—may be a symptom of trouble, though not characterizable as a cause. Somewhat more important is a mother's history of seizures. The "single most prominent predictor of cerebral palsy," epidemiological studies reveal, is mental retardation in the mother. But no single factor plays a role significant enough to suggest it as *the cause* of the disease. And no factor related to labor and delivery is associated with more than 2 percent of the risk.[28] Cerebral palsy risk factors usually overlap, making it all but impossible to say which (if any) are causes, which are merely effects. In short, "[t]he evidence is very convincing that complications during labor and delivery are not responsible for the meaningful proportion of cases of cerebral palsy."[29] "We probably do not know what causes most cases."[30]

The best *guess* we have today is that cerebral palsy is almost always caused by events that began long before delivery.[31] In 1986, a noted pathologist suggested that oxygen deprivation plays an important role only when it occurs in the late second or early third trimester.[32] Other researchers surmise that a chronically pinched umbilical cord during pregnancy may be important.[33] Still others point to fetal infections and placental problems early in pregnancy.[34] Congenital or early-pregnancy factors may, of course, produce a host of problems later on, problems that first become evident at the time of delivery. Low birth weight correlates with cerebral palsy, but might reflect placental problems months earlier. Oxygen deficiency may likewise be a reflection of earlier problems.

If causes at the time of delivery have little or no effect on the risk, and we do not know where the main causes lie, obstetricians cannot prevent cerebral palsy. One would never know it from reading about the lawsuits, but the scientific consensus on that point is now quite solid. One medical study after the next has reached the same conclusion: "no foreseeable single intervention is likely to prevent a large proportion of cerebral palsy";[35] it is "naive . . . to assume that cerebral palsy derives from a single cause, or that it is amenable to a single form of intervention";[36] blaming events that occur during delivery reflects a "common failure to look behind the events of birth to the causes of those events."[37]

So how can electronic fetal monitoring prevent cerebral palsy? It can't.[38] Indeed, EFM is such an imprecise tool that it can't do much of anything, except serve as a cost-saving substitute for direct human supervision by doctors and nurses armed with stethoscopes. In one revealing study, twelve national EFM experts interpreted fourteen abnormal heart patterns. On average, two physicians disagreed one-third of the time in classifying the patterns as "innocuous," "nonreassuring," or "ominous," and disagreed with almost the same frequency about whether to continue monitoring or to deliver immediately.[39] Supplementing EFM with results from fetal scalp blood sampling *increased* the levels of disagreement. All this among the nation's top EFM experts; a much wider range of disagreement could be expected among obstetricians drawn at random. Small wonder, then, that EFM provides no measurable bottom-line benefits. As early as 1976, a team of researchers found that EFM was no better than stethoscope monitoring.[40] Since then, nine randomized clinical trials have been performed in Australia, Denmark, Ireland, Scotland, and the United States. Not one has found that EFM benefits infants,[41] not even in "high-risk" deliveries.[42] As a report by the Institute of Medicine concluded in 1989, "[t]he incidence of cerebral palsy, still popularly and erroneously believed by many to be the result of fetal asphyxia, has not been reduced by EFM."[43]

The crowning blow came in March 1990, when American and Canadian researchers released the results of the latest and largest EFM study, based on six years of data. Not only did EFM fail to improve premature infants' neurological development, but "in most comparisons the results of [stethoscope monitoring] . . . were actually superior." Infants monitored with a stethoscope performed consistently higher on mental and psychomotor development tests than EFM infants, and their births on average took less time than electronically monitored births. Astoundingly, one group of EFM children ran a 2.9 times *greater* risk of developing cerebral palsy than stethoscope-monitored children.[44] That number, however, is in all likelihood a pure statistical fluke.

So the vaunted fetal monitor, the first card, the trump card, quite often the *only* card, in the cerebral palsy litigation deck, is a joker. It delivers wonderful results for lawyers, but not for anyone else. The wonder is that some trial lawyer isn't now waving the Canadian-American study under the noses of some jury, demanding to know why this brain-destroying EFM technology had ever been allowed near the unfortunate child.

DANGEROUS THERAPIES

While it is inconceivable that EFM directly causes cerebral palsy, it is more than conceivable that the indiscriminate use of EFM impelled by litigation has caused much real harm. EFM tends to flag problems that aren't. Fear of liability then induces drastic intervention that does no good except in court. Many doctors have proved quite willing to be so induced. With a cesarean, after all, the mother is quiet, the baby is lifted quickly through a large passage rather than extruded slowly through a small one; all in all, from the right side of the knife, it really does look more genteel and efficient. Unsurprisingly, then, the rise of EFM has been accompanied by a dramatic increase in the rate of cesareans.[45] Cesarean delivery accounted for 5 percent of all deliveries in 1970; today, the United States has the highest cesarean rate in the world, about 25 percent of all births. A cherished if medically dubious rule of thumb also used to maintain that "once a cesarean, always a cesarean," so (for a time) many of the cesarean child's younger siblings were delivered by knife too.

And what of it? To begin with, cesareans are twice as expensive as normal deliveries, and now cost $3 billion a year. Infants born by cesarean generally score lower on postnatal tests; vaginal delivery may, in fact, help clear lungs and stimulate breathing. And cesareans pose real risks to the mother. A cesarean birth—which is, of course, serious abdominal surgery—is two to four times more likely to kill the mother. Even in the best of circumstances, the cesarean mother endures an unnecessarily alienating birth experience, a longer and more painful recuperation, and perhaps also suffers psychologically for her apparent failure of performance. Fearful of lawsuits if they don't intervene, some doctors have even begun to seek court orders to force cesareans on unwilling mothers carrying infants judged to be "in distress."[46]

If plaintiffs' lawyers have willingly (and very profitably) become parties to this injustice, so have quite a few doctors retained as expert witnesses. Some testify for the same financial reasons as the lawyers; far more testify in the sincere but mistaken belief that they know more than they really do. Is this to say that many doctors are bad scientists? So phrased, the question is misleading: most doctors are not scientists at all, but practitioners. And while the good ones learn from science, stay abreast of its developments, and maintain a strong faith in the scientific method, some less good ones don't. Like all other clinicians, obstetricians are constantly exposed to biased evidence that encourages false inference. Many are seduced, some so completely that they are then willing to testify under oath to all sorts of things. Heroic rescues are always easy to imagine. Things that exist only in the imagination can never, of course, be definitively disproved.

EFM makes the imagining all the more vivid. It offers doctors a psychological crutch, a pseudoscientific anchor in a turbulent sea of biological uncertainty, the appearance of control but not the actuality. The mainstream of the profession itself has recognized as much. In January 1988, a committee of the American College of Obstetricians and Gynecologists (ACOG) recommended altering its long-standing policy in favor of EFM for patients.[47] Low-risk patients could be monitored by stethoscope, while high-risk patients could be monitored by EFM, stethoscope, or a combination of both.[48] So far as medical science was concerned, the EFM saga was over.

Today, most obstetricians are well aware of this. But few dare take the lead in changing their ways. Why should they? Lawyers have discovered in EFM the perfect technological wand to wave before juries. For all practical purposes, EFM has become the legally established standard for prudent care. Even most of the ACOG panel members conceded they would continue using EFM themselves. As the Institute of Medicine tersely noted, "the current professional liability climate supports the continued use of EFM, despite overwhelming evidence that it does not improve neonatal mortality and morbidity rates."[49] What holds for EFM holds even more for cesareans. The woman given an unnecessary cesarean and delivered of a healthy baby is unlikely to sue. The "maximin strategy"[50]—which focuses obsessively on the worst possible outcome and relies on the most extreme and interventionist (though ineffectual) methods in an attempt to prevent it—has become the only legally safe course in modern obstetrics.

Yes, once in a great number of times there really may be a case where a cesarean might help prevent cerebral palsy, or an obstetrician's incompetence contribute to causing it. Perhaps some small fraction of that small fraction of deliveries produces a lawsuit that culminates in a well-deserved settlement or verdict. But for every such case, there are dozens of baseless shakedowns. This statement can be made with high confidence, given the current state of medical science. We know there are many thousands of new cases of cerebral palsy a year. Exact numbers are impossible to come by, but only a tiny fraction of those culminate in successful lawsuits. There is no evidence—none whatsoever—that the cases that come to court have lined up at all consistently with cerebral palsy–causing malpractice beforehand.

This is, indeed, the part of the story that jurists and legal academics have most inexcusably neglected to track. Obstetricians have capitulated to virtually every demand of the modern legal system. Birth trauma now occurs far less frequently than it used to.[51] Forceps have almost disappeared. EFM, unknown in 1970, is now used in at least three-quarters of all deliveries. Cesarean deliveries have increased fivefold. After two decades of high-priced help from their ranks, we may now ask the lawyers: Just what have you achieved on the cerebral palsy front?

If the lawyers had been right, the cerebral palsy problem should by now be abating, and with it the lawsuits. Nothing of the sort has happened. With one modest exception unrelated to litigation the cause and prevention of cerebral palsy remain mysterious.* Cerebral palsy is as common as ever,[52] perhaps even slightly more common as more babies who would once have died now survive.[53] There certainly is no firm evidence of any appreciable decrease in cerebral palsy in the past forty

---

*Some modest progress did come from the virtual elimination of one source of athetoid cerebral palsy, hyperbilirubinemia, caused by blood incompatibility between mother and infant or by newborn jaundice. Doctors now have effective means for dealing with these problems that they lacked thirty years ago.

years.[54] And though they are sued vastly more often, there is no evidence whatsoever that American obstetricians are performing any better than their foreign counterparts in other industrialized countries.

DON'T JUST DO SOMETHING

American lawyers engaged in this kind of litigation, by contrast, perform better than lawyers anywhere else in the world. Invoking a simple gadget and a sharp knife, they have cashed in munificently on the cure half of scientific credulity. In an earlier day, the magic cures had to be sold to the patient himself, who might at least pause as he reached into his own pocket to pay for the elixir. Juries reach elsewhere, which may explain in part why selling such cures in court has proved vastly more remunerative.

This is not to suggest that plaintiffs always win; they certainly don't. A few well-known jurisdictions are notoriously prone to handing out munificent verdicts in cerebral palsy cases, but many others hew more closely to the science.

After an eight-day trial ten years after the birth of one stillborn and one cerebral palsy twin, for example, both attending doctors were cleared by the jury.[55] A Michigan jury exonerated both the doctors and the hospital in a suit alleging failure to use EFM and undue delay in conducting a cesarean.[56] Another obstetrician won on summarily (that is, without the case even being put to the jury) against charges of undue delay in treating oxygen deprivation.[57] The defense won yet again in a case involving complicated labor and standard charges of fetal distress evident by EFM.[58] A New Mexico jury sided with the obstetrician and the manufacturer of Pitocin, rejecting charges that too-severe contractions cut off the infant's blood supply and that a cesarean was unduly delayed.[59]

But though defendants win a generous share of cases, the outcome is always hugely uncertain. Of course, the defending doctor may present the icy statistics in mind-numbing detail, lining up bean counters to testify that links between birth complication and cerebral palsy are almost unmeasurably weak. Of course he may summon top-flight members of the College of Obstetricians to declare that fetal monitors have proved completely ineffectual in preventing cerebral palsy. But testify as they will, the other side has the considerable psychological advantage of an incontinent child in a wheelchair. Yes, jurors, like scientists, may be able to sort out the facts notwithstanding sympathy, case-selection bias, and the powerful, intuitive instinct to view a vividly described sequence of events as cause and effect. But even trained scientists make the this-then-that mistake so often that they force themselves to follow elaborate, rigorous protocols to protect against it, and no such protocols must be followed by self-styled experts on the witness stand. The system is not inherently biased or unreasonable, but in practice it is just highly random. And when the stakes are so high, randomness is itself the epitome of injustice.

Sadly, there is still much that is random in reproduction and obstetrics too. The medical profession has never been omniscient, nor is it ever likely to be. Doctors made their share of mistakes in their overly hopeful pursuit of the causes of cerebral palsy. The legal system, however, positively distorted the science, and has made the mistakes all but impossible to correct. Far from accelerating the shift to better medicine, litigation has frozen in place an unhelpful techno-fix and contributed to the dis-education of medical practitioners. There is little doubt that the cumulative costs of this misdirected litigation are now measured in lost lives.

The serious pursuit of better medicine—which is to say, its pursuit outside the courtroom—now emphasizes less intervention, not more. "Don't just do something—stand there!" runs the new aphorism for obstetricians at Mt. Sinai Hospital in Chicago.[60] Is this insanity? Only so far as your legal adviser is concerned. From all other perspectives, it's better medicine. As documented in the *New England Journal of Medicine,* cesareans at Mt. Sinai have declined over two years from 17.5 to 11.5 percent of all births, "without any apparent detrimental effect on either maternal or neonatal outcome."[61] The use of medical instruments in delivery has declined, too. "We learned to take a more 'hands off' approach towards our patients in labor," declared one participant in the study. "Sometimes it takes the most experienced and best judgment to know when not to do something."[62] One way of "reducing the rush"[63] to unnecessary cesareans has been to rely more on midwives and nurse practitioners, as in Europe, where far fewer cesareans are performed. Despite all these changes, made at real legal peril to the doctors who endorsed them, there has been no rise in complications for either mothers or infants.

CHAPTER 6

No Immunity
Chemicals Cause Everything

This book is dedicated to all patients who have ever been called neurotic, hypochondriac, hysterical, or starved for attention while suffering from environmentally induced illness. —T. G. Randolph and R. W. Moss
An Alternative Approach to Allergies (1980)

Meet Bertram W. Carnow, M.D., of the University of Illinois School of Public Health. His twenty-two-page résumé lists some 145 publications, some of them never in fact published, at least not under his name. Carnow obtained his medical degree in 1951, but hasn't practiced medicine for twenty years. He registered for the board certification exam in internal medicine in 1957, 1958, 1960, 1961, 1962, 1963, and 1964, but withdrew twice and failed five times. He has since testified eight times, under oath, that he sat for board certification in internal medicine only once. "I had completely forgotten" the other tries, Carnow explained.[1] Today, Carnow heads up Carnow, Conibear & Associates—the Conibear being Dr. Shirley Conibear, Carnow's fourth wife. (Third, testifies Carnow.) The firm's best-known service is expert testimony.[2] The testimonial line is that the human body is under almost constant chemical assault, that chemicals cause almost every human affliction, their mechanisms wonderfully subtle but their effects readily ascertained. It is a line most commonly labeled "clinical ecology."

The modern roots of the theory can be traced to 1962, an interesting year for several reasons. By that time, traumatic cancer theories were on the wane. Doctors, public health specialists, and ecologists were scouting around for more plausible causes of disease. In *Silent Spring*, Rachel Carson had identified something important: pesticides accumulate in animals (like birds) at the top of the food chain, and cause real harm. And 1962 also marked the year that Dr. Theron G. Randolph published his *Human Ecology and Susceptibility to the Chemical Environment*, a book destined to become the standard text of clinical ecology.[3]

Like other great eccentrics, Randolph has some serious credentials. He is a Harvard-trained, board-certified allergist. By 1950, however, he had been dropped from the Northwestern University Medical School faculty, for what he later smilingly described as his "pernicious influence on medical students." But ostracism of this kind inspires rather than discourages the new-age Galileos. Randolph claims to have identified a new illness; he has created "a new specialty of medicine concerned with a shadowy area unexplored, forgotten and maligned by analytically oriented scientists."[4]

The human body, adapted for the Stone Age, is being assailed by toxins of the Space Age, Randolph reasons.[5] "If viruses and bacteria can cause illness, why can't phenol, formaldehyde, chlorine and pesticides?"[6] Cumulative exposures to the wrong chemicals, he concludes, induce a "susceptibility," defined entirely by the symptoms that a patient actually exhibits. Chemical vapors from plywood and plastic telephones, furniture and food, may all be implicated. They will trigger allergic symptoms, inflammatory diseases like arthritis or colitis, and neuromuscular disorders, headaches, wheezing, depression, and countless other symptoms. Seriously afflicted persons grow mentally exhausted; they experience what Randolph calls "brain-fag." He does not know what causes this "total-allergy syndrome"; he attributes its symptoms to some as yet undiscovered mechanism.

"To be truthful, the mechanism isn't understood or accepted," he has stated.[7]

Understanding may be a long time coming, but acceptance comes surprisingly quickly, at least at some fringes of the medical profession. The modern clinical ecology movement took shape in the two decades after Randolph published his first big book. The movement would grow to encompass a broad range of constantly shifting views, some of them much less diffident than Randolph's. Today's clinical ecologists are a varied group, a mix of general practitioners, psychiatrists, urologists, and pediatricians. Few have scientific training in laboratory or clinical research. The one conviction they all share is that lots of people are sicker than mainstream medicine admits, and that environmental chemicals are to blame. In *The Incredible Shrinking Woman*, Lily Tomlin gradually shrinks to doll size under the onslaught of household cleaners and other chemicals. Clinical ecologists believe that in such matters, truth is almost as strange, and much more grave, than the comic fiction.

Consider, for example, reports published in 1989 in the serious-sounding journal *Environment International*, by Sherry A. Rogers, M.D., a self-diagnosed "universal reactor" to environmental chemicals.[8] Rogers's patients arrive complaining of (take your pick) hoarseness, headaches, failing grades in school, or any number of ailments from the endless list. Such symptoms, Rogers reports, have "baffled physicians from many specialties." Rogers, however, notices that all the symptoms began some time (days, weeks, or months—it varies) after moving into a new house, or buying new furniture, or starting a new job, or doing something somewhere. She injects each patient with small amounts of formaldehyde. One promptly reports "a warm feeling, ringing in the ears, and achy joints." Another displays "visible flushing." Yet another "began laughing and rocking in the chair and thought she was Jesus' wife." Amazingly, these are exactly the symptoms the patients complained of beforehand. Injections of pure saline solution reportedly produce no effect, though Rogers is sketchy about all details. Sooner or later, declares Rogers, the astonishing discoveries of clinical ecologists will "unavoidably . . . usher in a new era of medicine."[9]

A medical breakthrough this grand requires more than un-baffled physicians like Rogers. It requires a theory. What exactly is going on? The clinical ecologists have much to explain, for their observations cover a lot of environmental and medical ground. The chemical culprits in the environment include almost everything: urban air pollution, fresh paint, pesticides, perfumes, household cleaners, felt-tip pens, and tap water. These irritants produce infinitely subtle and complex effects. Lots of effects: depression, irritability, poor concentration, poor memory, fatigue, diarrhea, constipation, cramps, asthma, headaches, joint pain, pounding heart, charley horses, cancer, and the common cold. Equally significant, however, are the symptoms *not* observed. Clinical ecology patients display no distinctive lesions on their skin, or lungs, or digestive systems. Nor do they respond systematically to any standard tests for allergy. There must be some deep, subtle factor at the edges of medical understanding, one that can be implicated in virtually all facets of human health. What could it be? The clinical ecologists gradually settled on the human immune system.

It is a convenient, perhaps inevitable choice. Beginning in the late 1970s, and accelerating rapidly in the 1980s, medical science made huge, genuine advances in its understanding of the immune system. The immune system, it turns out, consists of an army of cells and proteins, differentiated into many distinct battalions—macrophages, helper T cells, killer T cells, B cells, memory cells, and five types of antibodies. All can be counted and cataloged. The development of monoclonal antibodies, among the most subtle and advanced of biotech wonders, makes possible laboratory tests that can tag individual proteins on cell surfaces, and thus allow dozens upon dozens of different measurements. And all of this arcane detail is suddenly of enormous public interest because of a single, terrifying, immune-system disease called AIDS.

So the clinical ecologists latch on to a theory perfectly matched to a public whose health concerns have been defined by Rachel Carson and the bathhouses of San Francisco. They maintain that environmental pollutants of every description can subvert the immune system in just the same way as the AIDS virus. They claim expertise in immunotoxicity, which they also label "total allergy syndrome," "twentieth-century disease," or—best of all—"chemically induced AIDS."

The beauty of clinical ecology is its breadth. You have cancer? It's because your immune system's ability to fight off cancer has been impaired. You have nothing but the common cold? Same reason. You have unspecific minor aches and pains, backaches and headaches, problems of digestion, concentration, and excretion? Same reason. You have no symptoms at all, but are gravely worried that someday you may? Well, you have reason to be worried, for a crippled immune system is a cold or a cancer just waiting to happen. You want continuous medical monitoring? Monitoring is certainly needed.

The legal implications are enormous. For a time, legal scholars had dismissed liability for chemical pollution as a "phantom remedy."[10] It would generally be impossible, the pundits agreed, to prove any link between pollution and disease. But no one had reckoned on the clinical ecologists, or on the eroding rules of evidence that would allow them into court. The clinical ecologists can connect anything to anything. The legal stakes rise accordingly. The economic value of a chemical pollution case depends on the number of claimants signed up. "The 'going rate' for settlements," reports Yale law professor E. Donald Elliott, "is $10,000 to $100,000 per plaintiff."[11] Clinical ecology sucks in potential plaintiffs like some enormous, indiscriminate vacuum cleaner.

JACKPOT IN SEDALIA

We find Bertram Carnow in Missouri, in late 1985, testifying on behalf of thirty-two residents of the town of Sedalia.[12] At a nearby plant, Alcolac, Inc., manufactures specialty chemicals for soaps and cosmetics. Pollution from that plant is said to have damaged the immune systems of families who lived nearby. The trial will drag on for over four months. The jury will hear from 165 witnesses. The transcript will occupy ten thousand pages.

The plaintiffs will blame Alcolac's pollution for dozens of different afflictions, spanning nerve damage and heart disease, brain damage and vomiting, kidney infections and headaches. Young women report interrupted menstrual cycles. Others declare that dogs, cats, cattle, chickens, parakeets, and bee colonies died "unaccountably and without signs of predation."

Carnow has ordered exhaustive laboratory tests. He presents by-the-numbers reports of immune cell populations of various kinds. He has identified at least one abnormality (and as many as eight) in the immune system of every single plaintiff.

Carnow is backed up by Arthur C. Zahalsky, Ph.D., who teaches immunology to nursing undergraduates at Southern Illinois University. Zahalsky never actually studied immunology in graduate school; but he does claim to have audited immunology classes at Washington University in St. Louis. In any event, he is now a big believer in measuring immune system performance. He uses every gun in the battery of laboratory tests that have recently been developed to tag, count, and measure immune system cells and proteins. He runs test after test, records number after number. And then invariably finds something of deep significance in the results. The implications are always clear: chemicals have surely undermined immunity.

In the Sedalia residents he tests, Zahalsky finds "pervasive abnormalities" everywhere he looks. Some counts are too high—a surprising symptom for a disease described as an immune *deficiency* syndrome. Others are too low. In one plaintiff after the next, Zahalsky finds "a gross distortion in the ratio," an immune system "functionally wiped out," "out of whack," "a 'severe' form of chemical AIDS," or at the very least "moderate immune dysfunction" certain to "develop to the AIDS condition somewhere down the line." Zahalsky's prognosis, as later summarized by a court of appeals, is gloomy. "[The chemicals have] dampened the immune system so that the plaintiffs will become subject to a variety of diseases, neoplastic disease [cancer] included. The findings already suggest the possibility of leukemia."[13] There isn't a normal immune system in the crowd. Not a one.

The jury is convinced. It awards $6.2 million in compensatory damages plus $43 million to punish Alcolac for its iniquity. The trial judge concurs. So does the court of appeals. Its opinion runs 371 pages of bloated prose. Cut through the periphrastic verbiage, and the appellate court's logic is simple. Chemicals can cause harm. There were chemicals at Alcolac's plant. Carnow and Zahalsky take care of the rest. Only one small reservation at the end. The AIDS metaphor, the court of appeals concludes, is just too inflammatory to be used in front of a jury. So a new trial will be ordered for the sole purpose of recalculating damages.

SPINNING THE WHEEL

No, *Alcolac* is not a typical case. It is to tort law pretty much what the clinical ecologist is to science: an aberration, interesting because it is so peculiar. But if the clinical ecologist does not routinely deliver $49 million verdicts, he can quite often provide a fair shot at one. A busy witness can move from glory to disgrace and back to glory as fast as he can switch courtrooms.

Carnow, for example, fails to convince one court that a railroad employee's involvement in cleaning up a chemical spill caused his "multiple illnesses and diseases which have been progressive,"[14] and another court that the headaches, fatigue, heat intolerance, nausea, numbness, chest pains, and depression of another employee were caused by a liquid solvent.[15] More often, however, Carnow delivers at least a split. For example, he was on call in the main Agent Orange case, which settled for $180 million on the eve of trial;[16] the trial judge then ruled summarily against all remaining claims, on the ground that no serious science stood behind them.

Carnow appears again and again and again. His methods are, of course, much disputed: he uses such things as a knee-jerk test to establish general nerve disorder and a single urine sample to reveal probable bladder cancer.[17] A physician for the defense in one case testified that "no one educated after 1950 could possibly" have relied on the tests that Carnow used to diagnose liver disease.[18] Nevertheless, Carnow bats a pretty good average. In another Agent Orange trial: summary judgment for the defendant.[19] Chemical spill at Times Beach: $14.5 million settlement by two defendants, followed by jury verdict for other defendants.[20] Another dioxin case: jury award of $58 million, overturned on appeal, $22 million settlement.[21] Chemical spill after train derailment in Sturgeon, Missouri: jury buys immune system abnormalities; court of appeals orders new trial.[22] Trichloroethylene pollution in Dowagiac, Michigan, said to cause "chronic systemic chemical poisoning" and damaged immune systems: summary judgment against all claims of physical injury, but claims for emotional distress allowed to proceed to trial.[23] Colon cancer in asbestos installer, supposedly caused by fibers migrating from lungs: jury verdict for the defense.[24] "Chronic systemic chemical intoxication" in seven chemical workers: jury agrees but defendant wins on legal technicality relating to workers' compensation laws.[25]

Carnow is not, of course, the only player on the field. Other clinical ecologists come to the aid of a woman who has "suffered chemical poisoning and damage to her immune system" from formaldehyde vapors emanating from a carpet.[26] The trial judge bars the testimony, but a court of appeals finds that clinical ecology is good enough science for Texas. Clinical ecology is critical in keeping alive another claim brought by employees of Firestone in California.[27] Other courts in Louisiana,[28] California again,[29] and South Carolina[30] all weigh in on the side of clinical ecology in worker's compensation claims. One case arrives at a $3.9 million verdict,[31] another at $16.25 million.[32] Other clinical ecology–backed settlements for $8 million and $19 million have been reported.[33]

The clinical ecologists, though not always successful, routinely do manage to give the wheel a great big spin. And for repeat players, a spin is good enough. On the plaintiffs' side, there is little to lose and much to gain. The lawyers and their witnesses can be quite content if jurists remain zealously agnostic, let it all in, and wait to see just what comes out. If the judge is agnostic, clinical ecology goes to the jury. If the jury is agnostic, perhaps it will split the difference. The difference between nothing (as urged by the defendants) and everything (as urged by the clinical ecologists) may turn out to be a very large number

indeed, especially when "everything" encompasses all aches
and chills, constipations and cancers in a fifty-mile radius in the
last five years.

BEYOND THE PERIMETER

What do top-notch scientists from the mainstream think of all
this? One among them is Stuart F. Schlossman, Chief of the
Division of Tumor Immunology and Immunotherapy at the
Dana-Farber Cancer Institute, and Professor of Medicine at the
Harvard Medical School. Like Zahalsky, like Carnow, Schlossman studies and diagnoses the immune system. The similarity
ends there. When asked about Carnow, Schlossman responds
with a short chuckle and then a long sigh.

In print, however, Schlossman works with the swift, sharp
precision of a surgical knife. In 1989 he published a postmortem
on the *Alcolac* case. Day-to-day living, Schlossman explains, tests
the immune system constantly, and when the immune system is
really in trouble the symptoms are plain. Real AIDS patients all
suffer frequent, unusual, life-threatening infections. They are
not, however, unusually susceptible to run-of-the-mill infections
like colds, the flu, or bronchitis. Thus, as Schlossman points out,
"if a patient has the kind of routine infections common to most
people—even if he complains that he seems to develop one cold
or sore throat after another—the astute physician will be able to
conclude that there is nothing wrong in the immune system
without needing any laboratory tests to reach that conclusion."
With the exception of Mary Landon, a seventy-one-year-old cancer patient on chemotherapy, none of the *Alcolac* patients had
suffered from any kind of recurrent infection at all. "The inquiry
should therefore have stopped right there," Schlossman concludes. "Without any resulting infections, the finding of damaged immune systems—whether that damage be called 'dysfunction,' 'suppression,' 'depression,' 'total suppression,' or some of
the more colorful phrases makes no scientific sense."[34] Only the
elderly cancer patient on chemotherapy clearly *did* have immune
system problems.

In the great tradition of far-siders, Carnow has dodged and

bobbed his way around this simple, devastating point. In his *Alcolac* testimony, he has explained away the absence of infection with what Schlossman terms the "amazing contention" that B-cell deficiencies lead to recurrent infection but T-cell deficiencies don't:

Recurrent infection is the consequence of B-cell abnormality, since the B system is that arm of the immune mechanism which relates to infections. [Linda Sanders's] abnormality, as with most of the *Alcolac* plaintiffs, was to the T cells—and they tend to relate to very specific types of infections, like tuberculosis and things like that, and they relate more to destroying cancer cells.[35]

Here, in reply, is Schlossman:

This testimony is nothing more than scientific bamboozlement. Not only were all tests of Linda Sanders' T cells normal—and not only did she not have a "very specific type of infection like tuberculosis and things like that" (whatever that means)—but it is utter nonsense to suggest that an abnormality of T cells does not lead to recurrent infections. One only needs to think of AIDS patients to realize that. As a result of their loss of T helper cells, AIDS patients suffer many repeated and severe infections.[36]

And what about the piles of laboratory tests and pages of numbers? Laboratory tests of the immune system's condition commonly produce responses that vary from day to day, and from individual to individual, by 400 percent or more. There is no great significance in being on the edge here; the range of "normal" is too broad, the boundaries are too blurred. Few of the Zahalsky-Carnow tests were repeated, Schlossman points out, and of the few that were, none showed consistent abnormalities. Even the single readings presented no coherent picture of impaired immunity. Three claimed abnormalities involved trivial elevations, insignificant in themselves but in any event "clearly inconsistent with 'suppression.'" Nine other readings fell slightly below the "normal" range, but were still not remotely low enough to suggest immunosuppression.

There were, finally, the monoclonal antibody tests, so high-tech and exotic, so seemingly compelling, so tremendously significant in the eyes of Carnow and Zahalsky. Nine such tests had been used.[37] Not one, however, had been approved for diagnostic uses by the Food and Drug Administration; all, in fact, bore warnings that they were *not* suitable for any diagnostic purposes. Carnow and Zahalsky used them anyway. None of the results, according to Schlossman, "even suggest a suppression in any of the plaintiffs' immune systems. . . . [T]here was no overall pattern to the results as one would expect if the plaintiffs had all been affected by a common chemical exposure." On one test, nine plaintiffs had results above the reference range and four below the reference range. One plaintiff had a slightly elevated response to one test, a slightly depressed response to the next, "even though those two tests are supposed to measure the same thing—total T cells."[38] Two other tests were also supposed to measure the same thing—natural killer cells—but only one plaintiff had a result out of the reference range on both.

A similar degree of confusion surrounded another antibody test, which reportedly detected fourteen abnormalities. Carnow testified that one patient's results showed "immature, unprogrammed lymphocytes, probably pre-leukemic cells." Schlossman responds: "there is no monoclonal antibody yet developed which is capable of detecting 'pre-leukemic cells' in the peripheral blood."[39] There were other errors, ranging from trivial to gross. Natural killers, Zahalsky's statements notwithstanding, are not part of the T-4 population. HNK-L, Zahalsky notwithstanding, "is by no means a helper-cell antibody." And so on down the line, as Schlossman dismantles one mumbled, misdirected, mistaken claim after the next.

Schlossman writes with a certain quiet authority on the subject. Most of the monoclonal tests relied on by Carnow and Zahalsky had been developed by Schlossman's own research team at Harvard. Researchers in Schlossman's lab were also the first to describe the T4/T8 or helper/suppressor ratio, on which Carnow placed great emphasis. "[T]he expert testimony in *Alcolac* was not only outside the mainstream of science," Schlossman concludes, "it was outside its widest perimeter."[40]

ALCOLAC REDUX

So if it's all so obvious, why couldn't Alcolac's lawyers convince a jury? We will never know. But we do know what convinced the appellate judges. And their reasoning, set out at exhausting length, does show how intelligent people can sometimes slide helplessly into junk science's flaccid embrace.

Alcolac's biggest mistake seems to have been to rely for its side of the scientific story on a middle-of-the-road expert, inclined (like good scientists generally) to caution and understatement: Daniel J. Stechschulte, M.D., a board-certified immunologist and internist, and Director of the Division of Allergy, Clinical Immunology and Rheumatology at the University of Kansas Medical Center.

As any competent immunologist will readily concede, chemicals can harm the immune system. Drugs used in chemotherapy and for organ transplants certainly do. Very high exposures to chemicals in industrial accidents may on occasion have similar effects, though moderate and short-lived. Stechschulte is competent, and he was skillfully cross-examined. What about the specific chemicals used at Alcolac's plant? Yes, they might in some circumstances be toxic to human cells. And to immune system cells? Well, they could be toxic to any cells. And if plaintiffs aren't suffering from any unusual infections quite yet, mightn't those infections materialize later? Yes, disease might "be just later down the road." Meaningless concessions, because they are so sweeping and vague, but perhaps highly significant for someone who is eager to be persuaded.

The appellate judges, in any event, are persuaded. Immunologists for both sides agree that "toxic chemicals of the kind emitted by Alcolac can adversely affect the immune system." The numbers seal the verdict. What is outside the "normal" range is "abnormal." An "abnormality" is a disease—actual, incipient, prospective, or whatever, but an injury any way you slice it. No need, then, to dwell on the details, on dosages and exposure levels, on the vast differences between chemotherapeutic drugs and ambient pollution, on the vapid generality of such phrases as "can be toxic to cells." Pure oxygen or water, as any competent scientist would readily concede, "can be toxic to cells" too, but no matter. Just grab a few mildly general concessions from the defendant's side and run. The colorful confidence of a Carnow or a Zahalsky, their "completely zapped" and "chemical AIDS" diagnoses, their mind-numbing arrays of mumbo-jumbo charts, tests, and tables, overwhelm the diffidence of a serious scientist on the other side.

So the appellate judges go firmly on record—in 371 pages, no less—endorsing Zahalsky, Carnow, and the clinical ecology movement from beginning to end. On appeal, Alcolac's brief attacked clinical ecology as "pseudo-scientific flim-flam."[41] It's nothing of the sort, replies the appellate court. "[T]he methodology used by Carnow to arrive at diagnosis for each plaintiff here—that of differential diagnosis of risk variables and confounding factors as to each individual plaintiff—was the orthodox methodology of environmental medicine. . . . We reject, accordingly, the Alcolac contention that the diagnostic procedure [was] a new methodology not generally accepted 'in the relevant scientific community.' "[42]

VIEWS FROM THE MAINSTREAM

The relevant scientific community, however, has other views. Though the clinical ecologists say otherwise, their claims have not been ignored by mainstream science. Far from it—they have been reviewed in depth. The results have been remarkably consistent: clinical ecology is medical fantasy, not fact.

Most tellingly, the theory finds no confirmation in studies of people who have been exposed to chemicals at levels millions of times higher than those encountered through environmental pollution. Serious epidemiologists have studied immune system responses following high exposures to suspect chemicals after accidental spills in the United States, Italy, Japan, and Taiwan. Several of these involved enormously high exposures. Serious follow-up studies tracked various aspects of the immune system for many years. As of 1987, with data dating back forty years, "there had been no published evidence of disease resulting from impaired humoral or cell-mediated immunity in the subjects studied." A review paper thus concluded, "In light of the great excess of immunologic capacity in the human and the compensatory shifts in response to injury that are known to occur in the immune system, it is unlikely that significant irreversible damage to the immune system has occurred" as a result of any of these exposures.[43] Good science has quite firmly established that, though scads of toxins might theoretically harm immune system cells and proteins, only a very few, usually delivered intimately, knock out immune response while leaving no visible marks on other body systems.

In a systematic examination of fifty patients that clinical ecologists had diagnosed as sufferers, Abba I. Terr of the Stanford University Medical Center found that "[n]o pattern of symptoms emerged to define a disease or syndrome." Physical examinations proved completely normal in two out of three cases. Laboratory tests showed nothing out of the ordinary either. Thirty-one patients were found with multiple symptoms "most likely of psychological origin. . . . The circulating levels of immunoglobulins and lymphocytes in this subgroup of patients did not differ significantly from those in the other two subgroups or in normal persons when the effects of prior infections were taken into account." None of the patients was "cured" by the clinical ecologists' ministrations; "in fact, the number of symptoms reported by most of these patients significantly increase after such treatment, probably reflecting increasing fear of other possible environmental hazards."[44]

In 1984, a task force appointed by the California Medical Association conducted an independent review of the clinical ecology literature. Clinical ecologists presented their claims, and specifically identified three of the best papers in their field. Two of those papers, the task force found, failed to define the disease being diagnosed or treated, and failed to use proper controls. One claimed to have used double-blind testing but in fact did not. One reported results that had been crudely fiddled. And so on, through the three model papers and the rest of the clinical ecology literature. "There is no convincing evidence that supports the hypotheses on which clinical ecology is based," the task force concluded. "[C]linical ecologists have not identified specific, recognizable diseases caused by exposure to low-level environmental stressors."[45]

A 1986 assessment of clinical ecology by the American Academy of Allergy and Immunology reached similar conclusions. "The idea that the environment is responsible for a multitude of human health problems is most appealing," it acknowledged. But there is no "satisfactory evidence to support the actual existence of 'immune system dysregulation' or maladaptation. . . . Properly controlled studies defining objective parameters of illness, properly controlled evaluation of the treatment modalities, and appropriate patient assessment have not been done." The "diagnostic and therapeutic principles used to support the concept of clinical ecology" are "unproven."[46]

One by one, other mainstream medical journals examined clinical ecology and found no there there. *The Lancet:* "A flawed theory of immunodysregulation as the basis of leukaemia, that would be rejected if sent as a paper to a peer-review journal, is heard with respectful attention when promulgated from the witness box."[47] The *Journal of Allergy and Clinical Immunology:* "The failure of clinical ecologists to examine their methods and their theories by scientifically rigorous studies can no longer be tolerated. . . . There is no indication that patients with clinical ecology diagnosis of chemical sensitivity have immune deficiency, immune complex disease, autoimmunity, or abnormal functioning of their immune systems."[48] *Science:* "The clinical ecologists have few friends, even where one might expect to find them. Ellen Silbergeld, staff scientist for the Environmental Defense Fund and an advocate of strong chemical regulation, finds this group 'unspeakable.' "[49] And so on through the literature. "The entire scheme is designed to always provide an answer, always to find a cause." "No data are presented." There are "no controls." The "reproducibility of results [is] not established." The theory lies "outside the realm of current immunologic knowledge." It "lacks a scientific foundation." It is a "dogma" unsupported by any "adequate clinical and immunologic studies . . . [that] meet the usually accepted standards of scientific investigation."[50]

MIND OVER MATTER

So what *does* maintain the faith of the clinical ecologists and their patients? Some, especially among the patients, certainly have an eye on litigation. Terr's systematic examination of fifty consecutive patients referred for reevaluation of a clinical ecology diagnosis found that forty-three were pressing worker's compensation claims and two others were pursuing tort claims against chemical manufacturers.[51] Only five, apparently, had no specific financial interest in being sick, and one of those was involved in child custody litigation.

Other patients undoubtedly are sick, distressingly so, but the illness is not centered in their immune systems. A 1983 paper by the psychiatrist Carroll M. Brodsky describes her examination of eight clinical ecology patients. "[M]ost have a history of overt psychiatric symptoms," Brodsky reports; "all too frequently they are seen by the same network of physicians who subscribe to clinical ecology, and their self-perception and diagnosis of 'allergic' to most substances have become an organizing principle in their lives, central to their identity and life-style."[52]

So we find, in the end, that the afflictions addressed by clinical ecology are not new to our chemically polluted times. Indeed, they have been known for millennia. Hippocrates coined the term *hysteria* (from the Greek meaning "uterus") to describe multiple, amorphous medical complaints experienced (according to Hippocrates) primarily by women.[53] Jumping ahead a couple of millennia, we arrive at the nineteenth-century discovery of "neurasthenia."[54] An 1881 treatise on the subject, "American Nervousness, its Causes and Consequences,"[55] describes symptoms virtually identical to those in today's clinical ecology texts: mental and physical fatigue, pressure in the head, poor memory, inability to concentrate, irritability, poor sleep, and so on. The patients, the neurasthenists announce, are suffering from "special idiosyncrasies in regard to food, medicines, and external irritants." Five features of "modern civilization" are found to be responsible: "steam power, the periodical press, the telegraph, the sciences, and the mental activity of women."

Expensive treatments aimed at cleansing and resting the body are sold to those who can afford them.

A generation later, in the early 1900s, the vogue term has become "autointoxication"; the same amorphous symptoms are now caused by toxins from bacteria residing in teeth, sinuses, gall bladder, kidney, and the gastrointestinal tract. The clinician's emphasis shifts to pure foods, which just happen to be in the headlines of the day. A major book on autointoxication is published in 1906, the same year that Congress enacts the Pure Food Act. The immediate forerunners of present-day clinical ecologists appear in the 1950s and early 1960s. Then comes Randolph. Then the rest. And thus arose today's junk science pastiche of clinical ecology and chemical AIDS: a bastardized immunological theory, batteries of meaningless, high-tech tests with monoclonal antibodies, and a clever play on contemporary public paranoias.

Over the years, the fad terrors of the moment have shifted from "the mental activity of women," to impure foods, to environmental chemicals, to AIDS. That degenerate recidivist, "modern society," is always lounging about, blamed for neurasthenia in the late nineteenth century and for twentieth-century disease in the late twentieth. The most striking thing about clinical ecology is how old and familiar the story is. For a century or more, nothing but the vocabulary has really changed. Not the symptoms—which remain as endless as they are vague. Not the diagnostic methods—rich in rambling detail, but always lacking the rigor of real science. Not the treatments—which invariably require the patient to clean up (with a doctor's expensive help) and get away from it all. No other changes, in short, except in court. No neurasthenist ever extracted $49 million from a chemical company in Missouri.

Money surely contributes to clinical ecologists' zealotry, but it is probably not their principal incentive. What most clearly characterizes the clinical ecologists today is their activist faith. Carnow exhorts the modern physician to political action.[56] "Whether the defense or the plaintiff wins," admits another like-minded colleague, "we're going to be much more careful in the future about the way we use toxic chemicals as a result of my involvement in toxic tort litigation, and that's my purpose in this game."[57] Many concede, more or less directly, that faith must come before the facts. Carnow allows that "[a] heightened level of consciousness" about the links between environment and disease "is critical to considering the 'disease syndrome.' "[58] Anthony Z. Roisman, a plaintiff's lawyer, is just a shade more careful in his credo: "[D]o I believe that immune damage is caused by toxic chemicals for which plaintiffs can recover in court . . . [?] Believe in it? Hell, I've seen it done. I believe."[59] That is what clinical ecology comes down to. There is no science here, but none is needed. As one mainstream student of the cult has concluded, the clinical ecology syndrome "constitutes a belief and not a disease."[60]

Unlike his patient, or at least unlike his patient's immune system, the clinical ecologist himself is an outlier, an aberration, a living example of dysfunction and pathology. He is perfectly adapted, in other words, to modern-day testifying. He is adept at prevaricating, playing on credulity, scoring verbal points, forgetting inconvenient data, and dredging up convenient anecdotes. He has experience with persuading, for his clinical practice depends entirely on persuading patients first that they are sick, then that they have been cured. He has vast experience with conflict, for he is forever in conflict with his mainstream cousins. He survives only by hiding and feinting, for good science deals ruthlessly with error presented directly in the open. He is not about to be sandbagged on cross-examination, for he has survived that sort of attack countless times before. Through it all, he remains a "generally quite charming, often charismatic, reasonable sounding physician . . . with a definite evangelical bent."[61] He will be, in short, an excellent witness in court.

He will need to be. Let us visit with Bertram Carnow one last time. Yes, in court again—where else?—but this time appearing not as a witness but as a defendant. The plaintiff is one Paul L. Pratt, Esq., no stranger to courtrooms either, for Mr. Pratt is a plaintiff's lawyer and Carnow's one-time employer. According to published reports about the suit, Carnow "misrepresented to Pratt the number of times he failed the board examination in Internal Medicine and, in addition, lied under oath about it."[62]

Pratt claims that had he known the facts, he would never have hired Carnow. Since Carnow's credibility as an expert witness is now ruined, Pratt refuses to pay $643,935.20 in outstanding promissory notes to Carnow, demands reimbursement of payments already made amounting to $1,624,596.29, and seeks over $15,000 in punitive damages. Carnow, for his part, is suing elsewhere for full payment.

CHAPTER 7

Nausea

The Massed Legal Attack

They call them GOKs, that means 'God only knows,' but I know it's drugs, it has to be. I can convince juries because I'm sincere about what I do.
—Plaintiffs' attorney James Butler (1983)

The *National Enquirer* broke the story in October 1979: "[U]ntold thousands of babies are being born with hideous birth defects." Two infants are born without eyeballs. Another without a brain. There are "several thousand tragically deformed infants in the U.S. alone." It's a "monstrous scandal" that "could be far larger than the thalidomide horror." The cause? An over-the-counter drug—a "vicious, body-twisting crippler"—called Bendectin.[1]

At the time, Bendectin was widely used to treat the affliction that killed Charlotte Brontë. In 1855, the author of *Jane Eyre* literally died of pregnancy. Or, more precisely, she died of what modern medics call *hyperemesis gravida*—"morning sickness" to the rest of us. Most pregnant women suffer from it, and for most it's merely unpleasant.[2] For a few like Brontë, however, severe morning sickness threatens the health of both mother and child. In 1956, the FDA approved Bendectin as a therapy. Twenty-three years later, the *Enquirer* finally revealed the scandalous facts.

Merrell Pharmaceuticals,* the drug's manufacturer, of course denied any problem. But the case against Bendectin was clear, at least to the *Enquirer*. The paper quoted Alan Done, "one of America's leading experts on drugs and their effects on children," and William G. McBride, an Australian gynecologist renowned for having been among the first to suggest a link between birth defects and thalidomide in 1961. Bendectin, like thalidomide, had been used indiscriminately. Bendectin, like thalidomide, deforms babies. Bendectin, like thalidomide, stands for drug companies putting profit above all else, above even the well-being of unborn children.[3]

It's the "like thalidomide" part that's really chilling. As everyone knows, women who used thalidomide during pregnancy bore babies with dolphinlike flippers instead of normal limbs. "Teratogens" (literally the "creators of monsters") have preoccupied many medical scientists ever since. Other factors that produce similar effects have been identified. Some anticonvulsant drugs cause cleft palate. Age is a teratogen: babies of older mothers tend to have more birth defects. Maternal infections can cause birth defects, too. Alcohol, tobacco, and other drugs can have similar effects. About 100,000 newborns a year have birth defects of some kind. But despite the abiding scientific interest, most birth defects remain complete medical mysteries; no more than 2 percent have ever been reliably linked to environmental factors of any kind.

By 1979, the causes of the other 98 percent had occupied William McBride for two decades. On the strength of his thalidomide fame, McBride had set up his own research center, Foundation 41. As his fundraising radio jingle happily promised: "Foundation 41 will find the answers / Just you wait and see / For they'll fix birth defects / If you'll send in your checks / Foundation 41 must be."[4] After years of work, and several false starts, McBride turned his attention to Bendectin. By 1979, as the *National Enquirer* reported, he "flatly declare[d] that Bendectin [was] the cause of birth deformities." A year later he

---

*Richardson Merrell was the original manufacturer, but was later acquired by Dow. For simplicity I refer to the Bendectin defendant as "Merrell" throughout this chapter.

denounced Bendectin at FDA hearings.[5] Shortly thereafter, he published a paper describing laboratory tests on rabbits and chicks. Two of eight rabbits receiving higher doses of a Bendectin-like chemical produced deformed fetuses.[6]

Picking up on McBride's research, Alan Done developed what he calls a "mosaic theory" of the evidence against Bendectin. The individual pieces of scientific evidence don't prove too much on their own, Done concedes.[7] But considering McBride's animal studies, some scattered laboratory tests, and Done's own analysis of Bendectin's chemical structure—putting all these together in his mosaic theory—Done concludes that Bendectin is indeed a teratogen. A large volume of published epidemiological data has previously revealed no statistically significant association between Bendectin and birth defects. But though he has never found the time to publish his results, Done has reworked the data and concludes that they in fact reveal a clear connection.

The implications are staggering. Over a thirty-year period, Bendectin has been used by some 30 million pregnant women.[8]

DAVID MEKDECI

Melvin Belli, self-styled "king of torts," is to lawyering what the *National Enquirer* is to journalism: flamboyant, outrageous, and hugely successful. It was thus quite fitting that Belli was to take charge of the first major Bendectin case, which came to trial on January 24, 1980, in a federal district court in Orlando, Florida.[9] At issue were the malformed arm and caved-in chest of four-year-old David Mekdeci.

National Enquirer readers had met the boy just a few months earlier: a large photograph of David, smiling brightly, accompanied the Bendectin story. Come to think of it, readers had also met Belli's main witnesses, McBride and Done, whom the *Enquirer* quoted with high respect. A suspicious mind might suppose that David's story had been fed to the *Enquirer,* line by line, by Belli himself.

David's case was, in any event, a line-by-line replay of the *Enquirer* story. McBride testified that Bendectin had caused David's affliction. Alan Done accused Merrell of falsifying data to conceal a clear link.[10] The lawyers played on emotion, just like the tabloids. And on March 21, 1980, the jury awarded David Mekdeci . . . nothing. Bendectin was exonerated. But surely David's parents deserved something—$20,000, say—for their trouble, medical expenses, and such. A big company like Merrell could undoubtedly afford such a trivial sum. The jury gave it a whirl. The judge summarily threw out this sympathy verdict and ordered a new trial.

The Mekdecis, sincerely convinced they had been wronged, were ready to start again. So was Merrell, equally convinced that Bendectin was blameless. But the Belli team already had exactly what it needed: a first jury "victory." Granted, David himself got nothing. Granted, the gift to his parents was immediately overturned. But the atmospherics were still good, the publicity generally favorable, the client lists growing. The last thing Belli and company wanted was to jeopardize their "win" in a retrial. What they wanted was time to sign up new clients. "People power," another plaintiff lawyer noted, is everything in this kind of litigation[11]; what the ambitious lawyer wants is lots and lots of people. Alone, the Mekdecis were of small importance.

So (as a federal court of appeals would later note) the Belli team then did everything it could to "capitalize . . . on the claimed victory in the first [Mekdeci] trial in a rather obvious effort to attract other Bendectin clients." They traveled the United States and Europe, "trumpeting their participation in [the Mekdeci] trial and advertising for Bendectin mothers to contact them, ostensibly for statistical studies." Meanwhile, back at home, they complained of "irreconcilable conflicts" with Betty Mekdeci, David's mother. "The attorneys' various antics," the court of appeals would observe, "create the impression that they may have been more concerned with bettering their position in other Bendectin cases, rather than with fulfilling their professional responsibilities to the Mekdecis."[12]

An astonished Betty Mekdeci objected. Two separate district judges refused to let Belli and company cut and run.[13] The lawyers squirmed, twisted, appealed, and begged to be released. And by the time they were finally ordered to get on with the next trial, the squirming had achieved its intended purpose.

ANNE ELIZABETH KOLLER

Mekdeci, even the plaintiffs' lawyers were prepared to concede, had not worked out exactly as hoped. There were better prospects ahead, however. "[T]his case in Washington, that's the perfect case," they agreed.[14] And so they informed Betty Mekdeci. But their "perfect case" turned out to be a third-rate soap opera.

It began with Anne Elizabeth Koller, a desperately tragic child born with severely malformed limbs on the left side of her body and no limbs at all on the right. Her lawyers were unusually colorful, even for the profession where nothing succeeds like excess. For the defense: Lawrence E. Walsh, later a television superstar in the Iran-contra hearings, once described as "the ultimate hired gun."[15] For the Kollers: the Florida lawyers who had collaborated with Belli on behalf of the Mekdecis. Joined this time by James Butler, a flamboyant advocate with a gray beard, hair flowing around his shoulders, and unconcealed disdain for medical types who can't explain birth defects. Butler knows better; he, after all, is "sincere" about what he does.[16]

Something more than sincere, according to at least one account. Fetal limbs develop between the twenty-sixth and the sixtieth day of pregnancy, but available records showed that Anne Elizabeth's mother, Cynthia Koller, had not used Bendectin until later than that. Cynthia had an explanation, however. As an army nurse she had obtained the drug earlier, through army dispensaries. But the army's bulk-order forms for the key months of her pregnancy had vanished.

Up popped Krystyna Janowski, a former stripper, now working as a legal secretary for Butler. On December 22, 1982, Janowski phoned the defense team and announced breathlessly that Cynthia Koller was lying. When Cynthia had first approached Butler (Janowski claimed), she had filled out a questionnaire about her Bendectin experience. The lawyers took one look at it and immediately told Cynthia that her answer to the "most important question"—on what dates she had used Bendectin—was "wrong," that she wouldn't have any claim if she answered *that* way. The lawyers then helped Cynthia fill out a new questionnaire "correctly." They then (still according to Janowski) "arranged for the disappearance" of the hospital bulk-order records.[17]

The delighted defense lawyers took down Janowski's whole confession in a rambling, convoluted, 1,300-page statement. Confronted with it, Cynthia's attorneys denied every word, and immediately accused the defense of bribing Janowski to raise false charges.[18] At various points thereafter, Janowski would recant, then un-recant.

The media joined the fray. The trial judge, Norma Holloway Johnson, ruled that certain FDA reports would not be admitted at trial. Butler promptly handed them over to Morton Mintz of the *Washington Post*, who performed on cue.[19] The defense rushed to court, protesting that Butler had defied the court by using the *Post* to get the excluded evidence in front of prospective jurors.[20] Judge Johnson agreed. Between the Mintz affair and their attempts to silence Krystyna Janowski, Koller's lawyers had gone too far. The judge disqualified them from any further appearance.[21]

Meanwhile, the prestigious magazine *Science* reported that McBride had been paid $5,000 a day to testify in the Mekdeci trial.[22] McBride (represented by James Butler) sued the reporter and the magazine for libel, throwing in a claim against Merrell for good measure. He demanded $18 million in compensation. The *Science* article, McBride charged, was all part of a "campaign" to silence, "smear," and "destroy" McBride's "credibility and career." Merrell was behind the whole thing—it was a plot to keep Bendectin among Merrell's "leading money-makers."[23]

So what finally happened? Were McBride and the ex-stripper vindicated? Did Mintz win a Pulitzer? Did Anne Elizabeth, the quiet, helpless center of this storm, collect a huge award? Were the villainous—or, depending on your sympathies, heroic— plaintiffs' lawyers even allowed to represent her? As befits a soap opera, we shall postpone answering these questions for now. They are not urgent. The Koller case would take nine years to be resolved. Nor are the questions important: Anne Elizabeth Koller, like David Mekdeci, was of interest to her lawyers only as a pitiful promoter of publicity, a diminutive sign-up agent for other Bendectin claims.

MARY VIRGINIA OXENDINE

By January 1984, when Judge Johnson disqualified the Kollers' lawyers, the Bendectin litigation had shifted forums again. It had moved across one narrow street abutting Pennsylvania Avenue in northwest Washington, from a federal building to the District of Columbia's local courthouse, the equivalent of a state court.

The new suit was on behalf of Mary Virginia Oxendine, twelve years old, who was born with a shortened right arm and missing fingers. She was represented by a Washington lawyer, Barry Nace. And Nace had retained Alan Done. As we shall see, Nace and Done were destined to become the Simon and Garfunkel of Bendectin litigation, the poet and the one-man band, performing in perfect harmony in one courtroom after the next. The Oxendine trial was their first big concert, and it was a sellout. On the strength of his mosaic theory, Done concluded that Bendectin must have been responsible for Mary's problems. On May 27, 1983, Barry Nace had his first big win: a unanimous, $750,000 verdict.[24] Nace was immediately flooded with calls from distraught parents and other Bendectin lawyers.

The *Oxendine* verdict was not yet final; there were important new revelations to come, and appeals to be decided. Indeed, no court in the country had yet given its final word on Bendectin. Nor had any regulatory agency or scientific institution yet endorsed McBride's or Done's theories. But all of this was once again irrelevant to the lawyers, as was Mary Oxendine herself. With the Mekdeci aberration, the Koller circus, and now, at last, one substantial verdict, they had secured the only thing they really needed: enormous publicity.

From here on, the science of Bendectin, already overshadowed by sympathetic claimants, flamboyant lawyers, breathless ex-strippers, receptive journalists, and the rest, would become almost completely irrelevant. Simple numbers would take control. Millions of women had used Bendectin. A hundred thousand women bear children with birth defects every year. There was bound to be substantial overlap between the two groups, even if Bendectin was as innocuous as pure sugar. Once suspicions were raised and publicity generated, intuition would take care of the rest. New clients would pour in. New suits would be filed. And still more publicity would be generated. So again, let's forget about Mary Oxendine for the moment, and move on to where the plaintiffs' lawyers were headed all along.

CINCINNATI

They were headed toward Stanley Chesley, a Cincinnati lawyer, described in *Forbes* as "the wheelingest, dealingest tortster ever to belly up to the bar." A former shoe salesman, this "master of disaster" paraded the wealth wrought from years of monster lawsuits: a gold Rolex watch, a $60,000 Mercedes sedan, and walnut-paneled offices reputed to be among Cincinnati's most opulent.[25] He belongs to the tiny club of super-litigators, the Michael Milkens of torts, the venture capitalists and investment bankers of the litigation industry.

For a Chesley operation, the first step is to consolidate the action in a single courtroom. Sometimes, this will mean formally launching a class action, in which a handful of "named plaintiffs" become legal surrogates for thousands of others. If legal technicalities prevent this, Chesley will go for a "master complaint"—what has been described as "a kind of litigatory grab bag into which every conceivable charge or allegation is tossed."[26] This accomplishes a similar purpose, establishing a lead case around which others will then pivot.

However achieved, consolidating many claims generates huge publicity, attracts still more claims, and pushes the financial stakes to stratospheric heights. Nothing else is needed. Smarter plaintiffs' lawyers don't want a trial; a trial, after all, carries with it the risk of losing everything if the theories of a William McBride or an Alan Done don't quite persuade. But defendants don't want any part of a huge trial either, partly because legal fees in this kind of litigation are astronomical, partly because there's always some risk, no matter how solid your scientific case may be, that you will still lose.

By 1984, the Bendectin lawyers were consolidating on cue, under Chesley's deft direction. Half a dozen—Nace, Chesley, Butler, and a few others—were really active. Most of the rest—the stay-at-home lawyers, Chesley calls them[27]—were just signing up babies, the victims of terrible birth defects involving arms, hands, legs, feet, the heart, the head, the genital-urinary, gastrointestinal, musculo-skeletal, and respiratory systems, as well as blood disorders and cancer.[28] No substance known to medical science can actually cause such a range of injuries, but claims poured in and afflictions accumulated nonetheless.

On June 24, federal district Judge Carl B. Rubin consolidated some 700 of the outstanding claims into a single, massive proceeding in his Cincinnati courtroom.[29] All Bendectin claims not already under way in court were to be resolved here. Barely a month later, on July 14, Merrell offered $120 million to settle the whole affair.[30] The company, which by that time had won most of the few Bendectin trials completed elsewhere, still adamantly denied that Bendectin had ever caused a single birth defect. But the money on the table spoke louder than any denials. In the normal course of events Stanley Chesley and his colleagues would have pocketed $40 million or $50 million as their share of the take, and the rest would have been scattered around here and there, at about $100,000 per baby.

But was that enough? Barry Nace and James Butler, among others, thought not. "The money is just pathetically low when you consider the number of people involved and the severity of the injuries," Nace declared.[31] "You can make a real bundle by settling all these cases cheaply, and that is something Chesley has recognized."[32] For his part, Nace calculated that fighting claims one at a time might yield considerably more, at least if McBride and Done proved sufficiently persuasive. A big "if." "They say [Bendectin] was a nickel-and-dime settlement," Chesley would later remark laconically, "but to collect $120 million without proving causation is not half-bad."[33]

The dissenters, confident that the likes of McBride and Done could nail down the question of causation in court, prevailed over Chesley's better judgment. They appealed the order that had consolidated all Bendectin claims in a single courtroom. An appellate court agreed that Judge Rubin had exceeded his authority.[34] So the $120 million check was voided. Rubin recertified the class, this time as a voluntary rather than a mandatory arrangement. When the trial began at last on February 4, 1985, more than 1,100 plaintiffs had chosen to opt in.[35] Jerome Skinner, one of the many plaintiffs' lawyers, would describe the subsequent trial as "the biggest crapshoot that ever occurred in the American legal system."[36]

To the horror of the plaintiffs' lawyers, however, Judge Rubin resolved to run a trial, not a casino. The trial was going to address Bendectin, so Rubin banned the word "thalidomide" from his courtroom.[37] The trial was going to turn on science, not sympathy, so Rubin also banned all visibly deformed children. When seventeen parents and seven children staged a protest, Rubin ordered extra security guards, set up closed-circuit televisions for the demonstrators, and retained a staff of nurses to care for the handicapped children while their parents attended the trial. Finally, Rubin declared that the trial would be held in three separate stages. In the first, the jury would decide only whether Bendectin can cause birth defects at all. Only in the subsequent stages—if they were needed at all—would the jury consider whether specific children had been injured, and if so what they deserved in compensation. There would be no playing on juror sympathies until some basic scientific questions had been resolved.[38]

A total of nineteen experts testified. Both Alan Done and William McBride appeared for the plaintiffs. On March 12, 1985, it took the five women and one man on the jury just four and a half hours to conclude that Bendectin does not cause birth defects.[39]

Aghast, the plaintiffs' lawyers demanded a new trial. Rubin had unfairly created a "sterile or laboratory environment," they charged.[40] Well, yes, he had indeed, on the assumption that that sort of environment is most conducive to good science. The court of appeals saw nothing wrong in that.[41] The U.S. Supreme

Court refused further review.[42] And for 1,100 Bendectin babies, that was that.

CARITA RICHARDSON AND SEKOU EALY

If Judge Rubin's first order had not been appealed, the final legal word on Bendectin would have been: plead guilty, to the tune of $120 million. If the Cincinnati jury verdict had been dispositive, the final legal word would have been: not guilty at all. But the one thing Nace and the other holdouts had ensured was that there would be no final legal word at all; cases would continue to be filed indefinitely. Nace had already persuaded one Washington, D.C., jury to award $750,000 to Mary Oxendine. He still had 40 Bendectin cases pending and 150 additional claims ready to file.[43]

Undaunted, Nace pressed forward with the claim of Carita Richardson, whose tragedy was to be born with a deformed left arm, three fingers missing from her left hand, and no lower right leg. The Richardsons had been part of the Cincinnati class at first, but had opted out when the chance arose. Carita's eight-week trial got under way in the late summer of 1986.

As the trial judge would observe, the Richardson trial was a "virtual reprise of Oxendine." Only one critical difference, again: the across-the-street factor. The soap opera involving Anne Elizabeth Koller, the stripper-turned-secretary, and the purloined files had been conducted in a D.C. federal court. The *Oxendine* verdict had come in a local Washington, D.C., courtroom. Carita Richardson was back in federal court again. Alan Done appeared once again to testify for Carita. On September 18, 1986, the jury awarded Carita $1 million, and her parents another $160,000.[44]

Barry Nace's gutsy decision to sink Chesley's $120 million settlement deal was beginning to look better. When the next trial ended, it looked brilliant. That trial belonged to Sekou Ealy, who had been born on May 29, 1979, just a few months before the *National Enquirer* broke its Bendectin story. He was missing both thumbs and he could not bend his elbows. In the course of Sekou's trial, which dragged on for five weeks in the torpid Washington summer of 1987, he would testify sadly that he couldn't "throw good," that he could tie his shoes "but not tight, though," that his second-grade classmates "make fun of my hands."[45] Alan Done would testify about mosaics. The jury was utterly persuaded. It concluded that Merrell owed Sekou $20 million in compensation. Plus another $75 million as punishment for its outrageous misconduct. It seemed that Nace's patience was paying off. The per-baby stakes had been rising geometrically, from the $100,000 that Chesley had been willing to accept for each of the Cincinnati kids, to $1 million for Carita Richardson, to almost $100 million for Sekou Ealy.

Nace had made only one disastrous mistake: he had walked across the street again, on the wrong day. After his $750,000 win for Mary Oxendine in *local* court, he had won both *Richardson* and *Ealy* in *federal* court. And that was going to make all the difference. The Bendectin litigation balloon was now ready to burst.

AFTERMATH

Carita Richardson's $1.16 million award was thrown out by federal Judge Thomas Penfield Jackson shortly after it was entered. Yes, Jackson declared, Carita's federal trial had been virtually identical to the *Oxendine* trial conducted across the street in a local courthouse. Yes, federal courts in this kind of litigation are expected to track local law. And yes, the *Oxendine* verdict had been upheld, at least so far. But the *Oxendine* court, said Jackson, had completely failed to address "the significance of certain evidence bearing upon the current state of scientific knowledge. In consequence, it judicially reopened an esoteric twenty-year-old controversy which is by now essentially settled within the scientific community. . . . Though Dr. Done might disagree," Jackson continued, there is "now nearly universal scientific consensus that Bendectin has not been shown to be harmful." In short, whatever the local D.C. courts were doing with Bendectin cases, Carita Richardson's million-dollar verdict could not stand. There was "not a prayer" the ruling would be upheld, Barry Nace confidently declared.[46]

Too confidently. On September 27, 1988, a unanimous court of appeals upheld the ruling in every particular. "[S]ingly or in combination," the court declared, Done's mosaic theory was "not capable of proving causation in human beings in the face of the overwhelming body of contradictory epidemiological evidence." Done's chemical structure analysis, by Done's own characterization, "gives you a clue," "raises at least a flag," "indicate[s] a suspicion." But clues, flags, and suspicion have "extremely limited" value. The animal studies, in Done's own words, required Done "to accept the notion" that similar harm might occur in humans. Notions wouldn't do either. And the value of other laboratory studies was "extremely meager." Done himself had conceded that none of the published human data on Bendectin showed a statistically significant association between the drug and limb defects. Done had "recalculat[ed] the data" to support his conclusions, but the "recalculations," unlike the originals, had never been published in peer-reviewed scientific journals. Done, in short, could simply not be believed, the jury verdict notwithstanding.[47]

A "political decision," Nace bellowed. "Who are these three old farts in the Court of Appeals, who give us a 15-minute argument and obviously, despite what they say, did not read the record?"[48]

There was worse to come. Even as he continued to tout Done's "towering credentials," Nace knew—and others were fast discovering—that the Done tower had been leaning ominously off center for some time. Done, you may recall, had helped deliver the $750,000 verdict for Mary Oxendine back in May 1983. On February 12, 1988, after further legal maneuvering and appeals in that case, a new judge took another, careful look. Done's statements about his credentials, this judge declared, were "so deliberately false that *all* his testimony on behalf of [Oxendine] is suspect. . . . [Done's] lies went so much toward enhancing his status as a witness that he reeks of the hired gun who will say anything that money can buy so long as it is glibly consistent with his prior testimony in other cases."[49] With Done the only expert backing Mary Oxendine's claim, and

Done's credibility now in shambles, there was no alternative but to order a new trial.

Meanwhile, the world was also turning on Anne Elizabeth Koller's soap-opera dream case. When we last visited the set in early 1984, the presiding judge had just disqualified several of the plaintiffs' lawyers for hushing up the loquacious stripper-turned-secretary and leaking excluded evidence to the press. Later that year, a court of appeals would rule that the disqualification was too harsh a sanction. In June 1985, the U.S. Supreme Court overruled the court of appeals, on the ground that disqualification orders are not immediately appealable.[50] By this point, the *Koller* trial, originally touted as the perfect lead case to expose the Bendectin scandal, had been postponed five times. It would be postponed several more. Finally, in June 1989, Merrell would win on summary judgment[51]—the kind of ruling reserved for claims so insubstantial they do not even deserve to be sent to a jury.

The $95 million verdict for Sekou Ealy was melting away too. The trial judge had immediately overturned the $75 million punitive-damages component. On March 9, 1990, a federal appellate court threw out the rest, declaring that "the existing body of published epidemiological studies, all finding no significant statistical association between ingestion of Bendectin and birth defects, must be recognized as the measuring stick for the admissibility of expert testimony on this issue."[52]

We may end, finally, where we began, with David Mekdeci, the unfortunate youngster whose case had started it all. At last contact, the Mekdeci parents (though not David himself) had won and then immediately lost a $20,000 sympathy verdict. Belli and associates were off hunting for bigger, mass-tort game. In their attempt to unload the Mekdecis altogether, the lawyers swore they couldn't afford another trial, and vowed they would call no live witnesses if forced to conduct one. Two courts had agreed that regardless of what might suit the lawyers, the Mekdecis were entitled to a retrial; a court of appeals would later excoriate Belli's team and strongly suggest that its members had breached their contractual duties and engaged in malpractice.

Whatever the Belli team owed the Mekdecis, the upshot of the second trial was that Merrell owed them nothing. Betty Mekdeci "got exactly what I told her she was going to get," Belli manfully declared. Poor Betty Mekdeci was left baffled by the whole miserable experience: "[M]aybe I'm naive, but I hate to think these guys are as scoundrelly as they look on the surface. . . . I keep thinking there's got to be a reason for why [Belli] did it the way he did, [but] I can't think of one."[53]

And so the lead cases—Mekdeci, Oxendine, and Koller—collapsed into dust, and the million-dollar and hundred-million-dollar verdicts that had followed were gradually whittled away to nothing. In gestating the litigation monster, David Mekdeci, Mary Oxendine, and Anne Elizabeth Koller had never much mattered anyway, of course. They had performed exactly as required, dutifully delivering $120 million to their handlers. Only their handlers' surpassing greed had kept anyone from cashing the check.

WILLIAM MCBRIDE

In January 1988, Barry Nace would take to the legal press and launch a rhetorical diatribe against the judges who persisted in overturning the jury verdicts he was winning in Washington, D.C.: "Is this a racial dispute? Is it a coincidence that each of the trial judges were white? If it is not a racial issue, is it a 'social struggle'? Are the 'weak' not entitled to 'win' because they are weak? Are the trial courts loath to allow the powerful drug companies to lose?"[54]

Nace's timing was ironic, to say the least. Within a matter of weeks, a Washington, D.C., judge would blast Nace's star witness, Alan Done, for misrepresenting his credentials. And within a matter of months, William McBride, whose rabbit study had been the scientific cornerstone of every case Nace litigated, would be denounced for fraud.

McBride, the man of thalidomide fame, one of Australia's "tall poppies," the "hero to every mother," was to fall a great distance. Just what kind of science had he been doing since 1961? Indeed, just what had he done way back then to deserve such fame? In September 1989, *Australian Medicine* asked those questions and published the answers in an article entitled "McBride: Behind the Myth." McBride's 1961 contribution on thalidomide had been a letter to the journal *Lancet;* the real research had been done by Dr. Widukind Lenz, a West German geneticist and pediatrician.[55] History will also record that Lenz had testified *for* Merrell (and *against* McBride) in the first David Mekdeci Bendectin trial.[56] Thalidomide had nevertheless secured McBride's fame. Sheltered in his own, well-funded research organization, McBride had drifted away from the mainstream scientific community.

For years, "rumors of shoddy science or less than perfect practice had dogged his tracks."[57] In the early 1970s, for example, McBride claimed to have uncovered the next thalidomide—a widely prescribed antidepressant, imipramine. For thousands of women who used the drug it was shocking news. An investigation of McBride's evidence was ordered, and he recanted.

Bendectin was McBride's next big shot, and the rabbit studies were his prime evidence. In December 1987, a Scottish pediatrician and science journalist appearing on Australian television charged McBride with outright scientific fraud. According to two of McBride's own professional colleagues, McBride had not only named them as co-authors of the 1982 rabbit paper without their consent but had "altered results to strengthen inconclusive experiments with the rabbits."[58] McBride had not tested as many rabbits as claimed; he had not used controls; he had not accurately reported doses. An investigative committee appointed by McBride's own Foundation 41 and headed by a former Australian Chief Justice confirmed the charges in November 1988.[59] "The experiment mentioned in [McBride's] paper was not conducted in accordance with proper scientific method and was not honestly reported. . . . Dr. McBride was lacking in scientific integrity."[60]

By this point, the evidence that Bendectin does *not* cause birth defects was all but overwhelming. Over thirty epidemiological studies had concluded as much. Official government and international reviews of the data by the FDA, the World Health Organization, and other health agencies around the world concurred. The editor of the journal *Teratology* called Bendectin the "most famous tortogen/litogen and the best studied human non-teratogen."[61] There was, according to the director of science information for the March of Dimes Birth Defects Foundation, "a general consensus among teratologists that Bendectin was one of the best studied drugs of all time for use in pregnancy and the great preponderance of evidence generally exonerates it from any harmful effect."[62]

McBride was due one last indignity. Only a few months after the irregularities in his research had been exposed, the New South Wales Medical Tribunal began to investigate fifteen complaints accusing McBride of professional misconduct.[63] Six of the complaints involved charges of scientific fraud; among others was that McBride was performing cesarean sections in over half the deliveries he conducted at one hospital.[64] Meanwhile, McBride's libel suit against *Science* magazine had been dismissed,[65] then reinstated,[66] and then largely resolved by summary judgment against McBride.[67]

A TERATOGEN AT LAST?

Some will discern in the Bendectin story a fine vindication for the legal system. In the end, Done's credentials and theories were discredited. In the end, McBride's fraud was exposed—not by the courts, to be sure, but by the scientific community. In the end, Merrell won pretty much everything, if one shrugs off the many cases still pending and the small matter of $750,000 owed to Mary Oxendine. Stanley Chesley alone reportedly lost $1 million in backing the Bendectin horse.[68] Merrell, however, probably spent upward of $100 million for its vindication. But for the insatiable greed of the lawyers, Merrell would also have paid $120 million to put an end to the legal nausea.

On June 9, 1983, Merrell capitulated to the lawyers and pulled Bendectin from the market. In the eight years since, the birth-defects monitoring program of the Centers for Disease Control in Atlanta has found no significant change in the incidence of birth defects. "In particular, the incidence of limb defects has remained stable," says José F. Cordero, assistant director of the program. "If Bendectin were teratogenic, given its extremely widespread use, we would have expected to see a drop in the incidence of congenital malformations."[69]

So much for the Bendectin babies. What about the lawyers? Needless to say, the courtroom nausea, the hyperemesis of the legal kind, did not in fact end with the discrediting of McBride and Done. On August 11, 1989, notwithstanding Done's misrepresentation of his credentials, a Washington, D.C., court of appeals resurrected the *Oxendine* verdict once again.[70] By that point, the verdict had been approved three times (by a jury and two appellate courts) and thrown out twice (by two trial judges). As of this writing, the case is still open on the question of punitive damages. Other Bendectin cases were still inching forward elsewhere. Nace had won yet another jury verdict (for $300,000) that remained on appeal. Another case was still pending in Utah. And yet another in Massachusetts, and one in Oklahoma.[71] Judge Carl Rubin, who had overseen Chesley's class action suit in Cincinnati, was presiding over a second Bendectin class action. The betting was that many of these cases would drag on for years.

It is not an experience that anyone in the pharmaceutical industry cares to repeat. "We wouldn't bring Bendectin back," a Merrell spokesman declared, even "if we won every lawsuit."[72] No other U.S. pharmaceutical company is ever going to expose itself to such legal risks either, so private research into pregnancy-related drugs has virtually stopped.[73] "If you're suffering from morning sickness," runs one bitter joke in the industry, "go see your lawyer."

The story ends on the serious note of what may prove to be the real Bendectin disaster. It involves children, of course. Not David Mekdeci, Mary Oxendine, Anne Elizabeth Koller, or Sekou Ealy—no one can be quite sure what caused their heart-wrenching injuries, but it clearly wasn't Bendectin. The children at issue now are the ones who suffered at the hands of the lawyers.

First, the lawyers whipped up hysteria. The editor of *Teratology* reports he "personally was aware of seven tragic and unnecessary abortions" that occurred in the weeks following the Belli-

Mekdeci-McBride story in the *National Enquirer.* Then the lawyers drove Bendectin off the market. According to an official of
the American College of Obstetricians and Gynecologists, the
loss of Bendectin created a "significant therapeutic gap."[74]
There are still women today, like Charlotte Brontë in 1855, for
whom morning sickness is a debilitating problem. Excessive
vomiting starves the pregnant mother's body of normal nourish-
ment, and the body begins to metabolize its own carbohydrates,
fats, and proteins to nourish the unborn child. Toxic chemical
by-products of this self-digestion are known to cause birth defects.

The *Journal of the American Medical Association* reported in 1990
"a two-fold increase in hospitalizations caused by severe nausea
and vomiting in pregnancy since the disappearance of Bendectin." For the women affected, "[s]evere nausea and vomiting can
eventually cause dehydration and acidosis, which threaten the
health of the mother and the fetus. . . . [S]evere cases have led
to serious maternal nutritional deficiencies and nerve damage.
Birth defects may well increase."[75]

CHAPTER 8

The Paranoia Plebiscite

The Legal Pursuit of Fad Terrors

*The theories and dogmas of scientific men, though provable by scientific refer-
ence, cannot be held to be controlling unless shared by the people generally.*
—*Everett v. Paschall* (1910)

Ella Bowley's baby was born quite healthy and unblemished. But
for four months the pregnant mother had been intensely worried that her latest child would be "deformed or marked."
About halfway through her pregnancy she had gone on a car
ride with her husband to buy some groceries and to "give the
children an airing."[1] Mr. Bowley had run into another car. And
Mrs. Bowley, like many pregnant women of the 1920s, believed
that trauma during pregnancy caused birthmarks on the unborn
infant. She sued, demanding compensation for her months of
worry. A defense expert dismissed the birthmark theory as
"scientifically unsound." But science was irrelevant, the New
Hampshire Supreme Court ruled in 1923. It simply didn't matter that had Mrs. Bowley "been thoroughly versed in medical
science she would have known that her fears were groundless."

Other courts took quite a different view.[2] Fear, anxiety, worry,
and such might be compensated, but only within bounds established by solid science. Even an indisputably real injury would

not support open-ended claims based on scientifically unreasonable fears. You have been bitten by a dog and you greatly fear rabies. Very well, you are entitled to damages for the bite, and for the fear. But regardless of how long the fear may last in your mind, its legal life ends a year or so after the bite, since that's about the outer limit on incubation of rabies. Five years after the bite you may still live in mortal terror of rabies, and may present a dozen friends and psychiatrists to testify to how frightened you really are. No matter—your fear is no longer scientifically reasonable.

Or so many courts ruled, from the late 1800s until the 1920s, in cases involving fear of such things as rabies, tetanus, blood poisoning, and miscarriage. Pieces of glass are removed from a plaintiff's stomach and he is "restored to his former condition of health and vigor"; at that point, the Georgia Supreme Court ruled in 1905, "his fears, so far as a damage suit are concerned, should cease."[3] A woman falls ill after sitting in an unheated railroad depot on a drizzling, windy, cold day. She develops a cold, fever, stomach trouble . . . and then a morbid fear of tuberculosis, which recently killed her sister. In 1909, the Arkansas Supreme Court flatly rejects the fear claim pressed against the railroad.[4] A plaintiff injured on the hand may not present to the jury his fears of blood poisoning and amputation, the Kentucky Court of Appeals rules in 1923, when the hand has not become infected, and the fears, which have "never materialized," are in fact "altogether groundless."[5] As late as 1974, a hospital patient in Wisconsin would be denied fear-of-cancer damages after a catheter in his shoulder broke, leaving two pieces that could not be found. He genuinely feared cancer, the court accepted, but there was no actual risk to speak of.[6]

Surprisingly, cases involving no initial injury—and no claim for damages—proved more troublesome. In 1898, for example, a Maryland appellate court had to decide between Mary Sansone, a woman suffering from leprosy, and her frightened neighbors, who didn't want her lodging next door. The school-age children of the family Sansone was living with would meet others at school, the neighbors maintained, making Mary a "constant menace and peril." The Maryland court quite understood:

"Leprosy is, and has always been, universally regarded with horror and loathing. . . . In past ages its unfortunate victims, shunned and avoided by their fellowmen, viewed by all with superstitious dread, wandered about the open country naked and starving. . . . The horror of its contagion is as deep-seated today as it was more than two thousand years ago in Palestine." And what of the science? "There are modern theories and opinions of medical experts that the contagion is remote and by no means dangerous," the court conceded. No matter. The court would not be swayed by "a mere academic inquiry as to whether the disease is in fact highly or remotely contagious." The fear of leprosy "cannot in this day be shaken or dispelled by mere scientific asseveration or conjecture."[7]

Two decades after the Sansone episode came the case against Benjamin S. Paschall, who wished to board ten tuberculosis patients in his Seattle cottage. Paschall's horrified neighbors sued to have the operation shut down. "[T]here is no real danger," Paschall informed the trial court. "The fear or dread of the disease is, in the light of scientific investigation, unfounded, imaginary, and fanciful." Paschall was right. Tuberculosis is indeed "contagious," but that unadorned label has little scientific meaning. Measles is so contagious that one infected child breathing for half an hour in an auditorium can spread the disease to hundreds. Leprosy, the greatest contagious terror of antiquity, is in fact one of the most weakly contagious diseases known; years of exposure and contact seem to be necessary for its transmission. In the loosest sense of the word, cancer is contagious too, because some communicable diseases like hepatitis increase the risk of some forms of cancer. Even in Paschall's day, scientists well understood that risks of contagion vary widely, and can sometimes be eliminated through simple protections. Tuberculosis is spread by prolonged contact in close spaces, but not from one house to another.

The trial judge understood this, and agreed with Paschall that his boarders posed no significant danger. "[T]here exists a general public dread of tuberculosis . . . in the minds of persons ignorant of the true nature of the disease," the judge acknowledged. But Paschall was conducting his sanitarium quite safely.

"[T]here [is] no danger to persons living in the immediate vicinity," the judge found. And he would take no account of "a fear unfounded and unsustained by science, a demon of the imagination."

The unanimous Washington Supreme Court accepted every word of this except the last. "[W]e question our right to say that the fear is unfounded or unreasonable, when it is shared by the whole public. . . . The question is, not whether the fear is founded in science but whether it exists; not whether it is imaginary, but whether it is real in that it affects the movements and conduct of men. Such fears are actual and must be recognized by the court as other emotions of the human mind."[8] Since laypeople generally differ from scientists in this instance, Paschall's patients would have to live elsewhere.

No one can doubt that the fears of Paschall's neighbors in 1910 were sincere, even plausible, though mistaken. Tuberculosis was at that time responsible for one of every seven deaths. Of course people were frightened. Speaking generally, they had much to be frightened about. Speaking specifically, however, Paschall's cottage endangered no one but Paschall. The science was solid enough. But not popular enough, at least not for some judges.

Few judges, however, cared to put the matter quite so bluntly. So even as they brushed aside "academic inquiry" and the "theories and dogmas of scientific men," they also scrambled to suggest that science might really be on their side. Not the mainstream pundits, perhaps, but at least some from the fringe, or at the very least the science of intuition and common sense.

The *Paschall* court, for example, felt obliged to write a blustery paragraph demonstrating why fear is important, quoting such authorities as *Paris Revue* and Alfred Capus, a "psychological playwright." "Fear consists in capitulating to the instinct of self-preservation," the court solemnly explained. "[I]t is far from being unanimously admitted that fear is a ridiculous malady."[9] A few months later, the Kansas Supreme Court considered the construction of a cancer hospital in Kansas City. Some experts had been found to testify that cancer may be transmitted "by means of insects, and perhaps in other ways." Cancer is not

contagious, the defendants replied. The court looked around
for "the prevailing view in the medical profession." "From the
current literature of the subject," the court conceded, "it has
not been proved to the satisfaction of the profession generally
that cancer can be communicated from one individual to another." But the court did manage to locate a French study pur-
porting to identify certain "cancer houses" and suggesting contagious origins of the disease. "[C]ompetent investigators are
not lacking who believe that [cancer] is of parasitic origin and
in some degree infectious," the court continued. "Not lacking,"
it turned out, would suffice: "The question is not whether the
establishment of the hospital would place the occupants of the
adjacent dwellings in actual danger of infection, but whether
they would have reasonable ground to fear such a result." They
did. Cancer, then as now, inspired "general dread." So construction of the hospital would be halted.[10]

And thus there slowly evolved a judicial faith in the paranoia
plebiscite. Whatever science might say, fear would count for
legal purposes if it "affect[s] the ordinary comfort of human
existence as understood by the American people in their present
state of enlightenment," declared the court in *Paschall.* Mary
Sansone's court appealed to the views of "the people generally," the "judgment of reasonable men," the discomforts of
persons of "ordinary sensibilities." The Kansas court that en-
joined a cancer hospital pointed to the "general dread" inspired
by that disease. In Ella Bowley's case, what mattered was that the
connection between birthmarks and trauma during pregnancy
had been "uniformly accepted by the laity."

Groundless fears, in short, would be controlled by the courts
if shared by the teeming masses. The fear is irrational, granted.
At war with science, if you insist. But "reasonable" nonetheless.
How can this be? Only if science does not have the last word on
reason. Which is to say, only if views of "the people generally,"
with all their prejudices, superstitions, and inchoate dreads,
count even more. How are the views of the masses to be ascertained? The judge will conduct a straw poll, starting with the
plaintiff.

WELL GROUNDED, NOT JUST WIDESPREAD

Some judges will, but by no means all. As far back as the days of *Paschall* and even before, many, perhaps most, courts took a much more hard-headed view of public fear and how to address it—the same firm view many of them took in the cases involving dog bites and blood poisoning. To recover for fear, in these courts at least, you had to prove your case not once but twice, to the satisfaction of both the psychologist and the scientist. Neither the fearless stoic, indifferent even to real dangers, nor the hypochondriac, terrified by imaginary ones, could recover. This was certainly not the rule in all courts, as *Paschall* and its progeny abundantly demonstrated. But it was the dominant rule that held sway in many others.

One line of cases, like *Paschall,* came under the rubric of "nuisance," a legal doctrine with roots in medieval England. From the beginning, "terror" had indeed been part of the legal package. The early nuisance cases spoke of "filthinesses which are in the ways and lanes of the said city and the suburbes thereof, the air there is so much corrupted and infected, that a dreadful terror strikes the [populace]."[11] But terror alone generally did not suffice. Even the *Paschall* and *Sansone* courts had acknowledged an English decision from 1752, in which Lord Hardwicke had refused to stop the building of a smallpox hospital. "[T]he fears of mankind though they may be reasonable ones, will not create a nuisance," Hardwicke had declared.[12] In 1887, another English judge likewise rejected an attack on a smallpox hospital, accepting the defendant's argument that "the fears of mankind were not a ground for granting an injunction."[13]

This standard, adopted by many American courts of the day, required judges to take science seriously. For a heartening contrast to the windiness of *Paschall,* one may read another sanitarium case of the same era, a 1905 opinion by Judge Beitler of Pennsylvania. Experts who had testified on the danger of living near the tuberculosis sanitarium "covered the subject from one extreme to the other," Beitler noted. "Any one reading their testimony will be driven to the conclusion . . . that it is the part of prudence not to do so." For the *Paschall* court five years later, that would be the end of the case. But not for Beitler. He visited the sanitarium to ascertain "its situations and surroundings," and initiated his own correspondence with public health authorities, on the strength of which he concluded that "the sanit[a]rium, as conducted, constitutes no menace to the health of the neighbors." "But I am constrained to say," he added candidly, "that I have not sufficient faith in my belief to warrant me in selecting, if I were hunting a suburban home, a house in close proximity to the sanit[a]rium."[14]

So the dilemma was as sharp as could be. The common citizen—and even this uncommonly wise judge—remained anxious about contagion. Mainstream science, however, was reassuring. Wiser courts insisted that fears had to be "well grounded," not just "widespread." "It is true that there exists a strong prejudice on the part of some people against living in the vicinity of such an institution," a court acknowledged in a 1926 challenge to an isolation hospital. "But if there be no actual danger of infection . . . the mere fear of such a danger will not suffice."[15]

Courts gradually developed rules of evidence and standards of proof to ensure that claimed fears were both real and reasonable. They would come to emphasize one requirement in particular: initial "impact," "physical manifestation," or "concrete event." At a minimum, fear claims would be entertained only when there was something tangible behind them—a decline of property values in the *Paschall*-style nuisance cases, or some actual physical impact at the outset. Even if the neighbor's dog looked a trifle foamy, you could press your fear-of-rabies claim only after the dog bit you, not while he remained securely chained next door.

The impact rule worked double time in raising standards of proof. First, it weeded out fears that exist only for the purposes of litigation. Faking morbid fear of the dog next door is easy; faking a dog bite isn't. Second, the impact rule helped pin down many fears that are scientifically baseless. By insisting that the punch actually have landed before you can press a fear-of-cancer suit, courts give real science something concrete to challenge. We have seen just this sort of punch before, a good scientist can confidently attest, and we know that whatever else it may cause, it doesn't cause cancer. Even in the much vaguer circumstances of the contagion cases, the requirement of a concrete effect on something like local property values shifts the focus to the larger community—and thus makes it easier for a competent epidemiologist to assess whether the risk is real.

In retrospect, the line drawn in many of these cases seems remarkably solid. In the contagion cases, the judges who invoked mainstream science were putting their faith in a science that was still rather young. Other plaintiffs, having been bitten, poisoned, traumatized, and catheterized in diverse ways at the outset, had much to be paranoid about. No one questioned the genuineness of the fears in any of these cases. The psychologist's half of the case was convincing. The scientist's wasn't. Whatever claims might be allowed for the bite, poisoning, and so on, most judges held firm when it came to separate claims for irrational fear. Through the 1940s and into the 1950s, a growing number of courts gradually came to agree on the twin requirements of real and reasonable in all fear cases.

MODERN TIMES

In the late 1950s the trend was reversed. Courts came to believe that liability law should operate as a reasonably generous system of accident insurance. One by one, rules were adjusted to permit more recovery, more often. The most obvious place to expand rights of recovery in fear litigation was when there had been some concrete injury at the outset and only the risk of future disease was in dispute.

New York's top court handed down a landmark ruling in just such a case in 1958. A decade earlier, Eleanor Ferrara had been suffering from bursitis. Her doctor, Anthony Galluchio, prescribed a series of X-ray treatments, which burned and exposed the flesh on her right shoulder. One surmises that Galluchio's treatments were part of a junk science, X-ray-treatment fad among some medics of the day, and Ferrara may well have had a valid malpractice claim for the burns themselves. But she would claim a good bit more.

Her lawyer, when first consulted, promptly referred her to a dermatologist of his acquaintance, who advised Ferrara to have her shoulder checked every six months thereafter, to monitor for cancer. As a result, Ferarra would claim, she developed severe "cancerphobia," a neurotic anxiety that cancer was inevitable. Her "neuro-psychiatrist" would testify that her anxiety might be permanent. What no one would testify to, however, was that it was well founded. To the contrary: "[W]e are not making any claim that [Ferrara] is going to sustain a cancer," her lawyer conceded at trial. "We are going on a neurosis." The jury went along, awarding Ferrara more for the neurosis than for the burns themselves. Four justices of New York's high court affirmed the verdict. "It is common knowledge among laymen and even more widely among laywomen that wounds which do not heal over long periods of time frequently become cancerous," the majority explained. How did they know? "Physical culture lectures to high school and college students, radio advice from life insurance companies, newspaper daily articles by doctors— all give the same advice."[16]

Ferrara marked a major turning point in fear cases. The scientist-in-your-corner requirement quickly eroded. Many courts came around to the view that, at least in the aftermath of the bite, the burn, or whatever, fear of future disease is inherently "reasonable," with or without scientific testimony that it really is.

Thus, in 1962, the New Jersey Supreme Court would uphold an award to Theodore Lorenc, who greatly feared he would develop cancer as a result of a chemical burn to his hand.[17] The risk was in fact utterly remote, and could have been entirely eliminated by means of the skin graft that Lorenc had refused to undergo. By 1974, the Louisiana Supreme Court would display still less hesitation in blessing a fear-of-cancer award to a fifty-seven-year-old welder, Henry Anderson, who had suffered radiation burns to his right hand. Anderson's own doctor had not even discussed the future risk of cancer with him, because "the possibility was too remote." The state Supreme Court, however, reinstated the full jury award. "[T]o a scientist in his ivory tower the possibility of cancerous growth may be so minimal as to be untroubling," the court conceded. But "this real possibility to this worrying workman" nonetheless merited full compensation.[18]

Through the 1960s and the 1970s, courts steadily downplayed the science in fear cases precipitated by such things as catheters,[19] blades lost inside patients during surgery,[20] and stabbings in shopping-mall parking lots.[21] In due course, chemical toxins, electromagnetic fields, microwaves, and trace contaminants in foods would all be elevated to new legal respectability by similar appeals to fear rather than fact. Courts would spend more and more time canvassing the neighborhood, less and less consulting the National Academy of Sciences.

Inevitably, there came a case involving pure hypochondria. A Helen Stoleson had experienced chest pains after she had begun handling nitroglycerin in a government munitions factory. A federal district judge awarded her $53,000 in damages. All the experts agreed that her health problems ended when she left the job. Stoleson, however, remained convinced that she was permanently disabled. Her ingenious lawyer argued that because she was no longer physically sick, she deserved still more. Why? Because she had become a certified hypochondriac, as exhibited by her perfect health coupled with her paranoid fear. The claim did not survive on appeal, but only because of lame concerns that hypochondria is too difficult to diagnose.[22]

THE CANCER EPIDEMIC

By the 1970s, tuberculosis had largely succumbed to vaccines and antibiotics, smallpox was soon to be eradicated from the face of the planet, and leprosy had all but disappeared. Infectious diseases had given way to chronic and degenerative diseases, most visibly, cancer. There is in fact a cancer epidemic, of sorts, caused (ironically) by the vaccines and antibiotics. Cancer is primarily a disease of old age; the most certain way to avoid it is to die young. In 1910, one in seven people died of tuberculosis, often quite young; sixty years later, one in six died of cancer, usually quite old. When you adjust for longevity and strip out the effects of tobacco, the cancer epidemic evaporates.

But adjusting and stripping are the arcane statistical tools of an epidemiologist. What ordinary people see is their relatives and friends succumbing to cancer more often than ever before, often in great pain and lingering misery. The disease is every bit as mysterious as tuberculosis and leprosy had been half a century before. Inevitably it became the main new object of public dread.

The dread is compounded, not dispelled, when science begins to provide some inkling of what is going wrong. The tuberculosis panics of an earlier day followed the discovery that the disease was contagious; it had previously been thought to be hereditary. In the 1950s, the unraveling of the double helix worked a similar transformation: new insight into how life itself replicates quickly offered new insight into how replication can go awry, to produce a cancer cell or a birth defect. The new biochemistry of genes immediately suggests a new biochemistry of gene corruption—most obviously by other chemicals or energetic micro-projectiles from radiation. Most frighteningly, the corruption is completely invisible, occurring at the scale of individual atoms and molecules.

The toxic waste dump at Love Canal near Buffalo, New York, which captured the headlines in the late 1970s, gripped the public imagination. It seemed that toxic chemical wastes were becoming the new tuberculosis, a ubiquitous, insidious peril, striking indiscriminately, responsible for a new epidemic of cancer and birth defects. Actually counting those cancers and birth defects, or indeed proving that any had been caused at all, would turn out to be much more difficult than writing newspaper stories about them; the hazards were eventually found to be far less grave than many at first feared. But many still feared nonetheless. And for some, fears of toxic chemical wastes would soon eclipse all others. With or without an epidemic of disease, an epidemic of litigation was inevitable.

How were judges to react? For some time they had accepted the idea that fears are generally "reasonable" once you've been hit, bit, cut, or burned. So why insist on the hit or other battery to start with? Many people can find something to be fearful about long before the dog bites, the catheter is lost, or the vorpal blade cuts snicker snack. Especially in the age of microbiology. After all, the microscopic and invisible—in the form of pollution, pesticides, radiation, and the like—assail us continuously from all sides.

This logic seemed compelling when the toxic chemical cases began to be litigated in the early 1980s. Soon enough, some judges allowed the bark to replace the bite. It became a source of legal entitlement to be frightened by "little" impacts—from shock waves, chemicals in polluted water, impurities in drugs. Time limits on how long people could legitimately stay frightened eroded too. Rabies conveniently has an incubation period of a year, but as everyone knows, chemicals and drugs may work their effects over decades, even generations.

The "impact" rule was discarded first in the most sympathetic cases, indeed, in cases where there could be little doubt that an impact of some importance really did occur. Seven decades after *Paschall,* another tuberculosis case provided one court with the appropriate vehicle. As in *Paschall,* the case involved neighbors; these neighbors happened to reside in a federal prison. One of them, it turned out, had active tuberculosis. The others were dismayed to discover this, and sued their landlord, the federal government. None had in fact become sick, but some did test positive for exposure; without doubt, the tubercle bacilli had entered their lungs. In 1978, the prisoners' claim for distress was allowed to proceed. "Admittedly, the 'impact' of a tubercle bacillus does not entail the palpable physical shock of a highway collision," the appellate court reasoned, but "the effects of a concededly minute tubercle bacillus are potentially no less lethal."[23]

It was not a particularly difficult case. The prisoners were worried; a knowledgeable physician might have been too. But the upshot was that this court, like many others, would soon allow fear claims without any visible "impact" to speak of, and many of the fears in question would be grounded in bad science.

The legal logic that worked for the prisoners and the tubercle bacillus is equally good for an alpha particle of radiation or a molecule of dioxin. Science can speculate readily enough about a possible mechanism, but it cannot begin to connect up the alleged causes and the feared effects. Epidemiological studies detected little of any significance. But the public fears were real, sometimes acute. Since we can never be absolutely certain that there's nothing to fear, plaintiffs began to win at least the funds (often running into the millions of dollars) they would need to find out. That they never would find out was of small importance; money changed hands anyway.

There was much discussion in legal circles about whether it might perhaps be too easy for people to pretend to be terrified even when they really weren't. Endless pages were written on how a wise judge might smoke out the faked fears while still allowing the real ones. The legal opinions were still replete with language about how the fear had to be "reasonable," not "idio-syncratic," "natural," not "eccentric," of a kind that any "normally constituted person" would share in similar circumstances. The fear had to have induced observable physical symptoms, or at least had to have triggered anguished visits to a doctor. A fear-of-cancer claim by Gwendolyn Mink, a DES daughter, was apparently undercut when she neglected to see a psychiatrist about the fears she claimed to suffer.[24] It all sounded ever so restrained.

But it was mostly a great exercise in misdirection. The one really important restraint—the one requiring that fears be based in solid scientific fact—had been discarded. Without a well-defined impact at the outset, science cannot say whether any subsequent fear is reasonable. Good science cannot deal with excitations that are vanishingly small, or consequences that—if they exist at all—lie indefinitely far in the future. The courts thus slid back to 1910, and the one-stop, common-citizen test for when fears count. The scientist faded from the plaintiff's case, to be replaced by a team of psychologists. It was not an even exchange. Courts quietly reverted to the paranoia plebiscite that had dominated much legal discourse in the days of tuberculosis.

Legal pundits were generally delighted. A new wave of phobia litigation was to be encouraged, to provide "a vehicle for asserting a sense of dread in the face of uncertainty." "Scientists, like other professionals, can no longer lay claim to the argument that their special knowledge deserves complete autonomy." The courtroom may "serve as a stage for dramatizing the sense of dread attendant upon many risk-creating activities."[25] *Paschall,* seventy-three years old when this was written, was cited anew with warm approval. A few prisoners aside, most people were not alarmed about tuberculosis any more. But what worked to close a tuberculosis sanitarium can surely work now to close a chemical factory, a nuclear power plant, or a recombinant DNA research laboratory. So hooray again for the common citizen. Time, once again, to take his fears seriously.

As the common citizen rises, the good scientist falls. Keep hammering at the ubiquity, naturalness, inevitability of the public's fears, and after a while it seems unnecessary to talk about anything else.

THE NEW LEPROSY

The common citizen's gaze, however, will soon be fixed on a new star in the firmament of phobias. There arrives on the scene a bizarre, almost undetectable new toxin. It seems to be ubiquitous. Its effects are horrible. It soon ranks as the leprosy of a new age, a source of universal dread. It's called HIV, and it causes AIDS.

So what should we all do, learned judges and the rest, when the new-age Mary Sansone moves in next door? Or sends her HIV-infected hemophiliac child to the neighborhood school? Or sets up a hospice to care for the dying, who do indeed die with awful regularity, often in the most miserable ways imaginable? The common citizen will find his answer quickly enough, for it has scarcely changed in the seventy years since Mary Sansone was sent packing. Blessed, no doubt, are those who comfort the sick and tend to the dying, so long as they don't comfort and tend too close to me.

For these new Samaritans, 1988 is a fairly typical and busy year. In January, two parents of children at a Fairfax, Virginia, school declare they are "trying to get a petition together and find out how to get an injunction to prevent [an] AIDS child from returning to school."[26] In March, the Texas Association of Realtors tells its members to advise prospective buyers if a house for sale has been occupied by a person with AIDS, for if buyers find out later they might end up suing.[27] In April, prospective landlords in Dallas refuse to lease space to an AIDS patient day-care center, fearing lawsuits by others who fear contagion.[28] In June, an arson trial begins in Queens, New York, against defendants who feared that conversion of a local house to a city-run shelter would bring AIDS into their neighborhood.[29] Soon thereafter, one group of AIDS-fearing litigants procured the testimony of a family practitioner, who asserted that medical associations, federal public-health officials, and the attorney general of the United States were all lying to the public about AIDS, that studies have been falsified, and that unexplained cases supported his view that AIDS is transmitted by casual contact, sneezing, and coughing.[30]

In all of these instances, some of the litigants fear contagion, of course. Others just fear fear-of-contagion lawsuits by other students, tenants, or employees on the same premises. Even if the first fear is groundless, the second certainly is not. Say's Law springs into action: the supply of legal solutions creates its own demand, whether or not there are real problems to go along with them. All of this on the heels of a memorandum from the federal government—the Department of Justice, no less—to the effect that if you're honestly frightened about AIDS contagion, it's quite legal to act on that fear, to shun the sick and avoid the dying.[31]

So the common citizen's fears are legally preeminent once again. Yes, the scientists assure the few who care to listen, AIDS is "contagious," loosely speaking. Just as (loosely speaking) some chemicals are "carcinogenic," just as gas tanks "may explode," just as nuclear materials "may melt down." Sweeping language of this kind is always useful for inspiring fear. But God is in the details, and nowhere is this more true than with the Creator's immutable laws of science. The details of AIDS, so far as contagion is concerned, are not too complicated. AIDS contagion operates through body fluids, on the scale of millimeters, no further.

NOTHING TO FEAR

"[I]t is far from being unanimously admitted that fear is a ridiculous malady."[32] As we have seen, this trenchant insight seemed to be important to the Washington Supreme Court in 1910, in its ruling against Paschall. Indeed, fear is often not a ridiculous malady. The line between ridiculous fears and the other kind is the line drawn by medicine and science against ignorance and superstition.

It is thus a line that depends very much on the quality of the science at hand. The only way a fear can be "baseless" and "reasonable" at the same time is if one kind of science underlies the first label, and another the second. No judge will openly admit to embracing junk science on the road to compensating junk fears. But in one junk-fear case after the next, eminent jurists pay lip service to the serious science and then slouch off to embrace the junk. Thus, in 1986, an Indianapolis judge terminated a divorced father's right to visit his two-year-old daughter when the father tested positive for AIDS. "It's probably a small risk," the judge conceded, "but if there's even a 1 percent chance, I don't feel she should be exposed."[33]

In 1987, the courts did finally draw at least one solid line against similar abominations in the context of employment. The Florida schoolteacher Gene Arline had been fired after suffering a third relapse of tuberculosis within two years. She claimed discrimination, rendered unlawful under the federal Rehabilitation Act of 1973. And seventy-seven years after Benjamin Paschall closed shop, the United States Supreme Court finally added a last word on tuberculosis. Of course no one who is *in fact* contagious has a right to teach school. But, as the American Medical Association had argued to the Court, a decision on contagion must turn on "facts, based on reasonable medical judgments given the state of medical knowledge." Citizens enjoy a federal right to be protected from "discrimination on the basis of mythology" and the "complex and often pernicious mythologies about the nature, cause, and transmission of illness." Congress intended to prevent discrimination based on handicap. And "society's accumulated myths and fears," the

Court concludes, are "as handicapping as are the physical limitations that flow from actual impairment."[34]

Lewis Carroll could hardly have devised a better ending for the chronicles of tuberculosis in court. You are *not* contagious, and therefore not in fact handicapped. The common citizen believes that you *are* contagious, however, and you are therefore fired. So the Supreme Court of the United States certifies that you *are* handicapped, by virtue of the common citizen's irrational prejudices. Which means that you are legally entitled to be treated as if you were *not* handicapped. Which you aren't anyway.

But even so interpreted, federal antidiscrimination law covers a narrow range of acts directed against specific individuals. Countless other opportunities for junk-fear litigation against hospitals and hospices, factories, products, and power plants, remain at hand. After all, who can really say for sure that contagion—or chemical wastes, or nuclear reactors, or explosive materials, or violent prisoners, or well-sealed asbestos, or the HIV virus in AIDS-infected children—has ever been absolutely, categorically, forever contained? No one. And any court wishing to banish the container will quickly remind you of as much. Early on, the court will hastily acknowledge the views of mainstream science, the elaborate calculations of the engineers, the assessments of the public-health authorities. No, no, this chemical is not poisonous, that patient not contagious at all. Probably not. But then again, who knows? What about the flies and the mosquitoes? Or the patients who might wander off unsupervised? Or the schoolchildren who might bite? This is the jurist's version of nudge-and-wink science. The appeal is to science—junk science—but with enormous powers of suggestion. No, no, the experts tell us, the disease won't spread. But it *is* "contagious." And there are these flies around, you see. It is a sort of grown-up version of the campfire horror story.

The far-side scientists are in their element, for they are great masters at telling stories. Once they are welcomed in court, anything is possible. Of course they will be answered by mainstreamers, but what is a jurist to do, split the difference? Splitting the difference between a good scientist who says mosquitoes don't spread AIDS and a bad one who says they just might is to conclude that they just-just-might. Given the horrifying specter of AIDS, a just-just-might risk is something to worry about. The greater the spread between good science and junk, and the greater the common citizen's ignorance, the more superficially "reasonable" the ensuing fear becomes. And junk science can always gain more leverage in the split-the-difference bargaining by moving farther out into left field.

And so the verbal dilapidation of science proceeds. The judge of course notes the views of the "profession generally," as published in professional journals and aired at respectable symposia. But then there are also some "competent investigators" who disagree with the mainstream. And then the ubiquitous flies, so obvious that no scientific assessment is needed at all— even a humble judge can intuitively grasp their importance. Before you know it, you're just where you began: the "general dread" has become specific. It's in the mind of the judge, and that's one place where dread really counts.

So junk science, we discover at last, does address real injuries: injuries of its own creation. There may be nothing to fear but fear itself, but fear is good for a lawsuit, both coming and going. The falsehood comes first, the injury follows. The word becomes flesh. This new account of the coming does not include a parable of the Good Samaritan, however. The leper is sent elsewhere, and all too often Paschall's patients must find new accommodations.

CHAPTER 9

Harmonious Coupling

Ignoring the Environment

THEOCRATO: Henceforth, in all tort cases, cause-in-fact between defendant and
plaintiff is no longer a necessary connective for liability.
PRACON: Outstanding. Ridiculous, but outstanding. Are you with Critical
Legal Studies?
                                    —Ronald Lansing
                        The Motherless Calf, Aborted Cow Theory of Cause (1984)

Joan Berry's mistake, her lawyers said, had been to fall for
Charlie Chaplin. She was a naive young woman of modest
means. He was a wealthy and famous movie star, reputed to have
had many affairs. Sometime in December 1942, she became
pregnant. Not long after, she demanded that Chaplin pay child
support for her new daughter, Carol Ann.

It was a scandalous trial. Berry claimed she had slept with
Chaplin on December 10, 23, 24, and 30. Chaplin was required
to parade in front of the jury beside Joan and her infant child.
Chaplin's butler agreed there had been a meeting on December
23. Chaplin himself admitted a liaison with Berry before March
1942, but denied all the December trysts.

It emerged, however, that in November, and again the following January and April, Joan had traveled to Tulsa, Oklahoma,
where another male companion had wined and dined her, taken

her to the theater, and then joined her at her hotel. She had also spent time with another man in Los Angeles, twice visiting his apartment. And in the spring of 1943 she told Chaplin's butler that she had married an army captain and was going to bear a child. The jurors nevertheless sided with Joan and Carol. Chaplin would have to pay.[1]

On appeal, a California appellate court acknowledged Chaplin's objection that marching him around the courtroom beside Joan and Carol had "caused compassionate visualization of the ancient masterpieces of 'Madonna and Child.' " But "the character of the evidence," the court concluded, "kept the minds of the jurors fixed on the unspiritual and terrestrial affairs of the mother and defendant." "Perhaps the jurors thought that the biological connection was less critical than [Chaplin's] exploitation of the woman and the fact that he easily *could* have been the father," one legal scholar recently speculated. After all, "[s]he became responsible for a newborn and was stuck with expenses while he continued his glamorous life. Or they may have felt that it was time for him to 'pay' for the numerous affairs he was believed to have had."[2]

THE MOTHERLESS CALF

This story brings us, appropriately enough, to the theory of harmonious coupling. We owe its most candid exposition to the legal scholar Ronald Lansing, who presents it as a Socratic dialogue in his clever article "The Motherless Calf, Aborted Cow Theory of Cause." "For reasons known only to the cow," the protagonist Theocrato begins, "she will not tend to any calf but her own. She will reject that which she did not cause." The result: "calves whose mothers have died will also die on the range while the mothers of stillborn calves look on." Fortunately, there's a simple remedy: "To fool the aborted cow, the cowboy will drape the motherless calf in the hide of the stillborn calf. The cow's senses are thus misled, and she will give suckle. Everyone is happier for it even though there is no biological cause." Tort law, Theocrato maintains, should operate just the same way. There's no reason to cling to "umbilical instincts for actual cause connections"; connecting this and that should be largely a matter of administrative convenience.

Not, Theocrato concedes, to the point where anyone can sue anyone for anything. The cow, to start with, must somehow deserve to be milked—it must have acted negligently, or with the intention of causing harm. The calf must be thirsty and in need of a parent. And finally, there must be "harmonious coupling" between the two. The injury must be "sequential, contiguous, and consistent with the defendant's tortious behavior," "compatible with the kind of injury suffered by the plaintiff." Such requirements are maintained not for any reasons scientific, but for "orderly convenience" and administrative simplicity. We cannot, after all, just sue the strawberry jam manufacturer whenever any regular user gets sick.[3]

Theocrato's vision is in fact modern liability science pushed to its logical end. Guido Calabresi himself argued that liability should be based not on "cause" but on "causal linkage," something weaker, though how much weaker remains unclear.[4] The legal retreat from the *Frye* rule on expert testimony slackened things further; it allowed "cause" to be defined by the fringe of science rather than the mainstream. Theocrato, in short, is singing in perfect harmony with the massed choruses of modern American law.

There are the law's parentless calves, to start with, who, like Carol Ann Berry, have either too few fathers or (what amounts to the same thing) too many: the children with missing limbs or cerebral palsy, the targets of runaway cars, the "completely zapped" victims of chemical AIDS. And somehow or other, some milky miscreant is always to be found near at hand. Whether you design cars, sell drugs, or deliver babies, it is *always* possible to conduct more tests, furnish more warnings, try other designs, or emit less pollution. So every cow this side of heaven deserves to be milked, at least for a cup's worth.

How about harmonious coupling, the sequence and contiguity that substitute for cause and effect in Theocrato's courtroom? Broadly speaking, drugs are always "consistent with" birth defects, pelvic disease "consistent with" use of an IUD, car engine microprocessors "consistent with" car acceleration.

Broadly speaking—which is the only kind of speaking supplied by the likes of Arthur Zahalsky—exposure to chemicals is "consistent with" immune system impairment. Theocrato insists that he does not intend to "deny the scientific or common sense notion of cause and effect." But he offers science and common sense as alternatives. Speeding trucks are not "consistent with" lung cancer, Theocrato allows, but he makes no mention of the many judges and juries whose common sense has indicated otherwise. And truth be told, Theocrato doesn't really much believe in science at all: "We don't know what *was;* we don't know what *probably was;* we don't know what *would have been;* but we do know what *could have been.* We know what was possible, so let cause-in-fact be damned." All we can hope for is some "reasonable possibility that [a] defendant could have been the cause." "As far as the jury is concerned," he declares, "their common sense notions of causation will do nicely."

THE IRRELEVANT TRUTH

Now this is convenient, at least for lawyers. Causes in real life are often jumbled and difficult to untangle. Especially in a Calabresian courtroom, where the search for cause extends to the far reaches of time and space, where causes small and large, certain and speculative, must be ranked by the omniscient economist according to how cheaply each might have been controlled. Opportunities for confusion abound.

Consider, for example, Margaret H., a Washington, D.C., secretary with medical symptoms typical of many victims of the Dalkon Shield intrauterine device: pelvic infection in 1970, scars in her right fallopian tubes diagnosed in 1973, and eventually a $1.3 million legal judgment, at that time the largest damage verdict ever returned in Wyoming history. But she hadn't used an IUD at all. She was suing, instead, A. St. George B. "Pony" Duke, heir to a North Carolina tobacco fortune, scion of the family that founded Duke University. Pony Duke had infected her with gonorrhea.[5]

Or consider Rose Cipollone, with medical symptoms typical of many victims of asbestos: degenerative lung disease, loss of one lung, then death from lung cancer on October 21, 1984, at age fifty-eight. She, however, had never been exposed to asbestos. Aspiring to be "glamorous or beautiful . . . [like] Joan Crawford or Bette Davis," she had been a steady purchaser of the Chesterfield, L & M, Virginia Slims, Parliament, and True brands of cigarettes for forty years.[6]

The subjects are impossibly delicate, tragic, and charged with emotion, but they cannot be avoided. Even asbestos and the Dalkon Shield have become part of the junk science story.

From the beginning of World War II through the 1970s, about ten million people were exposed to high levels of asbestos in the workplace. Today, good science confirms that heavy exposure to asbestos multiplies the lung-cancer risks you otherwise face by roughly five to seven times. The Dalkon Shield plays in similar leagues. Soon after worldwide marketing began in 1971, doctors observed that its users were developing pelvic inflammatory disease (PID) six to ten times as often as other women. Both Robins, manufacturer of the Shield, and Manville, a major supplier of asbestos, were driven into bankruptcy. As any knowledgeable scientist will attest, both sold products that caused great harm.

But there is ample room for junk science even when one is dealing with real hazards and grave harms. With asbestos and the Dalkon Shield, junk science served to minimize the role of other, even more important and widespread causes of identical injuries.

Start with PID. The problem is one of *infection,* and infection is tragically common, with or without IUDs. Most cases of PID are caused by sexually transmitted organisms; others, by abortion and various diagnostic procedures. The infection may cause scarring, which may lead to infertility, spontaneous abortion, or life-threatening tubal pregnancy. When the Dalkon Shield was introduced, the best-understood precursor of PID was gonorrhea, which was spreading rapidly as sexual mores relaxed in the late 1960s. A second venereal epidemic, then unrecognized, was also unfolding at the same time: chlamydia trachomatis. Today, chlamydia causes some four million new pelvic infections a year, twice as many as gonorrhea.

Pelvic infections often show no visible symptoms at the time they are contracted. About three-quarters of women exposed to gonorrhea become infected, and of those, nearly half develop PID. And about one in ten women who recover from a single episode of PID becomes infertile. The full consequences were not understood until years after the Dalkon Shield had been removed from the market, as women who had been sexually active settled into stable relationships and sought to conceive. No doubt about it: the Dalkon Shield contributed to PID hazards. But with or without the Shield, PID rates were rising geometrically because of the sexual revolution.

As Dalkon Shield litigation cranked up in the early 1980s, six years after the Shield had been pulled from the market, Robins of course focused its defense on something it had never sold to young women: sex. In one early case, the company's lawyers demanded the names and addresses—and other details—of every sex partner a claimant had had from the age of fourteen on. The questions, the lawyers insisted, were not designed to embarrass and intimidate; Robins was just trying to track down causes. In a friend-of-the-court brief, the Women's Legal Defense Fund objected strenuously. It was opposed by Robins's lawyer, a woman who had in fact been one of the Fund's own founding members. "[G]iven the medical realities, [Robins] is on very strong ground," she declared. In another case, an Iowa woman and her husband, questioned in each other's presence, were asked about her sexual relations before their marriage— ten years before she was fitted with a Shield, and fifteen years before the pelvic infection she believed had caused her problems. Another plaintiff, who had been asked what sort of pantyhose she wore and what kind of fabric was in the crotch, likened the questioning to "an obscene phone call."[7]

The debate might have continued for years, woman by woman, uterus by uterus, with clinical dispassion that would have outraged and offended many. In all likelihood, the pattern set in some early cases would have continued: some settlements, some verdicts, and a range of payments, modest to women who might well have suffered PID before or after using the Shield, much more substantial to those who most probably had not. But before long, the embarrassing and painstaking medical inquiries were swept aside by appalling new revelations. High officials at Robins had known about the Shield's problem well before the information was made public. The ensuing furor swept everything else aside. Before long, all serious legal inquiry into the varied causes of PID had ended.

The asbestos story unfolded along similar lines. Use of asbestos rose in parallel with use of tobacco; most of the World War II asbestos workers were also heavy smokers. Roughly speaking, heavy smoking multiplies the lung-cancer risks you otherwise face by about eighteen times. Together, asbestos and cigarettes can increase lung-cancer risks by multipliers of roughly five (asbestos) and eighteen (tobacco) for a devastating ninetyfold increase.

Like Robins, the asbestos companies did what they could to fill in the tobacco part of the picture, and at first some juries did listen. But experience had already shown that suing tobacco companies directly was next to impossible. Blaming chain-smoking asbestos workers for their own foolishness would be almost as difficult, given the often tragic circumstances by the time the issues came to trial. So asbestos defendants and their insurers tried to blame tobacco without quite blaming either the smoker or the seller of smokes. Plaintiffs' lawyers quickly learned how to blunt this defense very effectively. One, for example, would place a carton of cigarettes in an empty chair in the courtroom, and then mock the defendant's attempt to put nobody on trial.[8] Before long even the mockery became unnecessary; charges of coverup by asbestos manufacturers once again eclipsed an even-handed consideration of the science. By the time Manville filed for bankruptcy in 1982, the scientific inquest in the courts had, for all practical purposes, been closed. Asbestos was culprit enough.

Both scripts might have been pulled straight out of Theocrato's files. IUDs sometimes caused PID; asbestos sometimes causes lung disease. Robins and Manville had obviously done serious wrong in covering up hazard, or so many juries concluded. And with that, other causes of PID and lung disease became all but irrelevant.

They have remained so ever since. The landmark Wyoming verdict against Pony Duke was knocked down on a technicality; it turned out that the amorous and peripatetic Duke had had occasion to infect his lover in Virginia, New York, Pennsylvania, Iowa, and Nebraska, but had somehow missed Wyoming, the one state where Margaret H. had chosen to sue him. Rose Cipollone's husband likewise convinced a jury but still lost the case. A $400,000 verdict in his favor was overturned on appeal, and as of this writing the case is still languishing in the courts.[9] No jury had ever awarded damages against a tobacco company before, nor has any since.

SCIENCE WITHOUT THE DETAILS

What Theocrato prescribes for modern liability is armchair science, the layman's science of gut feel, the lawyer's science of hunch and impression, science that ignores dosage and timing, science without numbers, science without rigor, science without the details. The loss of important detail is convenient: it simplifies things, and it produces results. It also corrupts science. As Ogden Nash once reflected, the tortoise is a turtle, or is it that a turtoise is a tortle?[10] This difference is detail, of course, but detail spells the difference between zoology and nonsense poetry.

There is no scientific doubt, for example, that high exposures to asbestos are dangerous. But what crystallized in the courtroom, and then in the public consciousness, was the notion of asbestos as a uniquely potent poison, the exclusive or at least principal cause of lung disease whenever it's on the scene. Lawyers were then perfectly positioned to unleash a second wave of lawsuits, against companies that had supplied asbestos used in building materials, car brakes, and home hair dryers, and unleash it they did. Good science, however, was moving in precisely the opposite direction. The grave risks from high exposure to asbestos in the workplace were systematically distinguished from the comparably insignificant risks of environmental asbestos in buildings. A major review article published in *Science* in 1990, for example, would find that asbestos levels in U.S. schools and buildings were "minuscule"—typically 10,000 to 100,000 times lower than occupational levels known to cause disease.[11] Moreover, asbestos comes in two quite different kinds, and the one found in most buildings, it transpired, is probably much less of a hazard—if it's a hazard at all—than the one used so cavalierly in World War II shipyards.

Dosage is certainly one detail commonly ignored in court; timing is another, and sometimes both are misconstrued together. Consider once again the antics of our old friend, Dr. Arthur Zahalsky—in particular, his performance on behalf of unfortunate Michelle Graham. Shortly after being vaccinated against whooping cough, three-month-old Michelle was diagnosed as having suffered severe brain damage from stroke. Zahalsky blamed the injury on Wyeth's vaccine, four times more toxic (said he) than alternative vaccines. The jury awarded Michelle $15 million. Only on appeal did the other critical details emerge. Several weeks *before* her vaccination, Michelle's pediatrician had noted a worrisome fixed-right gaze in her eyes and referred her to a pediatric ophthalmologist. When the ophthalmologist was later shown results of a CT scan of Michelle's head, he concluded at once that her eye problem had in fact been the first visible sign of the tragedy, though originally misdiagnosed because stroke is very difficult to detect in infants. Incredibly, the trial judge had barred this ophthalmologist's testimony, reasoning that the vaccine was on trial, not the stroke. More incredibly still, Zahalsky had relied on data that overestimated toxoid levels in Wyeth's vaccine by between five and fifty times. Zahalsky, the court of appeals noted, had "significantly recanted much of his testimony" elsewhere. "[W]hen I did the calculation," Zahalsky's collaborator would concede in a later deposition, "I must have missed a zero."[12]

A zero there, a zero here; it may just be detail, but as they say in Washington, soon you're talking real money. Another common mistake is to ignore details of mechanism. For example, the nylon filaments on the Dalkon Shield's string rotted on prolonged exposure to body fluids, creating a porous highway for bacteria. Other IUDs did not share the problem, and in time were vindicated through methodical epidemiological studies. But plaintiffs' lawyers went after the other IUDs anyway, and blurred the mechanistic details so successfully that for a time even safe IUDs were driven off the market. The causes of cancer likewise depend on detail: chronic irritation (as may be caused by asbestos in the lungs, for example) *can* cause cancer; simple trauma cannot.

The art of junk science is to brush away just enough detail to reach desired conclusions, while preserving enough to maintain an aura of authoritative science. Some chemicals, at some dosages, can depress the immune system; indeed, transplant patients wouldn't survive without them. Some immune system effects, mostly modest and reversible, have been observed after high-exposure industrial accidents. From this base of real science, the clinical ecologists leaped to a national epidemic of "chemical AIDS." Yes, stray radio signals might possibly be doing wild things to the Audi's cruise control, but it is a matter of detail to work out that (a) they aren't, (b) even if they were, the brakes would still easily overwhelm the accelerator, and (c) there is a more straightforward (if less welcome) explanation for what is going on. Dosage is the often the most critical variable of all in assessing poisons, but also one of the most easily ignored or misconstrued.

In matters of contagion, pollution, and such, what usually limits dose is distance. In December 1942, Charlie Chaplin's testes, like those of every other man on the planet, contained biological products in quantities sufficient to impregnate every woman on the planet, but for the most part the containment systems that men and women maintain against such hazards worked. The important detail with AIDS contagion is that outside of blood banks, body fluids are usually transferred only over millimeters, in harmonious coupling of the sexual kind. Distance quickly attenuates the risks of radiation, noise, shock waves, chemical pollution, and tuberculosis, often for straightforward reasons rooted in euclidean geometry and the laws of conservation of mass and energy. But the junk scientist spends little time pondering such details. The difference between *near*

the sanitarium, the factory, or the power plant and *not near* is
detail. In court, just as Theocrato urges, vaguely defined contiguity is often quite enough.

In the worst cases, brushing aside detail will mean mixing up
risky problems and risky solutions. Your polio vaccine occasionally triggers polio itself, and I've been vaccinated; we're harmoniously coupled, even if the wild virus was epidemic when I
rushed to the clinic to receive your vaccine. Your whooping
cough vaccine may cause swelling, fever, irritability, and crying
spells, though almost certainly not encephalopathy, paralysis, or
death; whooping cough (which the vaccine prevents) can cause
similar symptoms, *including* the grave ones. No matter: the vaccine is always "consistent" with all the symptoms. Exposure to
X rays is consistent with causing cancer; if X rays are applied in
massive doses to *treat* a cancer, any later recurrence, manifestation, or growth of the tumor will be harmoniously coupled with
the therapy. With the original cancer too, of course, but the
treating physician may not seek refuge in details like that. By
alleviating serious morning sickness, Bendectin may actually
prevent some birth defects, but drugs generally are consistent
with birth defects, and the rest is irrelevant detail.

Junk science not only neglects typically salient variables like
dosage and timing, it is commonly embarrassed by them into a
luxurious exfoliation of theory. Are claims about effects of low-
dose radiation or magnetism not borne out by epidemiology of
highly exposed workers? Then uniquely toxic effects must take
place at low doses only. Do some victims of carpet off-gassing
fall sick at the time of exposure and then recover when the
stimulus is removed, while others suffer permanent symptoms,
and yet others fall sick only later? Then off-gas toxicity is triply
hazardous. Do no extra cancers show up within a mile radius of
a nuclear power plant? Still, we must worry about a two-mile-
radius study with a disturbing data point.

Junk science can always build in this way, on out-of-context
factoids like "tuberculosis is contagious," or "chemicals cause
cancer." Such assertions contain no verifiable statement of
probability—that's detail. Dosage and exposure levels, incubation periods, disinfectants, and containment systems make all

the difference. Tuberculosis *is* contagious; to say so is not to embrace junk science. But what of it? Until amplified with the how, where, and when, the statement just doesn't mean very much. Probabilities matter; time and space matter; so does the intensity of the light. "Sunlight is the best disinfectant," intone lawyers when it suits their purposes. In fact, that metaphor comes to us from the days of tuberculosis, when sunlight really *was* the best disinfectant available, when a few yards of fresh air and open space made all the difference so far as contagion was concerned.

But in court, detail of this kind is enormously difficult to convey. Unnecessary, in fact, if Theocrato's description of how the law should operate is at all close to how it does. And without doubt, Theocrato's rough-and-ready rules on how we should connect this and that in court are pretty fair approximations of how we in fact do. The approximations are science without the details. Otherwise known as junk science.

THE CAUSATION PACK

Amid the great jumble of possible causes that *don't* much matter because the dosage is too low, or the timing is all wrong, or some other critical detail doesn't jibe, there are some things that plainly *do* matter a great deal. Over the years, good science has successfully identified quite a few of them. Unwelcome though the news may be, most are simple matters of lifestyle. Tobacco smoke from your own cigarettes, or from those of your spouse, parent, or fellow employee, completely dwarfs risks from video displays, magnetic fields, factory smokestacks, furniture solvents, pesticides on apples, and dozens of other headline-grabbing sources. The key risks of pelvic and other infectious disease depend far more on sexual habits than on contraceptives. Alcohol is such a large factor in car accidents that if it is found in either driver of either car, any further inquiry about car design, potholes, city lights, hedge trimming, or anything else is a complete waste of time. And what does the Surgeon General identify as the six top priorities for saving lives and preventing disease? Stop smoking. Cut alcohol consumption. Eat less and

eat smarter. Exercise. Have periodic checkups for major disorders. Use seat belts and obey the speed laws.

One might have supposed that the new-age Calabresian lawyer would be delighted to learn that science has pinned down
so many important causes so solidly, with such high confidence.
The idea all along, after all, has been to send bills to the right
place; at the very least, those who wish to *deter* risky behavior will
want to be certain not to *reward* it. One might therefore expect
to find the modern law littered with strong presumptions that
the smoker and the tippler, the bed hopper and the glutton,
have no one to sue but themselves.

The presumptions of the modern law, however, point almost
uniformly in the opposite direction. And let's face it: we know
why. Liability science is all very well as a rationalization for
changing standards of liability and stretching rules of evidence,
but few practicing lawyers are really that interested in working
out which risks are large and which are small. They are interested in which risks belong to someone who can pay; cheapest-
cost-avoider runs a distant second to most-solvent-payer-of-
bills. If that means systematically transferring responsibility
away from important causes and toward trivial ones, that is what
lawyers will strive to do. They often succeed, and modern legal
rules do much to help them.

A first, traditional principle of tort law is that the defendant
"takes his plaintiff as he finds him." More colloquially, this becomes: don't blame the victim. So when asbestos came to court,
the defendants failed miserably in their efforts to blame the
asbestos workers' own smoking habits. The IUD litigants performed no better when it came to a Shield user's sex life. With
the IUDs, as with asbestos, personal choices that drastically
increased the risks involved were simply not given serious, evenhanded attention.

The modern law also expects remarkably little in the way of
active self-protection. What do risk experts have to say, for
example, about the safe design of cars and motorcycles? Well,
different designs certainly do make cars more or less crash-
worthy, and bikes more or less easy to control. But all else pales
beside the seat belt and the helmet. As a first cut, better than any

other simple rule of thumb anyone can propose, the "cause" of *every* road fatality for an unbuckled driver or an unhelmeted motorcyclist is the unused belt or the absent helmet. Obviously "every" goes too far, but it is so close to right that only a tribunal of very experienced experts is likely to hit on a better answer more often by assuming otherwise. And in court? In court, belt and helmet are usually minor factors among many others, almost never dispositive defenses, and in some trials cannot even be mentioned at all.[13]

The law likewise prefers not to lay blame on the victim's immediate colleagues or collaborators. If the Washington secretary is not to be blamed herself for the pelvic infection, Pony Duke is the next most likely candidate. If the smoker himself is not to be blamed for his lung disease, then perhaps the tobacco company is. But somehow the legal gaze usually remains fixed beyond such targets too. Few who study the case reports and law reviews will learn that the risks of secondhand smoke in buildings are hundreds of times higher than the environmental risks from asbestos in ceiling tiles and thermal insulation.

The law is more capricious still in its selection of risks from what Theocrato calls the "causation pack." As Theocrato explains (with a lawyer's simple clarity), some injuries depend on "multi-production, fungibility, dormant incubation, synergy, market mingling, body tolerance, and a whole host of ponderables and imponderables that lie between the truth and the detection of cause."[14] Theocrato advises ignoring the pack entirely; plaintiffs should be allowed to select target risks as they please. Of course, Joan Berry's case involved market mingling, dormant incubation, and such, so if Theocrato really means what he says, the other cads from Los Angeles and Oklahoma are to be ignored when Charlie Chaplin is on trial. But the crowds Theocrato is really after congregate outside the boudoir. And to a considerable extent, modern liability law treats them just as he advises, by ignoring the herd and searching for a single, milk-filled cow.

To start with, causation-pack logic helps elevate small risks of human creation above large risks of Nature. The background levels of radiation that assail us from below (radon) and above (cosmic rays) far exceed anything released from Three Mile Island, but in practice that's of almost no consequence when TMI comes to court. All-natural birth defects are far more common than those caused by drugs or medical malpractice, but the money and therefore the lawyers are to be found clustered around obstetricians and drug companies.

If it is relentlessly hard on the one steer in a hundred that happens to be pursued, Theocrato's theory is again wonderfully forgiving about the rest of the causation herd. Perhaps some cars do take off suddenly under their own initiative, but then some drivers (as *Car and Driver* delicately put it) just barely "earned their place behind the controls by paying some DMV drone five bucks and holding still for a picture."[15] Medicinal drugs cause some injuries to unborn children, but pregnant mothers relaxing with a stiff drink (or drugs more recreational still) cause many more. Maybe Charlie Chaplin was the father of Joan Berry's child, but then maybe the father was her beau in Oklahoma. In practice, however, none of the "but thens" seems to matter very much, especially not those within the thirsty calf's own choice and control. Nor should they, if the causation-pack theory applies.

Similar logic has blunted serious legal inquiry into the perplexing science of synergy. What is the "cause" of the concert at Madison Square Garden: Mick Jagger, or the wall of amplifiers and loudspeakers behind him? The audience comes to hear Jagger, of course, but without the electronics they wouldn't hear much of anything. The Dalkon Shield was a powerful amplifier of another cause—sexually transmitted disease. Much the same was true of asbestos and tobacco. But sober, evenhanded exposition of these synergies proved impossible in court. So much so that sometimes the science was turned completely on its head. The most powerful scientific claim *against* the Dalkon Shield belonged to women who had been the *most* sexually active while wearing it. The more songs Mick Jagger sings, after all, the more opportunities for the amplifiers to do their stuff. A monogamous user of the Shield who subsequently discovered she was infertile in fact had the *weakest* claim against Robins; her infertility most likely derived from appendicitis, endometriosis, abortion, or any number of other causes. And the questions posed by the Robins lawyers that were considered the most outrageous—questions about sexual practices long before and after the IUD was used— were in fact also the most medically reasonable. The one woman whose fertility definitely cannot be harmed by Shield-promoted PID is the one already sterilized by PID beforehand.

Causation-pack theory serves junk science best, however, whe· sed to cover up smoking, our most routine form of suicide. The asbestos experience is repeated daily, as plaintiffs' lawyers and their pocket experts grope for distant targets through a thick fog of their clients' own tobacco smoke. The pill, for example, *does* increase the risk of coronary problems, but principally for women who smoke. This conjunction has produced a cascade of lawsuits, despite abundant warnings that the pill and tobacco are a dangerous mix. Women working at video display terminals *do* experience more miscarriages than their stay-at-home sisters, and a fistful of lawsuits have been launched by that correlation alone. VDTs almost certainly do not cause miscarriages, but smoking increases the risk tenfold, and women who work outside the home smoke (or sit near a smoker) much more than others. Even moderate smoking presents a lung-cancer threat twice that of heavy exposure to asbestos on the job.[16] Smoking likewise multiplies the risks of workplace hazards in coal and metal mining,[17] petrochemicals, pesticides, cotton textiles, chemical dyes, and foundries. Smoke particles apparently do for airborne poisons much what the Dalkon Shield's wick did for venereal bacteria. But once again, the litigation is directed elsewhere.

At their silliest, causation-pack analysts cannot even distinguish between smoke started with a Zippo and smoke supplied by the community arsonist. Here, for example, is Bertram Carnow, testifying for Richard Ernzen, who has lost his job with the Batavia, Illinois, fire department after experiencing severe dizzy spells. Ernzen is suffering from inadequate blood supply to part of his brain. It's because on-the-job smoke narrowed his arteries, says Carnow. But Ernzen carries most of the smoke he breathes in his shirt pocket, and on top of this, X rays reveal a congenital arterial abnormality. Carnow nevertheless convinces a trial judge that Ernzen is owed a disability pension.[18]

Another firefighter smokes a pack a day for forty-two years. He dies of lung cancer, and his wife collects death benefits on the theory that the workplace smoke was really to blame. Burning tar in buildings "may well" release the same carcinogens as burning tar in cigarettes, an expert testifies. The verdict for Ernzen is later overturned on appeal, but the second verdict is upheld by the California Supreme Court. The burning buildings could have caused the cancer, might perhaps have been a "contributing cause," and that is sufficient.[19]

Predictably, the clinical ecologists have managed to twist even cigarettes to their own advantage. Here, for example, is Alan S. Levin, M.D., the man who "gladly" accepts credit for having popularized the term "chemical AIDS."[20] He is testifying in court on how best to prevent that same disease. "The primary treatment is alteration of the environment, in other words getting away from the chemicals and by that I mean avoiding exposure to things like cigarette smoke." Pretty good advice, even if chemical AIDS is a figment of Levin's imagination. But Levin is not the least bit interested in saving people from tobacco, it turns out. His crusade is against "things *like* cigarette smoke"—which for Levin means "scented agents like perfumes and deodorants," "cleaning compounds," "foods where there is all sorts of preservatives and food coloring," "liquids that are stored in plastic bottles," "new carpets and drapes and wall paneling," and "the plastic covering on new cars." Thus, the well-lubricated tongue slides from cigarettes to car seats, and the real perils of tobacco become the imaginary perils of perfume. And Levin can now explain why a smoker's lung problems are really caused by chemically induced "immune disregulation." "[T]he disease process is very common in smokers," Levin smoothly concedes, but it is still "reasonable to conclude that chemical exposures caused this precipitous change in [the victim's] status or well-being."[21]

Evidently, Carnow and Levin do not always convince juries or jurists that packaged smoke is irrelevant compared with other environmental factors. But they do often neutralize what should be an open-and-shut defense centered on the plaintiff's smoking. Before long, the cigarette becomes part of the invisible, no-one-to-blame background, like unbuckled seat belts, obesity, alcohol, or venereal disease. Any defendant may talk about such things, and all do. Judges and juries listen politely. And then give equal time to the view that deodorants are "things like cigarette smoke." The Laurel and Hardy of tobacco—the smoker and the seller of smoke—are quietly absolved from responsibility. What then is the "cause" of the piano dropping out of the second-story window? Probably the building architect or the buzzing fly, the man who waxed the floors or the caretaker who sneezed, or some other marginal or irrelevant player, tapped at the last moment after the real comedians are given an excuse from their lawyer.

It is certainly much easier to ignore lots of things, or better still, to pretend they don't matter even when they do. No one can doubt that by doing this so casually, so often, in so many different ways, Calabresian jurists can greatly simplify the world they set out to control. Suing one wealthy (though distant) defendant is both simpler and more rewarding than suing a nearby crowd of indigents. It is equally certain, however, that only junk science will be comfortable with this approach to pinning down cause. The junk scientist, most especially when backed by the ambitious lawyer, will happily seize one risk from the causation pack and build a career attacking it. Good science, unburdened by concerns about what is fair, just, reasonable, or socially acceptable, attends patiently to details, even when they come in packs.

Sorting out the causation pack is in fact the fundamental challenge of all epidemiology. Obscene-phone-call questions may be forbidden in court, but any competent gynecologist will certainly ask them, and even more so any competent epidemiologist. The elements of the causation pack—including sex habits, fat feet, tobacco, alcohol, and the rest—have to be taken on together, evenhandedly, or the scientific judgments that emerge will be junk. Before good science writes a word about how A causes X, it must write a volume on *ceteris paribus* ("other things being equal"), systematically determining just which other things amplify or reduce the A-X link, and which cause X quite independently.

But modern tort law disdains *ceteris paribus* at every turn. Sometimes the *ceteris* are ignored for arcane legal reasons— because contributory negligence just shouldn't count in strict liability. Sometimes it's familiarity that breeds legal contempt for other causes on the scene: smoking, incautious sex, obesity, and unbelted driving are so common that they just somehow escape notice. Some causes like sex habits or smoking aren't counted because counting them just doesn't seem fair. No doubt the more spectacular judicial exhibitions of junk science involve affirmative falsehood, to the effect that a slip-and-fall causes breast cancer, or a spermicide causes birth defects. The errors of omission are more subtle, but far more common and grave. Lifestyle factors are brushed aside, empty-chair defenses are overwhelmed, the causation pack is ignored. With the camels legally invisible, the gnats become a terribly strained federal case.

And so the law takes leave of good science yet again. Good science would dictate an all but absolute presumption that the pregnant mother who smokes, snorts, pops, or tipples has no one but herself to blame for problems in pregnancy. No such presumption will be found anywhere in the legal literature, however; birth-defect litigation in fact looks mainly to Bendectin, fetal monitors, and obstetricians too slow with the scalpel. To judge by what it finally achieved, the legal system was quite unable to disentangle the important causes of PID. The manufacturer of the Copper 7, a much safer IUD, did indeed escape bankruptcy. But the Copper 7 was nonetheless driven from the market, though by all serious medical accounts it was a superior contraceptive option for many women. Wherever the law may ramble in its search for causes, good science and medicine quickly focus in on chain smoking and the unbelted driver, caloric desserts, and helmetless motorcyclists. Minimizing, discounting, overlooking, or omitting the effects of self-poisoning and self-destruction has become the great genius of the American legal system. It is only by sweeping aside the environmental underbrush that we can go after the stray, milk-filled cows.

Cause in court comes down, in the end, to vocabulary, not science. Causes that don't count are matters of privacy, addiction, handicap, or hypersensitivity. Causes that count are matters of negligence, incompetence, defect, or coverup. With two-tone vocabulary like this, causes can be wheeled in and out like magic. Motes and beams can be all mixed up, to the point where half the time the courts are completely blind to huge risks, and half the time they discern tiny ones with eagle-eyed acuity.

Responsibility thus drifts, like secondhand smoke, away from the smoker, away from the Pony Dukes and their paramours, away from the slothful, the gluttonous, and the self-indulgent, and toward all manner of others downwind. Sometimes the downwinders are asbestos companies, with air-fouling products of their own. Sometimes they are the most innocent victims imaginable, like underweight newborns and the obstetricians who scramble to keep them alive. In medicine and epidemiology, lifestyles are the headline, the big factor, the prime suspect. In the law, they have become barely a footnote, all but lost in the fast shuffle of paper and money. The law selects its prey from the causation pack by looking for milk-filled stragglers. The main herd—the pack of causes that are part of the normal, ubiquitous, taken-for-granted landscape—ambles off untouched. The risk that is most common and familiar, the risk most immediately controlled nearby, will usually count the least in court. Such things, after all, are normal. Joan Berry, baby in arms, is terribly sympathetic; Chaplin is rich; and the man from Tulsa is nowhere to be found.

MILK AND BLOOD

Theocrato's prescription of how the courts should connect up this and that is thus a pretty good description of how they in fact do. Look for suggestive sequences in time—from which we get decades of junk science litigation on traumatic cancer and cerebral palsy. Look for some vague, general "consistency" between the alleged risk and the claimed injury—from which we build monsters of litigation against Bendectin and the Audi. Contiguity in space? An infected uterus and an IUD are close enough; so are shattered lungs and asbestos, give or take a two-pack habit; so are clusters of any disease that will be found, if you look far enough, around some bowling alleys, amusement parks, and chemical factories. Causation packs? Brush 'em aside. By Theocrato's standards, Charlie Chaplin was about as harmoniously coupled as a man can be. In the right bed, at about the right time. And there's no doubt about it: screwing around is "consistent with" paternity.

Curiously, however, one judge filed quite a vigorous dissent when the verdict against Chaplin was affirmed on appeal. "Time was when the courts could rely only upon human testimony," Justice McComb argued. "But modern science brought new aids. . . . [New] scientific means and instrumentalities have revised the judicial guessing game of the past into an institution approaching accuracy in portraying the truth as to the actual fact. . . . If the courts do not utilize these unimpeachable methods for acquiring accurate knowledge of pertinent facts they will neglect the employment of available, potent agencies which serve to avoid miscarriages of justice."[22]

What exactly did McComb have in mind? Almost half a century before, in 1901, Landsteiner had discovered the ABO system, which classifies blood according to the antigenic characteristics of red blood cells. The antigens are genetically determined; the A and B antigens don't occur in a child if they don't occur in at least one of the parents.

And amid all the confusion about just who had slept with whom in which cities on which days, amid the Madonna-and-child staging of the unwed mother and the randy movie star, the scientific evidence presented by Chaplin's lawyers was not in any serious doubt. Joan Berry had Group A blood. Her daughter, Carol Ann, had Group B blood. This meant that the father's blood must have been either Group AB or Group B. Charlie Chaplin's was Group O. As three physicians testified at Chaplin's trial, to no avail, Chaplin was not in fact Carol Ann's father.

PART III

THE RULE OF FACT

CHAPTER 10

The Cargo Cult

Does Liability Science Work?

Permit me to decline totally your proposition to cooperate in this simplistic experiment; the phenomena are much too delicate for that. Let each one form his personal opinion about N rays, either from his own experiments or from those of others in whom he has confidence. —René Blondlot (1906)

In *Cows, Pigs, Wars, and Witches*, Marvin Harris describes a magnificent jungle airstrip in the mountains of New Guinea, manned around the clock by natives. Bonfires burn as beacons. The natives "are expecting the arrival of an important flight: cargo planes filled with canned food, clothing, portable radios, wrist watches, and motorcycles. . . . Why the delay? A man goes inside the radio shack and gives instructions into the tin-can microphone. The message goes out over an antenna constructed of string and vines. . . ."[1]

The Nobel physicist Richard Feynman picks up the story.

During the war, they saw airplanes land with lots of good materials, and they want the same thing to happen now. So they've arranged to make things like runways, to put fires along the sides of the runways, to make a wooden hut for a man to sit in, with two wooden pieces on his head like headphones and bars of bamboo sticking out like antennas—he's the controller—and they wait for the airplanes to land. They're doing everything right. The form is perfect. It looks exactly the way it looked before. But it doesn't work. No airplanes land.

One finds many similar airports at the edges of the scientific community, Feynman observes, "theories that don't work, and science that isn't science. . . . I call these things cargo cult science, because they follow all the apparent precepts and forms of scientific investigation, but they're missing something essential, because the planes don't land."[2]

SLOUCHING INTO COURT

We may smile at the cargo cultists of New Guinea, but their ways are not so different from our own. Remember the witch hunters? They too were obsessed with things that flew, and the bonfires they lit were not just beacons. We too, in our own time, have often let our eagerness to control race far out ahead of our ability. In our obsessive pursuit of distant and mysterious causes of our afflictions, we ourselves have often attended to scientific cranks, iconoclasts, and eccentrics who go through all the right motions but cannot land any real airplanes.

Many a trial lawyer will of course indignantly answer that the "cranks" and "pseudoscientists" diligently promoted in court have contributed greatly to the advancement of science in modern times. Remember, after all, asbestos, the Ford Pinto, the Dalkon Shield, Rely tampons, DES, and thalidomide. Real risks, every one of them, first exposed by (at the time) "maverick" experts first located by lawyers. Lawyers are good at finding scientists who just happen to be at the cutting edge of things, and society benefits accordingly. Or so the lawyers maintain.

History records otherwise. The pathbreaking scientific work on asbestos was conducted in the early 1960s, and was accepted soon thereafter in mainstream scientific publications and symposia.[3] But the lawsuit that launched asbestos litigation was not filed until October 1969,[4] and four more years would pass before appeals were resolved. The Dalkon Shield's serious problems were recognized by physicians soon after Robins launched global sales in 1971; at the FDA's behest, Robins halted sales in June 1974. The litigation did not get under way until the 1980s.

In 1968, at almost exactly the same time that Robins executives were planning to launch the Dalkon Shield, Lee Iacocca, then a Ford vice president, initiated design of the Ford Pinto.[5] NHTSA had already promulgated one crashworthiness standard for rear-end collisions, and would promulgate others in 1975, 1976, and 1977. In 1977, NHTSA also initiated an investigation of Pintos already on the road; in May 1978 it formally concluded that Pintos had serious problems,[6] and a month later, under strong pressure from the agency, Ford initiated a recall. Where were the lawyers? In February 1978, a California jury returned the landmark $127.8 million verdict in Richard Grimshaw's suit against Ford. In September 1978, an Indiana grand jury indicted Ford on three counts of reckless homicide. But it took another two years for the Indiana criminal trial to be resolved—in Ford's favor.[7] In May 1981, a California court of appeals finally upheld $3.5 million of the *Grimshaw* verdict, emphasizing in its opinion the Pinto's shortcomings as against NHTSA's 1973 standards.[8] In May 1982, Richard Grimshaw finally settled his claim against Ford while the case was still under appeal. By this time, Lee Iacocca had left Ford and was president of Chrysler.

Time and again, the scientists and regulatory agencies have uncovered and addressed real problems long before the litigators. The key scientific discoveries on DES were published in the *New England Journal of Medicine* in 1971.[9] Serious litigation developed only in 1980.[10] The swine flu vaccine was distributed in 1976;[11] the key study linking the vaccine to Guillain Barré Syndrome was published by the Centers for Disease Control (CDC) in 1979.[12] Again, the litigation developed later. Procter & Gamble first test-marketed the Rely tampon in 1974.[13] Toxic shock syndrome (TSS) was first described in the *Lancet* in November 1978,[14] first linked (by the CDC) with menstruation in May 1980, and with Rely users in August and September of that same year.[15] The manufacturer withdrew Rely from the market immediately. The first TSS trial was not even held until 1982.[16] A last word is in order on thalidomide. More than one prominent U.S. lawyer has had the gall to claim thalidomide as yet another success for the investigative sleuths of the American plaintiffs' bar. In Europe, some 6,500 children were victims of the drug before its teratogenic properties were confirmed in 1961 by German scientists. Happily, however, the drug never received FDA approval in the United States.

No doubt plaintiffs' lawyers and their experts do sometimes congregate around real, cargo-filled planes, but only after someone else has landed them. Key scientific and engineering investigations are completed and published long before the legal claims are pressed or decided. Almost always, these same discoveries also trigger appropriate reaction by the EPA, NHTSA, the FDA, or the industry itself years before trial lawyers achieve anything at all.

The one race that the lawyer-discovered experts have won repeatedly is the one with no prize at the end for anyone but litigants. In 1985, for example, lawyers won a spectacular $5.1 million verdict against the Ortho Pharmaceutical Corporation, largely on the strength of a single study that had very tentatively suggested that spermicides might cause birth defects.[17] A year after the verdict, however, the several authors of that study spoke out again. One acknowledged that their work "was not corroborated by subsequent studies," and that their "study's definition of exposure to spermicide near the time of conception was grossly inaccurate." Another frankly conceded: "I believe our article should never have been published. In our present litigious environment, the reservations and qualifications written into a published report are often ignored, and the article is used as 'proof' of a causal relationship."[18] Two independent physicians from the National Institute of Child Health and Human Development noted that "the overwhelming body of evidence indicates that spermicides are not teratogenic."[19]

The legal disaster of the pertussis (whooping cough) vaccine unfolded in much the same way. The vaccine has virtually ended the 265,000 cases of pertussis and 7,500 pertussis-related deaths recorded in the years before 1949, the year the vaccine was first licensed. But a 1984 English study, serious and cautiously phrased in itself, suggested that the vaccine's use (extrapolated to the U.S. population) might be causing twenty-five cases a year of serious brain damage.[20] American lawyers responded with an avalanche of litigation, blaming the vaccine for brain damage, unexplained coma, Reye's syndrome, epilepsy, sudden infant death, and countless other afflictions.[21] Horrified pharmaceutical companies bailed out, and at one point it appeared that the last U.S. manufacturer of the product would be leaving the market.[22] More solid scientific evidence slowly accumulated.[23] Then, in March 1990, a report of a huge study of 230,000 children and 713,000 immunizations concluded that the vaccine had caused *no* serious neurological complications of any kind, and no deaths.[24] "It is time for the myth of pertussis vaccine encephalopathy to end," declared an editorial in the *Journal of the American Medical Association.* "We need to end this national nonsense."[25]

Without doubt, the lawyers and the idiosyncratic experts who backed them did lead the charge on clinical ecology, sudden acceleration, and the teratogenic effects of Bendectin. Of course they led the charge. To out-of-court, mainstream scientists, the factual claims looked dubious all along. So the hired testifiers took a big lead, and declared many a victory against runaway cars, cerebral palsy, and cancer. The real scientists arrived later on only to establish that nothing had really been won at all.

MALPRACTICE ON THE WITNESS STAND

As experience now richly demonstrates, the incentives for the lawyers today are simple and compelling. If the consensus in the scientific community is that a hazard is real and substantial, the trial bar will trumpet that consensus to support demands for compensation and punishment. If the consensus is that the hazard is imaginary or trivial, the bar will brush it aside, and dredge up experts from the fringe to swear otherwise. Even when lawyers pursue certifiably real hazards, there will be a strong incentive to stretch claims to the margins of validity and beyond, to reach not just dangerous IUDs but also safe ones, not just serious exposures to asbestos but also trivial ones. If the law allows a lawyer to put just about anybody on the witness stand, she is going to search far and wide for any expertise, real or otherwise, that is congenial to her case.

It is a deep irony that the one place the law tolerates this sort of thing is in court. The professional seated in the witness box, alone among all other obstetricians, engineers, chemists, or pharmacologists, is above the rules. Or, to be more precise, he is often not subject to any rules at all. Malpractice by scientific and medical professionals is not only tolerated but encouraged, so long as it is solicited by lawyers themselves.

The law has always been ready enough to impose standards of competence on quacks outside the courtroom. Negligence law requires every doctor to "have and use the knowledge, skill and care ordinarily possessed and employed by members of the profession in good standing." If there are contending schools of thought in the profession, a malpractice defendant may be given the benefit of the doubt if he favors one school rather than another. But as a leading legal treatise hastens to add, this does not mean "that any quack, charlatan or crackpot can set himself up as a 'school' and so apply his individual ideas without liability. A 'school' must be a recognized one within a definite code of principles, and it must be the line of thought of a respectable minority of the profession."[26] The designer of a product is likewise expected to have used "state of the art" materials and technology.[27]

Often the law demands even more. In a famous 1932 decision concerning a tugboat called *The T. J. Hooper* which (like most other tugs of the day) was not equipped with a radio, Judge Learned Hand sonorously declared that "in most cases, reasonable prudence is in fact common prudence; but strictly it is never its measure."[28] A court may thus require tugboat operators or doctors to surpass even accepted industry standards and consensus norms of the profession.[29]

From 1923 until the mid-1970s, the *Frye* rule made some attempt to hold expert witnesses to similar standards. Certainly not to anything better than mainstream scientific norms, but the rule did at least refer to competent science as defined by the consensus views of a profession. Under *Frye*, the expert witness could report only learning that was "generally accepted" in his scientific discipline. Negligence, incompetence, irresponsibility, reckless disregard for professional standards, and every other variation on professional malpractice were as unacceptable on the witness stand as they were anywhere else.

One might suppose that this sort of symmetry would be a matter of fundamental fairness. If an obstetrician is to be judged guilty of malpractice, it will be on the say-so of some other doctor sitting in the witness box. A similar showdown between professionals decides every challenge to the design of a contraceptive or a Cuisinart. Seated at Audi's table are the engineers who built a real car. Seated in the witness box is William Rosenbluth, who contends he could have done better. The jury must choose between yesterday's expert, who designed the morning-sickness drug or delivered the baby, and today's, who claims that the job was botched. Incredibly, many courts today enforce serious standards of professional competence only against defendants, not against their accusers.

The standards for medical witnesses are more biased still; the hermit clinician can usually testify to anything if he holds an M.D. and is willing to mumble some magic words about "reasonable medical certainty." Malpractice by mouth from the witness stand is thus not subject to any control at all. Any old résumé qualifies someone to be a witness, but only those who comply with the mainstream standards of professional medicine are good enough to escape liability.

The fringe theories and fanciful methods used to condemn experts in malpractice and product-design cases surface in other cases to explain disease. In the *Alcolac* litigation, for example, Zahalsky and Carnow based their chemical-AIDS conclusions on tests conducted with monoclonal antibodies. The antibodies, however, were not approved by the FDA for any diagnostic purposes at all. Used in a clinic as a basis for treatment, such methods would have been actionable malpractice.

Our pursuit of incompetence among scientific and medical professionals is now often led by incompetents from the fringes of those same professions. Courts too eager to chase after distant and mysterious causes willingly attend to far-out pseudo-scientific mystics. In our eagerness to suppress inept, irresponsible, or fraudulent practice everywhere else, we have embraced inept, irresponsible, or fraudulent practice on the witness stand.

THE DEPENDENCE EFFECT

During the Inquisition, the more witches were hunted, the more witches there seemed to be. As Harris recounts, witch-hunters were required at the outset "to increase the supply of witches and to spread the belief that witches were real, omnipresent, and dangerous."[30] "The harder the Inquisition looked," observes W. C. Clark, "the bigger its staff, the stronger its motivation, the more witches it discovered."[31]

We are caught in a similar, self-spinning vortex today. The enormous financial stakes of litigation transform some accidental ripple of scientific error into a whirlpool of self-deception. A few fringe scientists believe at the outset in sudden acceleration, clinical ecology, or a fetal-distress theory of cerebral palsy. They are located by some hopeful lawyer, displayed in a dozen or so different courtrooms, and sooner or later they deliver a favorable verdict. This supplies some instant respectability, which encourages more data dredging and funds further speculation.

When conditions are just right, the scientific nonentity who would never be funded by the National Science Foundation, who would otherwise languish in tweedy isolation in some third-rank school of public health, suddenly finds himself in the casino, tweeds traded for a tuxedo, avidly courted by the high rollers, and richly paid for his services. Instead of penury and obscurity, the far-sider now has wealth, publicity, a consulting firm, a research staff of his own, and the resources to publish all sorts of pseudoscientific pulp. Of course there is now controversy within the scientific community. Lawyers themselves have paid dearly for it.

Useless or even dangerous techno-fixes trigger similar, self-sustaining cycles of litigation. Northwestern University law professor Mark Grady describes how the steady proliferation of safety-related knobs and dials, bells and charts, increases the likelihood that the jet pilot or heart surgeon will overlook something and then be blamed for negligence. But in technology-intensive professions like medicine or aviation, there will *always* be a spare high-tech instrument, heroic procedure, or exotic medicine lying around that could have been tried, that might conceivably have made things turn out better. Grady conveniently assumes that "courts do not err" in defining what is useful and what isn't; his article would doubtless have been too short to publish if he had assumed instead that "doctors do not err" in delivering babies, or that "pilots do not err" in landing planes.[32] But courts sometimes *do* err, sometimes *do* embrace ineffectual new tests, or useless bits and pieces of new hardware. The cautionary CAT scan or cesarean, the amniocentesis, blood test, or fetal monitor can be certified as essential by lawyers much faster than by scientists. These tests and gadgets then accumulate in the cockpit and the operating theater, because not having them on hand has become legally risky. As the unnecessary or unreliable tests and technologies multiply, so do the opportunities for ignoring them in the heat of a crisis. Which creates opportunities for still more legal action.

Legal process can couple with the mass media in much the same way. Respected judges do for a Carnow, Zahalsky, Levin, Rosenbluth, or McBride what Nancy Reagan did for Joan Quigley: astrology suddenly became a more serious (or at least much more profitable) business when it was taken seriously in the halls of the White House. "60 Minutes" and the *National Enquirer* served the Audi and Bendectin lawyers wonderfully well, and the lawyers returned the favor. The media coverage attracted more complaints, and the deluge of complaints provided fodder for new stories.

All of these effects converge in litigation that turns on unadorned fear. Revolving as it does around word-of-mouth exchange and the made-for-theater anecdote, junk science is perfectly adapted for both the courtroom and the *National Enquirer.* In the beginning, there's just a spark of anxiety in the air, but nothing to burn so far as good science is concerned. Somewhere or other, a credulous jury and judge take the far-sider seriously, raise the common citizen's doubt higher than the good scientist's assurance, and grant relief anyway. The common citizen infers that there must be at least a bonfire behind the legal smoke. The next court will then find it easier to issue another order. The common citizen now discerns a two-alarm blaze behind the legal smoke, and soon there's conflagration of anxiety. The common citizen believes that what courts take seriously *is* serious. When courts declare, in turn, that what the common citizen takes seriously *is* serious, the it's-serious-if-you-say-so logic becomes completely circular.

It is with fear, where the passion to control is strongest and reason weakest, that the legal dilemma reaches its climax. What should the courts do about the local tuberculosis sanitarium, or AIDS hospice, or perhaps something even more scientifically unlikely, that frightens people out of all proportion to the actual risk? No one can doubt that irrational fear is often real, as are its costs. And how can such costs be cheaply avoided? By removing the cause, of course. Shut down the sanitarium, send Mary Sansone packing, destroy the witch, and the fear will be allayed. The right response to irrational fear, in short, is unconditional capitulation. Liability science, that happy marriage of good science and sound economics, ends up prescribing resolute surrender to the irrational.

THE COSTS OF ACCIDENTS

The cargo-cult controller cannot land planes, but he can misdirect enterprise, waste resources, and even cause accidents. A junk science verdict is an accident in court. It is a defective legal product, designed by incompetent legal engineers, assembled by ill-trained laborers. It represents a failure of supervision in both planning and production. The packaging is deceptive, the public warning delivered by the verdict misleading, often dangerously so. Such accidents are harmful. No one should understand this better than good Calabresians, who are committed to reallocating the costs of misadventures with cars and planes, chemicals and contraceptives, football helmets, diving boards, insulators, and peanut butter—accidents of every description, it would appear, except accidents manufactured by lawyers themselves.

The most obvious victims of legal accidents are those on the losing side of baseless verdicts. Wyeth Laboratories pays for a case of polio in fact caused not by Wyeth's vaccine but by a wild strain of the virus; the taxpayer pays a swine flu verdict for "serum sickness" not in fact caused by the vaccine. Audi loses two-thirds of its U.S. business on the strength of publicity and verdicts about defects that don't exist. The manufacturer of a spermicide pays more than a year's worth of profits for a birth defect it did not cause.

Consumers at large are victims too. Junk science verdicts raise prices, lower production, and deter consumption. Pregnant women lose when they can no longer buy an effective therapy for severe morning sickness, when obstetricians disappear from rural areas, when electronic fetal monitors are used indiscriminately at delivery, and when cesareans come to be ordered with an enthusiasm unmatched since the days of Jack the Ripper. Car buyers lose when one of the safest cars on the road is driven off the market by junk litigation, and owners of the car lose both confidence and resale value. The best guess we have today is that the Bendectin lawyers may have marginally *increased* the incidence of birth defects, because severe, untreated morning sickness can be a teratogen itself. While we cannot name the victims, it is statistically certain that real people have died because misdirected litigation encouraged them to switch from an Audi to a less safe car. Cesarean sections are far too common because they are safer in court, though more dangerous in the clinic. Liability lawyers almost drove the whooping cough vaccine off the market, and the publicity they generated about deaths and acute brain injury certainly curtailed its use. The best evidence today, however, is that the vaccine does not cause any deaths or permanent injuries; there is certainly no doubt that it prevents a considerable number.

Even the ostensible beneficiaries of junk science verdicts can pay a heavy price. It is no kindness to inform a retirement-age asbestos worker that his main problem is asbestos if in fact it's smoking; past exposure to asbestos cannot be altered, but future exposure to tobacco can. According to one psychiatrist who has studied their sad plight, clinical ecology patients rely on a "support system of lawyers and physicians" to support their withdrawal from work and life and maintain their identities as disabled persons.[33] Vietnam veterans who might otherwise have moved beyond their memories and fears to resume a productive life may be tempted to sit back as invalids, so certified by Agent Orange litigators. If the placebo effect is real, as it certainly is, so too is its mirror image, hypochondria. Junk science verdicts may promote and sustain illness even when the electric fields, the microwaves, the trace pollutants, or the all but unmeasurable radioactivity have caused nothing but the verdict itself.

Verdicts speak to the public at large, too, and people tend to believe what the courts say, especially when they say it with large amounts of money. The casual follower of jury verdicts might easily conclude that most pelvic disease is caused by IUDs and tampons, most lung disease by workplace dust and building asbestos, most road injuries by defects in car design, and most miscarriages, birth defects, and cancers by medicinal drugs, pollution, or obstetrical incompetence. But they aren't. By far the most important keys to safety and good health involve tobacco, alcohol, seat belts, diet, and sexual habits—matters well within an individual's own reach and control. Pandering to junk science that asserts otherwise is dangerous.

In the end, junk science weakens the courts themselves. Today, all serious observers recognize that only junk science supported the countless claims of traumatically induced cancer in the 1920s and 1930s. Few doubt that junk science produced the settlements and verdicts against Agent Orange, the Ortho-Gynol spermicide, and Bendectin. The pages of *Science* magazine calmly recount the courts' rising susceptibility to junk science claims from clinical ecologists and other fringe experts attacking the U.S. contraceptive industry.[34] But public acceptance of judicial power ultimately depends on our shared confidence that courts will get the facts right.

It is popular to believe that one should err on the side of safety. Many lawyers maintain that this means one should tolerate even fringe science when it calls safety into question. But however rationalized, junk science on safety matters is dangerous. For many years, anti-vaccinationists railed against the idea of deliberately introducing disease into the human body.[35] They were right that, as a general principle, one should not make a practice of infecting oneself with disease, but they were wrong about the details and their mistake was fatal for many who embraced it. It is precisely because junk science can be dangerous that we ban the teachings of quack diagnosticians and snake oil salesmen from the doctor's office, the itinerant peddler's push-cart, and the thirty-second TV spot. Before we condemn the Audi pedal configuration as more dangerous for inexperienced drivers who are shifting out of park, we had better be very sure that these pedals are not safer for any driver moving fast on the highway. Today, not-quite-right science in court impels many to rip well-sealed asbestos out of buildings when it would be safer for all concerned to leave it alone.

It goes without saying that all human institutions are fallible. To demand perfection is of course unrealistic. Plaintiffs' lawyers are often the first to mention this when confronted with some of their more embarrassing junk science triumphs. And the argument is quite valid, even if unexpected from people with little tolerance for imperfection when it comes to lawn mowers rather than lawsuits. Nonetheless, the runaway potential of junk science in court presents an especially grave problem, not to be brushed aside as one of the ordinary and inevitable incidents of human imperfection. Because courts are tremendously powerful, the accidents they precipitate can be unusually costly.

Let us revisit, one last time, the problem of junk science in one of its most tragic modern contexts. How many young women in the 1980s, and perhaps to this day, believed what the courts implicitly declared, that the PID problem is the IUD problem? All we know is that fifteen years after the Dalkon Shield was pulled from the market, four years after the Copper 7 was withdrawn, PID rates—and PID's side effects of infertility, ectopic pregnancy, spontaneous abortion, and the rest—are as high as ever, and perhaps still rising.

There is also wide agreement among medical professionals today that, the Dalkon Shield aside, IUDs are superior contraceptive options for many women. The pill, highly effective, protects against cancer of the endometrium and the ovary but increases cardiovascular risks in older women, and perhaps also the risks of chlamydial PID by affecting the chemistry of the uterus. Barrier methods of contraception provide the best protection against venereal disease, but certainly not the best protection against pregnancy. Abortion is riskier than almost all forms of contraception, and also carries an extra burden of emotional and physical distress. Pregnancy is riskier still—but having children reduces a woman's risk of breast cancer later in life. Those same risks are increased by living in complete chastity. No one who has followed the IUD litigation chronicles can believe that litigation successfully provided an evenhanded, sober exposition of these difficult trade-offs.

Let me state once again that Robins sold young women a dangerous bill of goods, and that many were gravely injured as a result. But the courts are influential sellers and teachers too: they teach not only by their decisions but by the attention they give to various problems, by how seriously they consider competing claims and defenses, and by which experts they listen to. The history of Robins's miseducation of young women is well documented. Too easily forgotten is how much the courts have done to miseducate women a second time, matching Robins's junk science optimism about the Shield with what has become, for all practical purposes, a blanket legal pessimism about all IUDs. Thanks to the courts, every educated woman today knows that IUDs have been linked with pelvic disease. Thanks also to the courts, far too many undoubtedly believe that IUDs are the main problem. Of those, many have turned away from all IUDs, including the safe ones. Many have doubtless returned to the pill, which for older women, especially those who smoke, is a more dangerous option.

Returned to the pill? Yes, that is what many of them had been using until the early 1970s. Many switched in the first place because of trials of another type, conducted in 1970 by Senator Gaylord Nelson, in the form of widely publicized congressional hearings. No doubt with the best of intentions, Nelson used his hearings to orchestrate a major attack on the risks of oral contraceptives. The dramatic testimony, based on preliminary reports and studies that have since been largely repudiated, was extensively covered by uncritical journalists and eagerly noted by some ambitious lawyers. Millions of young women began searching for a safer contraceptive option.

One of the first star witnesses at Nelson's hearings, one of the most persuasive about the pill's risks, one of the most credible on the possibility of safer alternatives, was Dr. Hugh J. Davis of Johns Hopkins. Four years earlier, he had in fact developed one of those supposedly safer alternatives. It came to be called the Dalkon Shield.

CONTROL, Q.E.D.

For legal purposes, Calabresi declared, "the cause" of tuberculosis depends not on how much we understand but on how much we can control. So much for liability science. In science of a more conventional stripe, control is usually considered later rather than earlier in the proceedings. Forty years after Curie, we had sufficient control of radioactive elements to make an atom bomb. Thirty years after Watson and Crick we were ready to engineer DNA for human therapy. Sometimes control never comes at all. The astrophysicist must be content to observe, analyze, and explain, for she can no more control the star's destiny than the star can control hers. So a lawyer may breezily announce that only the "prospect of genetic engineering" makes it "meaningful" to "speak of genetic predisposition as a 'cause' of [disease],"[36] but a good scientist will vomit at the thought. Causes exist quite independent of what can or cannot be controlled by humans. Control follows good science; it does not lead.

Control nevertheless *is* important in science—tremendously so—not as an end but as a component of proof. The ability to control is the strongest possible demonstration of true understanding. Many doubted whether Becquerel, Curie, Bohr, Oppenheimer, and the rest really understood what causes what inside the atom. But after July 16, 1945, when the day dawned prematurely to the northwest of Alamogordo, at White Sands,

New Mexico, no one could possibly doubt any more, for the atom bomb was plainer than the sun. With a demonstrated ability to control, the good scientist may sign off like the mathematician at the end of a proof: *Quod erat demonstrandum.*

It is by putting control back where it belongs that one puts liability science to its one serious test. Do the planes ever land at this particular airport? It might seem that liability science can boast of many successes. Lawsuits against drunk drivers may perhaps help run them off the road, if the drivers are not dead already. But simple cases of this kind, in which it's quite easy to say just what went wrong, are also cases in which traditional legal principles and standards of evidence, proved by long experience, make ambitious modern theory superfluous. To test the power of the cargo cult, one must travel to the South Seas; to test modern liability theory, one must look to where it has been most enthusiastically applied.

If any planes have ever landed in these scientific jungles, no one has ever reliably logged their arrival. There is no systematic empirical evidence—not a shred—that liability science applied to anything but the utterly obvious case has in fact improved the efficient control of accidents. Decades of traumatic cancer litigation have of course had no effect on cancer rates. Despite a huge legal assault on the contraceptive industry, the incidence of pelvic inflammatory disease has not abated. Bendectin is gone but the incidence of birth defects is unchanged, if not actually rising. And despite a great surge in litigation against obstetricians, despite the proliferation of fetal monitors and the multiplication of cesarean sections, the incidence of cerebral palsy has not changed. Nor is our rate any lower than Europe's or Japan's, where liability science is as yet unknown. Americans file vastly more lawsuits against doctors and drug companies, manufacturers of cars and contraceptives, municipalities and midwives than do the citizens of any other country in the world. But by every objective measure, the safety of our medical care, cars, contraceptives, and workplaces falls in the middle of the pack.

Some bad products have been effectively attacked now and again in the American courtroom. But the attack usually comes late in the day, after others have discovered the hazard, and after other effective controls have been put in place, both in the United States, where liability scientists roam, and abroad, where the species is unknown. And for every anecdote about liability well aimed, there is one where the shooting was wild. There was a Ford Pinto, but there was also the Audi 5000, which was in fact an exceptionally safe car. There was the Dalkon Shield, but also the Copper 7, a good contraceptive option. There was thalidomide, but also Bendectin, a valuable therapy. According to studies conducted by George Priest of the Yale Law School, how much we sue has no observable effect whatsoever on how safe we are. Accident and mortality rates in small planes, on the job, and elsewhere have been declining steadily for many decades. Lawsuits have surged only in the past ten or fifteen years. There has been no observable countersink in accident rates.[37]

The growth in litigation has not tracked a rise in accidents any more than it has forced a decline. Infant mortality has been on a steady decline for fifty years—the sudden burst of malpractice litigation against obstetricians in the past fifteen years has effected no visible change. Small plane fatalities have likewise been on a steady decline for a long time—yet liability payouts by plane manufacturers took off abruptly in recent years. The safety of contraceptives and vaccines has increased steadily and substantially for many decades—yet litigation against such products has increased dramatically (even putting aside the Dalkon Shield) in the space of a single decade.

That no beneficial effects can be measured from our enthusiastic dabbling in liability science is not surprising: so many causes affect the rate of birth defects, pelvic infection, lung cancer, and runaway cars that the few occasionally targeted in court are just lost in the causation pack. The fog is so thick, the unidentified flying objects so numerous, that no one has the slightest idea if any planes are landing at all.

THE LAWYERS' BANQUET

The few with blind faith in liability are often richly rewarded. Junk science, to put things bluntly, has become a very profitable business. Not profitable for society as a whole, of course—junk

science does not cure chemical AIDS, or prevent sudden acceleration in the Audi, or deliver healthier babies—but profitable
for those who peddle junk science through the courts. Those
with the staying power to outlast the many juries who decline to
buy can still make quite a profit on the few who buy all too
eagerly.

Modern lawyers will quickly understand—though only slowly
admit—how profit can corrupt their own endeavors, for they
spend much of their time explaining how profit has corrupted
everyone else's. The hunted and the hunters, it turns out, have
far more in common than the hunters care to admit. True
enough, a defense witness for Robins was caught claiming he
had personally conducted experiments that in fact were conducted by others, though he was acquitted when later tried for
perjury.[38] But then, a mountain of Bendectin litigation was created by one scientist who had faked experiments and another
who misrepresented his credentials. There is profit in lying on
both sides of the courtroom, and the margins and markups are
quite comparable.

Yes, the scientists at the drug and chemical companies may
sometimes advance the interests of their employers by shrug-
ging off serious scientific evidence of real problems. But litigation is a business too, and the captains of this industry maintain
their own stables of tame scientists. If one side has an incentive
to scoff at solid evidence of hazard, the other has an incentive,
at least equally large, to dignify junk. Larger, in fact. Unlike the
manufacturer of a dangerous product, who may simply not care
about relevant scientific evidence, trial lawyers gain a positive
advantage by concocting scientific falsehood. Outside the courtroom, moreover, there are some strong incentives to get the
science right. The pilot is always the first one at the scene of the
airplane accident, the expensive plane is usually a total loss, and
the ensuing publicity is terrible for business. Few people who
sell lawn mowers or deliver babies build sustainable businesses
by slaughtering their customers. But the more successfully lawyers sell junk science, the more customers they will have.

The phenomenon is not new to our time or place. In the days

of the Inquisition, the law of Spain provided that the property of a convicted witch could be confiscated by the Church. As Harris recounts, the witch's family was required to pay for the services of the torturers and the executioners, the cost of the faggots for the fire, and the food for the judges' banquet after the burning. "Considerable enthusiasm for witch-hunting could be built up among local officials, since they were empowered to confiscate the entire estate of any person condemned for witchcraft."[39] When Alonso Salazar y Frias revoked the law on confiscation of property, the rate of witchcraft accusations plummeted, and many witch-hunters were forced to seek other employment.

THE IRRELEVANT PRISM

The liability scientists began with a grand theory. Rules of evidence were modified accordingly. Experts of every stripe would congregate in the courtroom. Liability would expand and more money would change hands. According to theory, all of this was going to accomplish good for society: the costs of accidents would be reduced. The experts did congregate. Liability did expand. Vastly more money did change hands. But no one, nowhere, has ever systematically observed any beneficial effect on the costs of accidents. Many believe, many see, many buy, many swear high and low. But the controller is wearing headphones of wood and the antenna is bamboo. The planes don't land.

So liability science, one discovers in the end, is like the science of Blondlot's N rays at the turn of the century. After Blondlot's claims were challenged, it was proposed he apply his methods to identify the N-ray source in one of two sealed boxes. At length, he responded with the language quoted in the epigraph to this chapter: the effects of N rays were "much too delicate" for such a "simplistic experiment."[40]

This, for the most part, is how our lawyers respond too. The rays at issue here supposedly emanate from the courtroom. They are supposed to have all sorts of effects on accident rates, birth defects, life expectancy, and public health. But the effects, it turns out, are just too delicate to be detected systematically, at least when the tests are conducted in an objective way by someone who does not already know the answer. One need not rely on a skeptic to remove our liability prism surreptitiously: similar social experiments are being conducted around the world without it. By all objective measures, the rest of the industrialized world is quite as safe as ours, if not more so. Liability is supposed to brighten the safety spark, but only American lawyers, it turns out, have the acuity of vision to detect any change. No one else in the world discerns any positive effects.

And yet the form of American liability science is perfect. There are appropriate scientific experts on the one hand, to tell judges just where and how accidents might be avoided. And accountants and economists on the other, to compare costs of various options. Yes, science on the left, science on the right, science as far as the legal eye can see. To the uncritical eye, most especially to the eye of a lawyer doing tolerably well out of the system, it certainly inspires confidence.

Outside the legal system, the confidence is not widely shared, and for good reason. We discover in liability science that every ill has a distant cause, most often technological or chemical. The critical doses in liability therapy are uncalibrated, the responses unmeasured. All learning comes from the uncontrolled, idiosyncratic case study. When therapy is administered, the dosage varies wildly from one day to the next. The science is assertive, far-reaching, and confident. It can diagnose every ill and cure every affliction. It has all the trappings, formalism, and solemnity of science, but none of the substance. Nothing is verified empirically; the effectiveness of the system is a matter of theory and faith. True believers believe, but no outside observer ever does. Where have we seen such science before? Among the traumatic oncologists, the clinical ecologists, the sudden accelerationists, the fetal-monitor cultists, and the Bendectinists, that's where.

Modern liability science is cargo-cult science, nothing more. Both are impelled by zealotry and profit, not by science. Both aspire to control wisely and effectively, but neither demonstrably do. Both are willing (like Calabresi) to set aside "seemingly significant philosophical questions" as "irrelevant."[41] For the true Calabresian, like the South Sea islander, the mind is set too firmly on the ultimate objective of control. Bring down the cargo; the rest is detail.

CHAPTER 11

Stopping Points

Confronting Malpractice on the Witness Stand

[M]ortality and sickness . . . are constant in the same circumstances, varying as the causes favorable or unfavorable to health preponderate.
—William Farr (1836)

Today, judges across the country confront a terrifying new threat. They recognize that "deep anxieties and considerable hysteria" afflict a small community in Florida as much as a large one in New York. The fears are undoubtedly real, but most judges refuse to be swayed by "theoretical risk," "future theoretical harm," "pure speculation," or "irrational and unsupported belief." Almost without exception, judges brush aside popular fears and stake everything on real science. They empathize with those who are frightened but find themselves "duty bound to objectively evaluate the issue . . . and not be influenced by unsubstantiated fears of catastrophe." "Little in science can be proved with complete certainty," a California judge concedes, but decisions cannot turn on some tiny, unerasable, shadow of doubt. Judges must rely instead on "[t]he overwhelming weight of scientific evidence," the "clear weight of the expert medical evidence and opinion," "reasonable medical knowledge," and the consensus views of expert agencies and public health authorities.[1]

What could possibly elicit so much good sense in so many different quarters? Certainly not "chemical AIDS," the clinical ecologist's junk science alternative to the dread disease. At issue is AIDS itself, the new leprosy. More specifically, the issue is whether AIDS can be transmitted by casual contact. The argument is always the same: Since we don't know absolutely for sure, shouldn't we err on the side of safety? It is the same argument that we have seen raised in connection with tuberculosis, electronic cruise controls, morning-sickness drugs, contraceptives, vaccines, and industrial chemicals: better to banish the small risk than to hazard the large harm.

But in answering this tired and superficial argument in the context of AIDS, courageous judges call the science straight. They side with doctors against a New York landlord who does not want them to treat AIDS patients on his premises, with AIDS children who want to attend schools in New York City and Florida, and with young Ryan Thomas, who begs leave to attend kindergarten in California.[2] Predictably, the California school district does manage to dig up a Dr. Steven Armentrout, who opines—correctly, no doubt—that there is a tiny possibility that AIDS could be transmitted through as yet undiscovered vectors.[3] But five experts, backed up by prestigious medical journals, present strong evidence that AIDS is not transmitted by casual contact, and that is enough.

And now a strange thing begins to happen: as one judge after another affirms the solid science and rejects the paranoid speculation, the courts help to educate the public and allay some of its most acute but least well grounded fears. By refusing to take the junk science of AIDS seriously, wise judges help put a stop to it.

Why have courts been willing to rein in destructive legal speculation on genuine AIDS, when they are so reluctant to do the same when it comes to "chemical AIDS" or the other bogeys of junk science? One reason, no doubt, is that a young Ryan Thomas with his heart set on kindergarten is a much more visible and sympathetic victim of junk science than a faceless, deep-pocket corporation called Alcolac. But giving in to scientific nonsense entails costs in either case. A rational court system can and should vindicate good science not just as an occasional excursion into sense where the stakes are especially high and poignant, but as an everyday matter for every kind of litigant.

SCIENCE AS CONSENSUS

But what *is* good science? How can we identify it? The trial lawyer and his acolytes will never tire of telling stories about how high priests of science have been proved badly wrong by "cranks" and "mavericks" in times past. Galileo, the patron saint of all heretics, figures often in such stories. Let's not ostracize the "mini Galileo," pleads a plaintiff's lawyer; the legal system must be "capable of advancing."[4] Honor the expert "at the edges of the bell curve," advises the chemical-AIDS maven Alan Levin, "as was Galileo and as are other people at the frontiers of medicine or science."[5]

No doubt about it: the views of the establishment *are* sometimes wrong, in science and medicine as in law. Galileo gained fame by challenging one orthodoxy but eventually became part of another: he refused to believe that the moon caused tides, or that planets moved in ellipses, as the upstart Johannes Kepler maintained. Eighteenth-century astronomers stubbornly refused to believe that stones fell from the sky. Darwin's theory was dismissed initially by physicists who calculated (correctly) that ordinary combustion could never have kept the sun burning over the Darwinian millennia. Ernest Rutherford's views on the radioactive transmutation of elements were attacked for sounding too much like alchemy. Albert Einstein never was reconciled to quantum mechanics. When the great Hungarian clinician Ignaz Philipp Semmelweis discovered the antiseptic properties of chlorinated lime in 1850, his findings were met with deep skepticism from many in the medical establishment. True enough, the isolated scientist, the iconoclast, the maverick, crank, or congenital rebel has sometimes been proved right.

But science has changed profoundly since the days of Galileo and Semmelweis. This is most particularly true of medical science. Until the late seventeenth century, as the historian James Burke recounts, a medical career "flourished or foundered according to the relationship the doctor managed to strike up at the bedside." The doctor would emphasize his "heroic and secret" insights into disease and its cure. Each individual's illness was thought to be a unique condition. Each doctor "would claim that all other doctors were quacks and their remedies ill-advised or dangerous."[6] Doctors believed that every disease could exhibit every symptom. Therapies were correspondingly quirky. The patient's own view of what kind of treatment he needed was often the main basis for recommending a cure.

In 1800, the French surgeon Xavier Bichat demonstrated that disease is a specific phenomenon peculiar to certain lesions or tissues. Doctors began to recognize that disease itself presents a specific and concrete target that transcends individual patients. As medicine raised its sights from the idiosyncratic and particular to the regular and general, it converged with statistics, a new branch of mathematics that was evolving during the same period. The foremost French physicist of the age, Pierre-Simon Laplace, would show how statistics could systematically improve observation, establish the reliability of experimental results, and reveal hidden regularities. The center of medical learning shifted to the hospital, where patients could be studied in still larger numbers. As Burke recounts, "Bedside secrets gave way to a desire among doctors to share techniques and information."[7] Medical journals proliferated.

When cholera struck Europe in 1829, the hospital was overtaken by the city. William Farr, appointed Controller of the General Register Office, set out to conquer cholera with a radically new medical instrument: the biometer. The biometer was pencil and paper—a life-table that insurance company actuaries had been using for years. Farr systematically analyzed who was dying and where. The most important things he discovered were negative. Wealth didn't protect you from cholera. Nor did occupation, or residential proximity to the sea. What mattered was how high above the Thames you lived. Farr concluded that cholera was caused by the river's awesome stench. He was wrong, but only in this single, last step of the analysis. It was left to another English physician, John Snow, to make the right connection in 1853. The key was not dirty air but dirty water;

the London sewers emptied into the Thames, so the farther down-sewer you lived, the more likely you were to drink foul water. A few years later Parliament passed legislation to rebuild the sewers, and cholera disappeared from the city forever.

The story of cholera is the story of how medicine was transformed from black art to science, from a pseudoscience of the individual to a science of groups. The difference between the clinician who cures and the clinician who quacks is the difference between the intellectual hermit and the member-in-good-standing of a community of scientists. For the one, medicine is shaped by an endless series of peculiar and individual cases; for the other, by broad perspective and consensus conclusions. One espouses fictions as changeable as the individual patient and doctor; the other, truths that apply to many people, not just to one. The rise of modern medical science, with its astonishing capacity to diagnose and cure, can be traced to the decline of individual eccentricity on both sides of the stethoscope.

Medical science is not unique; all modern science has similar origins. Many Renaissance scientists lacked any cohesive social structure or professional journals; Galileo had limited opportunity to belong to a larger community of scientists, though one should not forget that his heresy was to agree with Copernicus. But in 1660, there was established the "Colledge for the Promoting of Physico-Mathematicall Experimentall Learning," which became London's Royal Society.[8] The original Royal Society boasted such luminaries as Charles II, Christopher Wren (who gave the society's first lecture), Samuel Pepys, Robert Hooke, and Sir Isaac Newton (president of the Society for twenty-four years). Since that time, all science in the West has been built up through collegiality and consensus—and a concomitant decline in the role of the hermit scientist.

Modern science is thus a far cry from the science of centuries ago. It is no longer linked to any single theory or result; it is a process of replication and verification, a search for consensus. This is not to say that the new ideas are shunned; the truth is quite the opposite. As Gardner points out, "[t]he prevailing spirit among scientists, outside of totalitarian countries, is one of eagerness for fresh ideas. . . . If anything, scientific journals err on the side of permitting questionable theses to be published, so they may be discussed and checked in the hope of finding something of value."[9] But science centers on objective fact, and the only reliable test for objectivity is to determine what many different people can see in common, from different vantage points, in their waking hours. What individuals see alone, awake or in their dreams, is not science. A solitary white coat, test tube, and résumé are not science. Modern science is not a solitary undertaking.

Litigation is. Real science is the study of facts that are regular, of things that recur in patterns, but a courtroom trial is quintessentially singular. Science depends on placing facts in an orderly context, but a trial frames facts in isolation. Good science transcends the here and now, the individual and idiosyncratic, the single laboratory, the single nation, the single planet, even the single galaxy, but a trial typically examines a singular datum, and demands that scientific truths be rediscovered anew every time. Scientific facts emerge from many isolated observations, as data are accumulated, vetted for error, tested for significance, correlated, regressed, and reanalyzed, but trials are conducted retail. Good science is open, collegial, and cumulative, but the courtroom setting is discrete, insular, and closed—a one-shot decision.

The methods of science are so fundamentally different from those of litigation that scientific anarchy in court is inevitable if rules of evidence are not strictly maintained. Absent such rules, scientific facts remain perpetually in play. Each patient, each injury, each illness becomes unique once again—or so says the eighteenth-century doctor, on the payroll of the twentieth-century lawyer. Trials are not connected; the same question about Bendectin, the Audi, or clinical ecology can be litigated again and again. In the worst cases, courts drift through the degenerative sequence described by the historian Jerome Ravetz,[10] and thereafter elaborated by W. C. Clark. Tentative outlooks are often suppressed, views are quickly polarized, and a "great confidence game" replaces serious science. Recognition and money flow "to those making the first, loudest, and most frightening noises." The careful skeptic is rewarded with "accusations of corruption, cowardice, or insensitivity." There will be "an accretion of cranks and congenital rebels whose reforming zeal is not matched by their scientific skill."[11]

HOLDING WITNESSES TO A COMMON STANDARD

As we have seen, an accretion of cranks in court follows inevitably from the great paradox of modern liability science: in attempting to control quackery outside the courtroom, we invite quacks to the witness stand. If this degenerative process is to be halted, or better still reversed, judges must rediscover rules of evidence consonant with the essential collegiality of modern science. Such rules are not self-evident, nor can they be implemented mechanically, nor will they work their intended effect in the hands of jurists who hold science itself in no real respect. But rules can be formulated, and even modest rules, if enforced with evenhanded conviction and some measure of faith in the scientific method, will make a positive difference.

Whatever his credentials, publications, or affiliations, a scientist who becomes the alter ego of a lawyer is no longer a scientist. At the very least, rules to maintain some minimum separation of egos are thus urgently needed. They are not difficult to devise.

"Training is everything," Mark Twain once suggested. "The peach was once a bitter almond; the cauliflower is nothing but cabbage with a college education."[12] Many, like Twain, will suppose that the cure to junk science litigation is to have judges scrutinize professional credentials more carefully. It isn't; Twain was only half right. Strings of letters appended to last names do provide a useful initial screen against professional incompetence, but only a very coarse one. Even yesterday's stellar achievement offers little assurance that today's opinion is correct: many a great scientist takes off sooner or later on some foolish frolic. Isaac Newton, for example, ended up in alchemy. Johannes Baptiste van Helmont, the seventeenth-century scientist who invented both the term and the concept of a "gas," later extolled the curative powers of magnetic forces. David Starr

Jordan, one-time president of Stanford University, who coined the term *sciosophy* ("shadow wisdom") to describe the junk science of his day, was a dyed-in-the-wool eugenicist. The modern patron of clinical ecology is a Harvard-trained, board-certified allergist. Individuals change; yesterday's competent medical student or even Nobel-caliber chemist can become tomorrow's crank.

So while a résumé may be a necessary condition of expert competence, it is never a sufficient one. Twain's views notwithstanding, what defines a cauliflower is not its résumé but the views it shares with other cauliflowers. A cabbage with an M.D. is a still a cabbage. Science is likewise defined by a community, not by the individual, still less by a résumé. Lawyers already know this. Credentials are all but irrelevant when a doctor sits at the defense table rather than in the witness box, and so they should be. *Cucullus non facit monachum:* the cowl does not make a monk.

This was, indeed, the key insight in the old *Frye* rule. *Frye* directed the focus away from the individual, whatever his credentials might be, and toward the scientific consensus. Define the relevant community whose consensus views should prevail. Then require expert witnesses to report not their own, personal views, but the consensus views of that community.

Applying the test is not always simple; there will always be room for quibbling. Any definition of "the relevant scientific community" will be somewhat arbitrary. But despite what some lawyers maintain, it isn't terribly difficult to decide which community of scientists to consult on Bendectin, cerebral palsy, or sudden acceleration. Lawyers in fact define similar communities all the time. A long-standing principle of negligence law is that doctors are held to the standards of the medical community in which they practice; one standard for an urban specialist, another for a rural generalist. Class actions—a great favorite among many legal scholars who disdain *Frye*—operate on the theory that a few individual claimants can be identified as "typical" of many others; a few from the mainstream, the reasoning runs, will represent the interests of the rest quite adequately. Most of the time, common sense serves well enough in identifying a relevant scientific community, far better than it does in ascertaining the science itself.

The second step in applying *Frye*—determining just where the mainstream scientific consensus lies—is usually not all that hard either. Careful reviews of current learning on one subject or another are published in top-notch scientific journals all the time. Such journals have long track records of accuracy and insight. They are backed by established scientific institutions. What they publish is reviewed by other scientists. A judge need not know the slightest thing about traumatic cancer or electronic cruise controls to make sensible calls about who speaks for mainstream science on such issues and who does not. Even a person who knows nothing about hydrology can distinguish the mainstream of the Mississippi from stagnant pools near its banks.

As the legal scholar Bert Black has lucidly discussed, a sophisticated, modern application of *Frye* looks to the methods behind a scientific report, not to its finely detailed conclusions.[13] An epidemiological study will easily survive *Frye* even if it is the very first to report, for example, a link between Bendectin and birth defects, so long as standard protocols for conducting such studies have been observed and the data are reported with error bands, significance tests, and similar statements of caution suitable for a refereed professional journal. What should not survive, however, is a crude imitation of science, the unpublished hunch, the letter to the editor, the impressionistic "mosaic theory," in which the lawyer's science of harmonious coupling substitutes for systematic observation and analysis.

Lawyers should be the last to suggest that any of these ideas is radical or unreasonable, because lawyers apply every one of them to defendants, though not to witnesses. If the laws of negligence and strict liability can condemn doctors, chemists, pharmacologists, and car manufacturers for their ineptitude, it is because we believe that there *is* such a thing as ineptitude, that competence is ascertainably different from incompetence, that there are objective standards worth enforcing. But if people who really design cars or deliver babies are to be judged by professional standards in court, those who accuse them must be held to similar account. If the law is capable of holding defendants to professional standards, it is capable of holding witnesses to the same.

Judges, too, certainly live by *Frye* when their own, personal interests are at stake. The judge who currently sits back and allows the general practitioner's testimony on esoteric problems of pharmacology is the same judge who jumps on the next plane to the Mayo Clinic when he himself needs treatment.[14] If he is wise, he will also trust the Mayo Clinic doctors when they tell him which therapies *won't* work, and which treatments are *not* worth trying. He trusts the Mayo Clinic—for both positive and negative advice—not because he knows the individual doctors, or is impressed by their résumés, and still less because he really knows what ails him or what cure to accept. What he trusts is the institution, the process, the collegiality, the experience, and the track record. And this, of course, is just where he should place his trust when administering a legal process that establishes standards and prescribes therapies for everyone else in the world.

The consensus scientific community supplies stopping points in abundance for those who care to find them. An authoritative scientific pronouncement on Bendectin by the Food and Drug Administration might be one. Or a report by the National Institutes of Health on electronic fetal monitors. Or one by the Centers for Disease Control on the pertussis vaccine, or the causes of pelvic infection. Or the surgeon general's office on tobacco. Such institutions, established and funded to make difficult scientific calls, draw on the best and broadest scientific resources. This is not to suggest that they are infallible; of course they aren't. They are just less fallible—*much* less fallible—than a thousand juries scattered across the country grappling with the complexities of immune system impairment after being educated by the likes of Bertram Carnow or Arthur Zahalsky. Judges therefore have abundant reason to promote the former and to be far more cautious about admitting the latter.

Half the time, ironically, that is precisely what judges already do. If the FDA declares that thalidomide causes limb defects in the womb, there will not be a very long or complex trial if a drug company nonetheless sells the product and a child is born without arms. The case is easy not because the science is easy—it isn't—but because a much larger community has already thrashed out the questions and reached some consensus. But there is consensus with Bendectin too, yet Bendectin trials have lumbered forward, one by one. If the FDA says the drug is a teratogen, liability will follow almost automatically. If the FDA says it isn't, ask a jury. And then another, and another, as many times in succession as the trial bar may deem to be justified by either visceral conviction or speculative greed. We find, once again, that our modern liability system is all accelerator and no brake.

When definitive pronouncements of the FDA, CDC, or surgeon general are not at hand, the next best place to look for the consensus views of mainstream science is in the peer-reviewed scientific literature. There is, indeed, a straightforward test for judges to determine which methods, procedures, and theories have *not* been "generally accepted" by other scientists: the absence of peer-reviewed publication. Writing is the medium of science. As lawyers well know, writing imposes discipline and precision; it clarifies both the strengths and weaknesses of a claim. Modern science simply does not exist without it. Only a much firmer emphasis on the written word can bridge the wide gulf between oral testimony in court and the only medium accepted by scientists themselves for communicating important findings and theories. A witness whose views have survived peer review in a professional journal will already have been forced into a candid disclosure of cautions and qualifications; good journals won't publish without them. If the published claim is of any importance, publication will also mobilize other scientists to repeat, verify, contradict, or confirm. By requiring professional publication as a basis for expert opinion, judges will help line up the larger community of scientists to shadow the necessarily smaller community of expert witnesses.

One might expect judges to be very comfortable with such a write-it-down rule of scientific evidence, for they apply similar rules elsewhere. The "parol evidence" rule, for example, declares that a written contract trumps the verbal discussions that lead up to it; writing is likewise required by the law to make binding a will or a contract for the sale of land. If the law already recognizes that only a written document can be trusted to determine who gets Aunt Agatha's prized collection of china dogs, it is hardly excessive to require formal writing by anyone who claims to have identified the causes of cerebral palsy or chemically induced AIDS.

There is one final test of expert competence, one more difficult to articulate but of great importance nonetheless. Scientific study of the causes of injury and disease, like scientific study of anything else, looks for regularities, patterns, and recurrences. Modern science uses rigorous, systematic methods to locate such regularities, methods that are rooted in statistics and significance tests, blinded trials and especially epidemiology. Each human spirit may be individual and unique, but the frailties of human flesh are shared by many. Medical science has recognized this fundamental fact for the better part of two centuries.

Thus, any truly scientific claim about the causes of disease will be based on systematic observation of many patients or test subjects, not on off-the-cuff impressions developed in the course of clinical treatment. The skills required to diagnose cerebral palsy, or perform infant surgery, or treat leukemia, are not the same skills required to determine the causes of the afflictions in question. The difference between the clinician and the scientist is one that courts must learn to understand and affirm.

For there to be real science, the subjects of scientific study, like scientists themselves, must connect up with a broader community. Peer review places the clinician in the larger context of the community of clinicians; epidemiology and systematic clinical trials place the patient in the larger context of the populace at large. Both are enemies of bedside medicine. They force conviviality on the hermit scientist. They elevate learning from the specific to the general, from the singular to the plural—and thus from the idiosyncratic impression to something we call science. As solutions to a pressing legal problem, they may appear undramatic. But by systematically emphasizing such well-recognized instruments of mainstream science, judges can do much to reconcile science in court with science in the real world.

THE PRIVILEGED INTERLOPER

To hold experts to serious scientific standards is not to abandon venerable legal principle but to reaffirm it. The expert witness is the only kind of witness who is permitted to reflect, opine, and pontificate, in language as conclusory as he may wish. We give him the considerable license he enjoys because some facts are meaningful only in the context of those larger patterns of facts we call science. It's useless for a pathologist to describe in fine detail what he saw when the reagent was added to the blood sample, if he may not also explain blood types, genetic rules, and why harmonious coupling between Charlie Chaplin (Group O) and Joan Berry (Group A) could not have produced Carol Ann (Group B). The expert, in other words, is there to provide a bridge between the particular facts of a case and patterns of facts that can be observed and understood only through much wider study.

Once we recognize the expert witness for what he is, an unusually privileged interloper, it becomes apparent why we must limit just how far the interloping may go. A witness cut loose from time-tested rules of evidence to engage in purely personal, idiosyncratic speculation offends legal tradition quite as much as the tradition of science. Unleashing such an expert in court is not just unfair, it is inimical to the pursuit of truth. The expert whose testimony is not firmly anchored in some broader body of objective learning is just another lawyer, masquerading as a pundit.

The challenge, then, is to determine when the anchor is secure. The only possible test is to confirm that other boats have favored similar moorings. The only way to tell that expertise is based on objective experience is to see whether others with similar experience favor similar methods, adopt similar procedures, embrace similar theories, and reach similar conclusions. This is pretty much the standard articulated decades ago by *Frye*.

It is heartening to record that at least some judges have arrived at some of these conclusions in recent years. Something of a turning point in judicial attitudes came in 1986, in a much-cited opinion by federal appellate Judge Patrick Higginbotham. "Our message to our able trial colleagues: it is time to take hold of expert testimony in federal trials," he wrote.[15] A slowly growing number of able colleagues have taken these sentiments to heart.[16] Some have begun to emphasize that radical London novelty of 1660—the ‘professional society—and that radical Paris novelty of the 1820s—the professional journal and peer review.[17] Others have begun to emphasize the importance of solid epidemiological data.[18] Still others have concluded that medicine, too, is a part of science, and that medical experts can be screened along the same lines as all others.[19] Some have expressed mounting impatience with experts who wander far from their specialties, such as the plastic surgeon who wanted to testify on Bendectin although he admitted he had no knowledge of studies that had been conducted on that drug.[20] (The witness was confined to making mountains out of molehills outside the courtroom.) Others have revised rules to allow experts to be questioned about how much they are paid, how often they testify, and for whom.[21] Others have rejected testimony from witnesses who actually solicited their own employment.[22] Still others have refused to enforce contingency-fee arrangements made with expert referral agencies.[23] But, as we have seen, many judges still reject any such limits, or equivocate so much that defendants settle baseless claims rather than risk going to trial.

If judges will not screen witnesses retail, state legislatures can screen wholesale; it is encouraging to note once again that a few have recently done so.[24] In 1987, for example, Alabama passed a law requiring expert witnesses to have practiced recently in the same specialty as the doctor they charge with medical malpractice.[25] Colorado passed a law in 1988 restricting malpractice expert testimony to licensed physicians who can demonstrate "substantial familiarity" with the applicable standard of care and the procedure being litigated.[26] A recent Maryland law bars testimony from any malpractice expert who spends more than 20 percent of his time in court.[27] Kansas, Michigan, Maryland, Rhode Island, and West Virginia have developed similar requirements. Most of these states also bar from the witness stand academics who do not practice at all.

The strongest antidote to bad science in court remains one that most American judges are still regrettably reluctant to use. European judges routinely summon their own experts. Our judges have similar powers,[28] but few choose to exercise them.[29] Most trial lawyers vehemently oppose court-appointed experts, perceiving (correctly, no doubt) that consensus cannot be good for a conflict-centered livelihood. Lawyers will therefore assure you that there is no such thing as a neutral expert. But it is obviously possible to find knowledgeable scientists of high principle, and having a nonpartisan judge do the finding considerably improves the prospect of locating a less partisan expert.

None of these ideas is the least bit radical. What they all come down to is biblical wisdom on the punishment of harlots. If not certifiably free of sin, the expert witness who casts the first stone should—at the very least—not be a notorious patron of the local scientific bordello.

PUBLISH AND BE DAMNED

It has gradually dawned on professional societies that they too should be concerned about a legal system in which the worst doctors, engineers, or toxicologists are given a better than fair shot at prescribing standards of conduct for the rest. If X rays, CAT scans, and cesarean sections are proliferating in unnecessary (and even perhaps dangerous) excess, it is because too much obstetrics, oncology, and emergency-room surgery is conducted a second time in court, by second-rank doctors who understand law better than medicine. Witnessing can have far-reaching professional consequences. It is therefore a form of professional practice. Or malpractice, as the case may be.

While lawyers are uncharacteristically tolerant about this one form of malpractice among all others, professional societies need not be. The American Medical Association, joined by the American College of Obstetricians and Gynecologists and the American Academy of Pediatrics, recognizes the doctor's "ethical obligation to assist in the administration of justice," but insists that "[t]he medical witness must not become an advocate in the legal proceeding." Contingent fees for witnesses are flatly labeled "unethical."[30] Several engineering societies have taken similar initiatives. However much lawyers may wish otherwise, professional societies have a major role to play in maintaining sharp lines between the practice of litigation and the practice of medicine, engineering, or pharmacology.

Another, even more important challenge for professional societies is to maintain scientific candor. We can all sense that truth is in peril when witnesses say things in court they'd never dare say elsewhere. Sins of omission are less obvious, but no less common. Bad scientists routinely engage in "data dredging," a process by which observations that coincide with initial beliefs are carefully saved and recorded, while others somehow get lost.

The law grandly insists that individual witnesses swear to tell the *whole* truth, but modern rules of evidence in fact encourage dredging of an even more brazen kind. The lawyer dredges not for congenial data points but for congenial scientists themselves. The upshot of this degenerate process is a firm like the Medical Legal Consulting Service of Rockville, Maryland, which promises lawyers: "If the first doctor we refer doesn't agree with your legal theory, we will provide you with the name of a second."[31] This sort of thing corrupts not only the legal process but its scientific participants. As the physicist Richard Feynman once noted, this too is a form of scientific corruption, and perhaps an even more pernicious one. "If your answer happens to come out in the direction [those who solicited it] like, they can use it as an argument in their favor; if it comes out the other way, they don't publish it at all. That's not giving scientific advice." Good science, Feynman pointed out, demands "utter honesty," a "leaning over backwards" to be open and frank. "[T]he idea is to try to give all of the information to help others to judge the value of your contribution; not just the information that leads to judgment in one particular direction or another."[32]

Half the time, the legal system shares this view, but half the time is not enough. The sober scientist or doctor who works calmly day by day, meticulously recording all her observations and speculations, tentative, final, or otherwise, will end up seeing her every marginal note scrutinized in open court if something goes wrong. When Audi's engineers or Merrell's pharmacologists are summoned for trial, they will find the law to be limitlessly enthusiastic about candor and complete disclosure. Every doctor, druggist, or corporate defendant can be forced to empty all files and disclose every opinion and musing he ever recorded on the hazard now being litigated.

But once litigation begins, scientific inquiry suddenly becomes altogether private and confidential. Experts rounded up purely for the purpose of litigation are carefully sifted and sanitized, primed and primped. And these experts, the ones on the lawyers' payroll, are completely sheltered by a circus-tent privilege of confidentiality. Lawyers, it turns out, believe in complete candor for every scientist but their own. This, of course, allows them to shop around for divergent views, and then rehearse the one or two most perfectly congenial to the case at hand. But as Feynman points out, such shopping is just a sophisticated way of subverting integrity and objectivity through a sort of Darwinian selection. Lawyers will insist that the selection must be performed in complete secrecy to protect their confidential relationship with their clients. But a lawyer out angling for expert witnesses is not doing anything that deserves to be protected from public scrutiny, especially when protection has such antisocial consequences.

Feynman once suggested a pellucidly simple rule to protect against the subversion-by-selection that lawyers routinely practice. The honest scientist approached for his expert opinion must resolve at the outset to publish or at least disclose his conclusion, regardless of whose side it will benefit in the forthcoming trial. "If you don't publish such a result, it seems to me you're not giving scientific advice," Feynman wrote. "You're being used."[33]

The very thought that their own, duly hired and solemnly signed experts might feel free to publish findings beneficial to the other side would of course send trial lawyers into fits of blustery protest. But this should not deter professional societies from policing malpractice by their members wherever it may occur. Societies could accomplish wonders by requiring every member approached as potential witnesses to make a Feynman declaration at the outset: "In keeping with my professional responsibilities, I will promptly publish anything of scientific note that I may learn in our consultations, regardless of whose legal interests my findings may favor." Judges might achieve much the same result by forbidding lawyers to do what they now do, which is to conceal all but the most favorable of the fistful of expert opinions they may solicit. Or better still, by announcing that only experts solemnly Feynmanized on first contact would be allowed to testify at all. The ultimate test of a scientist's competence is her ability to publish in peer-reviewed journals. The ultimate test of her scientific integrity is her readiness to publish and be damned. *That* is one real lesson judges should have learned from Galileo.

GAVAGING THE RATS

Real science, science outside the courtroom, is an evenly balanced process of proposal and disposal. Science does, of course, require a steady supply of the new and different, the bold, the shocking, even the outrageous. But it requires even more a steady supply of replication, verification, and peer review, the patient development of consensus, the systematic weeding, pruning, and uprooting of spurious data and erroneous theory. Starting promising new lines of inquiry is important; no less important is stopping unpromising old ones. Beginning speculation may be more exciting than ending it. But good science depends quite as much on the patient, plodding rejection and elimination of bad data and mistaken theory.

Judges have understood this well enough when addressing unfounded prejudice against victims of AIDS. But when the targets of junk science are less sympathetic, and their pockets deeper, the legal record has been dismal. Let-it-all-in rules of scientific evidence have made it trivially easy to begin pseudo-scientific speculation in court and almost impossible to end it. Courtroom science has come to revolve around the opinionated eccentric, the go-it-alone maverick. It is heavily biased in favor of the impresario who begins speculation, and against the plodders who end it.

The vindication of good science in court requires precisely the opposite. Judges, like scientists themselves, will never pen a final opinion on the laws of nature, nor should they try. What they can do, however, is realign courtroom science with the science of scientists. This means giving much less attention to the self-proclaimed new Galileos, and far more to the reticent stalwarts of the mainstream scientific community. No doubt, trials will always depend on individual witnesses and personal credibility. But just who those witnesses are and what they testify to can be controlled. Lawyers and judges who claim so much aptitude in deterring incompetence and preventing accidents everywhere else can surely find the rules to deter and prevent them in court—if they can ever find the will. Until they do, courts will maintain their current renown for quixotic, pseudoscientific crusades, begun in haste and repented at leisure. Until they do, what passes for science in court won't be.

All science—all *real* science—contains what Karl Popper called "stopping rules." Statements of scientific fact are statements that could be systematically shown to be false (if they are false) after some finite, circumscribed inquiry.[34] Questions that are forever open, questions that can be answered only one way or not at all, are the domain of philosophy and religion, not of science. "Dioxin may be a human carcinogen" is not a statement of scientific fact, nor is "AIDS might be transmitted by flies." No finite number of tests and experiments could ever refute a statement of general fact couched in "mays" or "mights." No matter how far one searches, a weaker, as yet undetected effect may still be lurking just over the statistical horizon. The language of *could, possible, may, might,* and *maybe* that so often litters fringe testimony in court is not the language of science. Nor is science a business of completely open-ended speculation, where any idea can be floated but none can ever be finally brought back to earth.

W. C. Clark pursued the point in his scathing commentary on

what often passes for risk assessment, but he might equally well have been speaking about legal process:

> If rats cope with the heaviest dose of a chemical that can be soaked into their food and water, you can always gavage them. Or try mice or rabbits. . . . [T]he only stopping rule is discovery of the sought-for effect, or exhaustion of the investigator (or his funds). Many of the risk assessment procedures used today are logically indistinguishable from those used by the Inquisition. . . . Since neither is advancing falsifiable propositions, neither is capable of producing anything more than propaganda in support of its own prejudices.[35]

It is only in the most naive and uninformed views of science that every question is perpetually unresolved, that every theory is as good as every other, that every fact is forever in doubt. Real science has stopping points. Real scientists respect them.

Is this to say that their minds are closed? Yes. Closing the mind, selectively and carefully, of course, is the essence of most good science. Science is defined as much by what it rejects as by what it accepts. Indeed, much of good science, especially in the early stages of new inquiries, consists of proving negatives, of closing the mind to plausible but erroneous possibilities. Good science has closed the modern mind to perpetual motion, polywater, and N rays, and to the curative powers of Krebiozen, Radiothor, Galvanic batteries, and Laetrile. When a new disease like AIDS arrives on the scene, much of the critical early research is a process of elimination: the cause is *not* traumatic, *not* bacterial, *not* autoimmune, and so on. By knowing what it is not, one eventually converges on what it is. Although the point can easily be misinterpreted, closing the mind—to demonstrably incorrect claims and theories—is much of what science is about. If we no longer burn witches at the stake, it is because science has closed most modern minds to the possibility that certain women cause plagues, pestilence, and crop blight.

If courts are to assimilate good science in their proceedings, legal process must be equally symmetric. Judges must discover ways to cut off junk science as resolutely and reliably as they can affirm science that spotlights real hazards. If the only thing certain to stop Bendectin litigation is the disappearance of Bendectin itself, legal process has failed science miserably. If the law acts decisively (and remuneratively) against real hazards, and with perpetual indecision against fake ones, the upshot will be a corruption of science in court, a gradual, inexorable slide toward ignorance and paranoia.

Stopping the slide toward ignorance requires, at the very least, that incompetence not be unleashed against competence. The paranoia possibilities of junk science must be resisted more firmly still. Junk science's one very real power is to stir up fear. As a wise trial judge in Washington State recognized eighty years ago, there must therefore be cases of *damnum absque injuria*—harm without a legally recognized injury, harm without a right to recover from the person who caused it.[36] The miscreant in that case, we may recall, was Benjamin Paschall, and the harm he had caused was frightening his neighbors by opening his home to victims of tuberculosis. The harm was real enough, but only because the neighbors held fears out of line with scientific reality. Today, many judges confronted with similar AIDS cases have performed much more courageously than did the Washington Supreme Court in the Paschall litigation. When it comes to junk fear, a court either affirms good science or ends up increasing the very injury it seeks to redress.

Yes, the pained judge too often responds, but if only we had better science, more certainty, firmer answers. All these suggestive studies—with traumatic cancer, Bendectin, Audis, fetal monitors, and chemical AIDS—yet never anything absolutely, finally, completely positive. The scientists themselves refuse to speak in absolutes. How vexing for the nonscientific bystander, especially the one seated at the bench or in the jury box. Do another study! Still inconclusive? Then a major research program is in order. The problem isn't really too much bad science—it's too little good science. Until the balance is corrected, the courts just have to muddle along, resolving the uncertainty one way or the other, as the jury may see fit.

In fact, what is most desperately needed is almost the opposite of more research: not less research across the board, but reliable ways of saying that enough is enough when great and costly towers of litigation are being erected on the soft, ever-shifting sands of junk science. In law, as in science, not all frontiers are worth exploring forever. Not when exploration is so socially disruptive and expensive, and when there are other, manifestly more productive territories to be settled.

It is perhaps comforting to declare that we need more research. But that statement is always trite and often wrong. Worse still, calls for more research provide great comfort to junk scientists, who will find there subtle support for their own idiosyncratic crusades. Such calls legitimize and dignify the concerns that have been raised. Believers in Martian spaceships and astrology undoubtedly would welcome calls for more research in those fields, too. What takes more courage is to put an end to what, given a fair test of time, has proved to be fruitless, wasteful speculation.

CHAPTER 12

Science and Certitude

"Our freedom to doubt was born out of a struggle against authority in the early days of science," Richard Feynman once wrote. "It was a very deep and strong struggle: permit us to question—to doubt—to not be sure."[1] Science *does* search for absolute and immutable truths. The search *does* progress. But it does not end.

For just that reason, no one quite knows exactly what it is that science confirms or denies. We therefore have no precise definition of "junk science," "pseudoscience," "quack," "crank," "crackpot," or "snake oil." Nor, for that matter, is there a precise definition of "snake." As Martin Gardner points out in *Science: Good, Bad and Bogus*, there is "no exact way to define anything outside pure mathematics and logic, and even there some basic terms have extremely shaggy edges "[2]

Many a modern philosopher is so intrigued by the shag that she will deny the existence of the carpet entirely. There is simply no meaningful line to be drawn between pseudoscience and science unprefixed, she will assure you, or at least nothing that can be rigorously demarcated and defined. Are there then any real differences between astronomy and astrology, chemistry and alchemy, immunology and clinical ecology, pharmacology and homeopathy, mathematics and numerology? The zealous agnostic doesn't believe that she or anyone else can ever really know for sure.

Many trial lawyers embrace this philosophy with boundless enthusiasm. "[T]he courts are an institution established for the resolution of disputes, not arbiters of scientific truth," declares Russ Herman, president of the Association of Trial Lawyers of America. "History shows that many scientific 'facts' lack staying power."[3] The argument is by now familiar: Don't reproach us for getting the facts wrong; we're just here to settle disputes. We don't create them, we just resolve them. There's no such thing as objective truth anyway. A jury in old Salem, Massachusetts, that found a connection between old women and lunar eclipses performed its function quite adequately. It "resolved the dispute," another lawyer declares. "That society at that point in time was satisfied."[4] How satisfied the witches were is not reported.

It is, of course, very much to the lawyer's advantage to embrace the modern philosopher, to maintain that science is unreliable, to assert that nothing is really known for sure and that no one outside the courtroom is to be trusted. The more tightly law is bound to good science, the more orderly and predictable the legal process will become. Most people value order and predictability, but many litigators don't. "[L]itigators as a class are not disposed to value coherence in the law," observes federal appellate judge Laurence Silberman. "[T]he more uncertain the law, the more litigation will take place."[5] For litigators, if for no one else, it is a positive advantage to maintain that science, being undefinable, can supply no reliable truth, that facts (and law too) can never really be known, that true scientific expertise can embrace any view, just like the lawyer paying the expert's fee.

Disparaging science seems to suit the social engineers too. "[C]ausation is treated both in science and in law in accordance with the social purposes of the affected community," declares Yale law professor Jerry Mashaw.[6] As we have seen, the modern liability scientist defines *cause* by reference to what courts think they can control. Cause, it turns out, is something surpassingly vague; it has little to do with scientific fact and much to do with society, culture, and legal will. Much like the law itself, one is told. Nothing is neutral or objective, nothing is certain. One view is as good as the next. Law, science—they're all the same, just pliable figments of the social context. And courts *are* the social context. So on matters of fact, as on matters of law, courts may believe and assert whatever they please.

SCIENCE OR SOCIAL PURPOSE

No one can say whether the courts' single-minded pursuit of scientific truth will yield more cosmic justice than other approaches; cosmic justice is, after all, a difficult thing to measure. When ignorance abounds, as it still often does with cancer, contagion, birth defects, and many other dreadful afflictions, there is going to be injustice here or there, and nowhere is it written that injustice should fall on the small and weak rather than on the large and powerful. When Charlie Chaplin was appointed to serve as Carol Ann's father, blood-test evidence notwithstanding, the truth was undermined, but a young woman and her infant child undoubtedly won some help from a man who could easily afford to give it—and whose behavior, in any event, had been less than gentlemanly. Verdicts of this kind may perhaps help keep a few flies better zipped in Hollywood. By some measures, this is fine justice. By all measures it is appalling science.

The way courts view scientific facts profoundly affects the way they act. Indeed, it will often determine whether they act at all. Many important causes of accident and disease are either unknown or beyond practical control in court. Alcohol and unbuckled seat belts eclipse virtually all considerations of car design; smoking habits, virtually all issues involving dust in the air; causes unknown, virtually anything an obstetrician might do to prevent cerebral palsy. If we are determined to call the science straight, we will not normally have to look much farther when these familiar causes or mysterious effects are found on the scene. If, on the other hand, we are determined to shuffle around accident costs one way or another, it will always be possible to muddy the facts. The modern liability scientist can always find a reason to hunt far afield for more attenuated or speculative causes that are arguably cheaper to control. Downplaying both self-destructive lifestyles and the mysterious unknown—everyone knows *those* causes are not easily controlled—the liability scientist stretches instead to the limits of science and beyond in search of things that can be. A jurisprudence under full sail in the blustery winds of social engineering will travel quite a different course than a jurisprudence anchored in solid science.

Sooner or later, people in authority must choose, between the blood tests of paternity and the community benefits of fly-zipping, between affirming scientific fact and advancing social control. This is because social control is sometimes advanced by misrepresenting scientific facts. It is for just this reason that the junkiest of junk scientists gravitate toward the most socialist of social controllers: the grand Inquisitors, the Hitlers, the Stalins, or their small-time siblings in and out of court.

But falsehoods do not become truths simply because they advance social purposes identified by people in positions of power. Even if the "social purpose" of the affected community is to rid itself of elderly women, good science will not concede that they cause crop blight. Whatever the social purpose of the Church, it is the Earth that does most of the moving, not the sun; the Church's purposes notwithstanding, Galileo's *eppur si muove* ("nevertheless it does move") is what has endured. Whatever the social purpose of the Marxist state, Mendel was right and Lysenko wrong; when social purposes decree otherwise, the upshot is Stalin's Academy of Junk Science Genetics. National Socialism's purposes transformed Buchenwald medics into murderers; this did not change the nature of good medicine, it just increased the number of murderers. When Little Boy exploded over Hiroshima on August 6, 1945, it set back the social purposes of one affected community and advanced those of another. The bomb exploded oblivious to both, the causes of detonation rooted in science discovered and developed by physicists at Los Alamos.

In court especially, a clear distinction between science and social objective is essential, whatever the modern philosopher may say. As Horace Rumpole observes, the law should "represent some attempt, however fumbling, to impose order on a chaotic universe."[7] Indeed, the fundamental demand for government "of laws," not "of men," means government by rules that transcend individuals. We want courts to be independent, but we do not want legal anarchy. We want cases to be tried on their own facts, but we do not want facts themselves reduced to transitory, manipulable sound bites with no objective reality. The individual trial must somehow fit into a larger coherence, or all we have is despotism sold by the drink. Many activist legal bartenders may be comfortable with that notion, confident that their intentions are good and their judgment is wise. But those on the other side of the bench who prefer self-government to government by philosopher-kings will properly insist that judging be constrained by law and by fact.

On the legal side, law is (or at least should be) constrained by legislative pronouncement, by judicial precedent, by respect for convention and history. When it comes to deciding what the securities law on insider trading means on this fine Monday morning, good judges do not throw up their hands in despair, invite the parties to summon fringe legal experts from third-rank law schools, and then leave it to random panels of jurors to decide the question by majority vote. It would surely be a gripping spectacle if they did, especially for those immediately at risk of losing their reputations and fortunes. But it would not be something we could honestly characterize as law. Instead, good judges conduct a deliberate search for the most reliable description of the law they can find. This is not a surrender of judicial independence; it is its finest vindication.

The same is (or should be) true when it comes to the facts. The critical establishment will of course continue to maintain that facts are no more ascertainable than the law, that anyone should be allowed to testify to anything, that science should be approached as a chaotic heap of unconnected and contradictory assertions, that the best we can do is invite juries to decide scientific truth by majority vote. But anyone who believes in the possibility of neutral law, as many fortunately still do, must at the same time believe in the existence of objective fact, which ultimately means positive science. The "rule of law" is a completely empty promise if key facts are infinitely plastic, if there is no external and immutable reality. Neutral law without objectively ascertainable fact is as useful as a power steering wheel in the hands of a drunk. The mechanism itself may be an engineering marvel, capable of turning a ten-ton truck, but that ensures only that a random input will produce a random response.

No one should suppose that those who are liberal on consumer or environmental protection must therefore be especially liberal about what passes for science in court. If it is politically convenient for chemophobes to embrace the junk science of chemical AIDS, it is politically convenient for homophobes to embrace the junk science of AIDS proper. Indeed, outside the liability system, liberals will often find themselves the front-line defenders of science against the world.

In 1982, for example, a federal trial judge grappled with a line between science and nonscience not so different from those we have examined throughout this book. His analysis is a model of sense and clarity. Science is what scientists do, he concluded—the process and findings accepted by the scientific community. "Their work is published and subject to review and testing by their peers." Good science is falsifiable. But aren't the high priests of orthodox science prejudiced against important new ideas? No, he decides, the scientific community is dispersed, heterogeneous, and individualistic; it is "inconceivable that such a loose knit group of independent thinkers in all the varied fields of science could, or would . . . effectively censor new scientific thought."[8] In short, "creation science," which the Arkansas legislature wishes to see taught on an equal basis with evolution in public schools, is religion, not science. Despite affidavits filed by two scientists, two theologians, and an education administrator, the U.S. Supreme Court reached a similar conclusion, though less elegantly reasoned, in 1987.[9]

In another case, the question before the High Court was whether a certain brand of psychiatric soothsaying ranks as real science. The American Psychiatric Association declared that it doesn't, and all the Justices conceded that two-thirds of the predictions made by certain psychiatric prophets are wrong. No matter, a majority concluded in a dismal display of let-it-all-in reasoning: a jury can always be trusted "to separate the wheat from the chaff."[10] The chaff in this case was represented by a psychiatrist nicknamed "Dr. Death," a man who testifies frequently on the "future dangerousness" of capital defendants.[11] The upshot was that Thomas Barefoot, his future dangerousness suitably certified by a credentialed expert, was executed by lethal injection in Huntsvlle, Texas, just after midnight on Tuesday, October 24, 1984.[12]

In other courts, the question has been whether children should die for lack of a syringe. At issue in one case was the use of emergency blood transfusions, which (one side claimed) "involve certain risks, are of limited value, and [are inferior to] alternative means of treatment which makes the use of such therapy unnecessary and inadvisable."[13] A second child died of an untreated bowel obstruction.[14] A third of purulent meningitis.[15] Each of these children could readily have been saved by science, though not, sadly, by other forms of healing. When such deaths come to court, judges have little difficulty distinguishing the two. Thus, Christian Scientists and Jehovah's Witnesses are held accountable for the preventable deaths of their children; judges once again draw calm, firm lines between medical science and religious conviction.

One may believe, as I do, that no mother should be required to associate her child with schools that teach anything inimical to religious belief. But if we are to teach science in public schools while also maintaining separation of church and state, we will have to draw lines between science and religion. One may readily assume, as I do, that one brutal murder is sign enough of "future dangerousness," and yet still recoil at the thought that a junk science fringe of psychiatry—a squishy enough science in the best of circumstances—could decide who will be sent to the gallows. One may accept that many fathers are honestly terrified by the thought that their precious children might accidentally be exposed to AIDS at school, as I surely would be with my precious daughter. But if we are serious about preventing discrimination based on handicap, we will still have to draw lines between quarantines based on the science of contagion and those based on paranoia and prejudice.

And one may surely believe, as I emphatically do, and as most states legislatures have agreed,[16] that devoutly religious parents should be allowed the final say on the medical treatment of their children, and yet readily accept that it's a wrenchingly close call. But if there were really no definable difference between science and witchcraft, it would be abominable—not to mention grossly unconstitutional—for any state to elevate one form of witchcraft over another. Medical science is not just another kind of witchcraft or religion, however, as many a "liberal" jurist has understood when a dying child needs a blood transfusion.

THE RULE OF FACT

The scientific ideal stands in sharp contrast to the windy agnosticism of the modern philosopher, litigator, or social engineer. As one student of real science, Nobelist Sheldon Glashow, puts it:

We [scientists] believe that the world is knowable, that there are simple rules governing the behavior of matter and the evolution of the universe. We affirm that there are eternal, objective, extrahistorical, socially neutral, external and universal truths and that the assemblage of these truths is what we call physical science. Natural laws can be discovered that are universal, invariable, inviolate, genderless and verifiable. They may be found by men or by women or by mixed collaborations of any obscene proportions. Any intelligent alien anywhere would have come upon the same logical system as we have to explain the structure of protons and the nature of supernovae.[17]

This is not to say that modern scientists are dogmatic about their beliefs; far from it. As Feynman points out, modern scientists "have learned a lot from experience about how to handle some of the ways we fool ourselves."[18] When any competent modern scientist writes in a professional journal or reports findings and theories in court, he will also report error bands, acknowledge significant objections to his findings, and suggest ways in which they might be contradicted or confirmed. A generous measure of doubt and self-criticism is an integral part of modern science. The modern scientist is a credulous skeptic—skeptic in that he demands serious evidence and proof; credulous in that he concedes, not just offhandedly but very systematically, that every measurement, correlation, analysis, or theory may contain some margin of error, which may in turn conceal important but unrecognized new truth. There is thus, today, a science even to uncertainty, even to doubt, even to ignorance itself. Good science systematically allows for its own error, and remains expressly open to the plausibly unorthodox. Suspending judgment further than that does not make one more scientific still. It is possible to keep a mind so open that it is perpetually empty.

With science's own, systematic allowance for uncertainty and imprecision duly noted, science's definition of *cause*—arrived at without direction from politicians, philosophers, clergymen, or lawyers—is the only one that is objectively verifiable. This is an utterly safe statement: the domain of systematic, objective verification is by definition the domain of science. Social purposes are irrelevant. Our ability to control is irrelevant. Causation is not something that needs to be "treated," by Mashaw, Calabresi, or anyone else. Causes just *are*, whether or not we understand them, whether or not we can control them, whether they suit us well or ill. Lawyers and judges, lay and ecclesiastical, may use the word *cause* in other ways, but only because they, like Humpty-Dumpty, are masters of the words they use, so much so that they may decree, if they wish, that witches cause crop blight. The master of words, however, is not the master of crop blight, and has never yet been able to decree healthier crops. The witches may burn, but the wheat will still rot inexplicably in the fields.

The legal history of our dealings with witches is fundamentally important. The scientific ideal offers us our only real hope of social control that transcends the frailties of the controllers themselves. Science is indeed imperfect. Science does indeed offer less than absolute certainty. But it has proved to be vastly more accurate, reliable, stable, coherent, and evenhanded than the alternatives. In matters involving difficult science, courts will therefore control best when they forget about control and concentrate on scientific truth.

It is simply unacceptable for any judge to insist that there is no such thing. With or without the modern philosopher's blessing, courts must still make calls between the manufacturer of Bendectin and the child born without arms, between the woman with breast cancer and the operator of the streetcar. With or without a philosophically certain demarcation between science and pseudoscience, courts are still going to issue certain judgments. Judging is the ultimate exercise in positivism, a faith in facts strong enough to justify transferring fortunes, ruining reputations, and putting people to death. Anyone who does *that* for a living has a moral obligation to maintain faith in external, discoverable truth. Those who can't should practice their uncontained credulity elsewhere.

So in court, at least, lines can and must be drawn. We speak freely enough of "junk bonds," not because there are any exact definitions here either, but because, as we are reminded in *Liar's Poker*, bonds issued by IBM are fundamentally different from bonds issued by a Beirut cotton-trading firm.[19] Shaggy edges notwithstanding, we need similar distinctions—with straightforward terminology to match—between fact and fantasy. Claims dressed up in the form of serious science but lacking serious empirical and conceptual credentials will continue to be junk science. We do not hesitate to denounce charlatans and frauds when they peddle snake oil in country fairs or on network television. We need not hesitate to denounce them when they are primped and primed by lawyers and solemnly ushered into court.

Will the tyranny of a scientific priesthood then usurp the independence of judges and juries? Not really. Independence, like everything else, can be carried to oppressive extremes; in court we have a right to expect independence within a very clear matrix of rules. When a wise judge conforms to the dictates of external law, this does not mark a loss of independence, or at least not a loss that we should regret. The same is true for scientific facts. The judge who meticulously steers the search for the most authoritative, reliable assessment of Bendectin, or the origins of cerebral palsy, or the causes of sudden acceleration, is not surrendering her independence, she is vindicating it. In other circles, countless extraneous considerations might corrupt the inquiry into the facts. The judge's unique privilege and responsibility is to do her utmost to get the facts right.

In the long run, a judge's independence is increased, not reduced, by careful respect for external law, whether written by other judges, legislators, constitutional framers, or the still higher authority, beyond any appeal, that enacted the laws of nature. The hermit clinician may assert that every set of facts is different, that every case is unique, that truth is infinitely plastic, variable, and indeterminate. The wise judge, however, recognizes that scientific facts, like the law itself, exist and are ascertainable beyond the bounds of the individual courtroom.

The disciplined pursuit of scientific fact in court will eventually promote social control, of course, though not in the way the Calabresians have come to accept. It is a first step toward real control to admit we don't yet understand the major causes of cerebral palsy, though we do know that obstetricians are not among them. It is by asserting real facts—on causes of lung disease and pelvic infection, car accidents and AIDS—even when those facts translate into legal *inaction,* that we will build a solid foundation for doing something useful. We have had law for millennia, and for millennia the law's only visible contribution to public health and safety has been in restraining gross violence and irresponsibility. Today, for the first time in history, we have at hand tremendous new power to control accidents and disease, birth defects, even genetic disabilities. It is by affirming true science—and also by affirming what is still a matter of scientific ignorance—that we will get to real power all the faster. Courts are respected teachers. In matters touching on difficult science, the real power of the courts comes from proclaiming the facts as accurately and lucidly as possible, and least-cost social control be damned.

The implications for liability scientists are sobering. Broad social control may be law's inevitable end point, but it should not be its immediate objective. A legal system that sets as its paramount objective the finding of truth, the whole truth, and nothing but the truth, and crafts its evidentiary rules accordingly, will effect far more useful control in the long run, though occasionally less in the short. This kind of law will promote good science above all else. It will give full weight to lifestyle causes of disease, because those causes are far more important than most others. It will cut off liability sharply at the frontier of solid science. And it will categorically deny liability for irrational fear. Less money will change hands in court. But the truths proclaimed will be much more durable. The social control that emerges from such a process will be control of a kind that society really needs.

The rule of law is indeed a grand thing, but not half so grand as the rule of fact. Most will agree that in a capital murder case the judge should be unbiased, the jury randomly selected, the lawyers competent, and the definition of *murder* clear and precise. But everyone will agree that the innocent must not be executed. It is not enough for courts to give us evenhanded process conducted in earnest good faith: earnest people, it has been observed, often look on the serious side of things that have no serious side. We may prefer the law to be neutral, fair, reasonable, predictable, and governed by general rules rather than idiosyncratic individuals. But we should demand that the law get its facts right. Some part of those facts will depend on the laws of science, which, though we will always understand them imperfectly, represent the highest law of all. Resolving disputes is important, process is important, transitory social satisfaction is important—but facts are essential. Else Gwinner, the baker's wife and accused witch who was burned to death on December 21, 1601, in Offenburg, Germany, did *not* in fact have intercourse with the devil. As Marvin Harris reminds us, that is "not an uninteresting or uncertain conclusion considering the fact that she was carbonized for having done it."[20] Good judges will cherish the rule of fact even above the rule of law.

SCIENCE AND CERTITUDE

Science was powerless and unnecessary when gods were numerous, active, capricious meddlers in everyday affairs. Only a remote and jealously singular Creator leaves room enough for the relentless rationality of science. True singularities, the solitary footprint, are the domain of art. For obvious reasons, the litigator with a scientifically weak case would much prefer summoning artists rather than scientists to the stand. Art's one great advantage over science, after all, is that anything goes. But as Thomas Kuhn points out, a scientific "fact" is the collective judgment of a specialized community.[21] Good science is defined not by credentials but by consensus. Whatever her résumé may say, an expert who reports on views held by no one but herself, or on symptoms experienced by no one but one of her patients, is not reporting anything that can properly be called science. And the judge who welcomes her to court is allowing the pursuit of speculation and superstition to replace the pursuit of truth.

In so doing, the judge does no honor to the memory of Galileo. One way to dishonor Galileo is to imprison him for heresy. Another, quite as effective, is to teach his views side by side with those of astrologers and mystics. It is not liberal, open-minded, tolerant, scientific, or progressive to give equal time to astrology and astronomy. The modern judge who defers to mainstream science will at the same time defer to science's own, methodical acceptance of the possibility of error. To insist that things are more uncertain still is to deny things we know to be true, and to believe things we know to be false.

Unless we are all raging hypocrites, facts should be paramount in a process that repeatedly swears fealty to the truth and nothing but the truth. Presidents and legislators may twist and dodge the truth, but they can also be retired at the ballot box. We expect better of judges. Of all the despicable features of despotic governments, none is more despicable than the kangaroo court. The law, at least, should affirm something higher than raw will. The rule of law depends on both lucid rules and accurate facts.

This is much more than an esoteric issue of concern only to

lawyers; it is where Western civilization began. For the ancient Greeks, the physical universe—*physis*—supplied certainty in its scientific laws. In a similar manner, human convention imbues the moral or normative universe—*nomos*—with laws that are clear and coherent. Or these at least are the ideals—the antithesis of dissonant chaos—through which we will discover Truth, Justice, Beauty, Virtue, and Good. The alternative is radical subjectivism, which views the world as a fundamentally mysterious and therefore hostile place, where every rule of law and nature is quite as valid as every other, and the only authority is the tooth, the claw, or the sword.[22]

In the end, getting facts right is a fundamental requirement of morality. As Harris points out, "it is quite impossible to subvert objective knowledge without subverting the basis of moral judgment. If we cannot know with reasonable certainty who did what, when, and where, we can scarcely hope to render a moral account of ourselves." If we really can't say what is fact and what is fantasy, how can we challenge the next demagogue who declares that the Jews are plotting against the Reich, or announces that he holds in his hand a list of 205 Communists in the State Department? "We have to make up our minds about certain events," Harris concludes. If we really have no confidence in our ability to determine facts, "we must either advocate the total suspension of moral judgments, or adopt the inquisitorial position and hold people responsible for what they do in each other's dreams."[23]

Let us concede one last time that the difference between dream and reality is itself uncertain, that absolute certainty is always unattainable. This does not mean, however, that we should throw up our hands in despair and surrender to endless debates among legions of for-hire scientists from the fringe, who understand courtrooms far better than laboratories or clinics. It is precisely when there is uncertainty about the facts, Clark reminds us, that we most need serious rules about how to approach the evidence.

"[T]he data" are always insufficient to dictate unambiguous conclusions. . . . The debate therefore shifts away from a preoccupation with "facts" and their "proof." It turns instead to the careful development of rules for the admissibility of legitimate evidence, and for the form of legitimate argument. Such rules are known to be fallible—the guilty can be acquitted and vice versa—but fallibility is accepted as an inevitable consequence of our lack of omniscience. On the other hand, careful attention to developing mutually agreed-upon rules of evidence can create that essential willingness to proceed in the face of fallibility. . . . Perhaps most important, formal rules of evidence constitute formal hypotheses on how we can best cope with the unknown.[24]

It is not especially scientific to deny rules of evidence, to disdain the formalisms of serious science, to sit back, let everything in, and invite random groups of twelve stout citizens to vote as they please. Such attitudes serve no one but the lawyers who act as impresarios and intermediaries and the fringe scientists in their pay. An excess of credulity is not science.

"I define truth as the system of my limitations, and leave absolute truth for those who are better equipped," Justice Oliver Wendell Holmes once observed in an exchange with Judge Learned Hand. "Certitude is not the test of certainty. We have been cock-sure of many things that were not so."[25] Holmes was right, of course: certitude is not the test of certainty. The best test of certainty we have is good science—the science of publication, replication, and verification, the science of consensus and peer review; the science of Newton, Galileo, and Gauss, Einstein, Feynman, Pasteur, and Sabin; the science that has eradicated smallpox, polio, and tuberculosis; the science that has created antibiotics and vaccines. Or it is, at least, the best test of certainty so far devised by the mind of man.

NOTES

Introduction

1. *See, e.g.,* Rheingold, *It's Time to Change the System on Junk-Science, Quack-Expert Issues,* Manhattan Lawyer, November 1–7, 1988, p. 13.
2. *See* Digirolamo, *Judge Throws Out $986,000 Jury Award to 'Psychic',* United Press International, August 9, 1986; Fleetwood, *From the People Who Brought You the Twinkie Defense: The Rise of the Expert Witness Industry,* Washington Monthly, June 1987, p. 33.
3. O. Wilde, *The Critic As Artist in* The Portable Oscar Wilde 119 (R. Aldington & S. Weintraub, eds., 1981).
4. D. Hering, Foibles and Fallacies of Science 10 (1924).

Chapter 1: Liability Science

1. W. C. Clark, *Witches, Floods, and Wonder Drugs: Historical Perspectives on Risk Management* (RR-81–3) (Laxenburg, Austria: International Institute for Applied Systems Analysis, March 1981).
2. Epigraph quoted in M. Harris, Cows, Pigs, Wars, and Witches: The Riddles of Culture 217 (1989).
3. Clark, p. 289.
4. G. Calabresi, The Costs of Accidents: A Legal and Economic Analysis (1970).
5. *See generally* Weinstein, *Improving Expert Testimony,* 20 University of Richmond Law Review 473 (1986).

6. Ferguson v. Hubbell, 97 N.Y. 507, 514 (1884).

7. 293 F. 1013 (D.C. Cir. 1923).

8. Fed. R. Evid. 702.

9. Rubanick v. Witco, 576 A.2d 4, 15 (1990) (Stern, J., concurring).

10. In re Air Crash Disaster at New Orleans, LA. Eymard v. Pan American World Airways, 795 F.2d 1230, 1234 (5th Cir. 1986).

11. Elliott, *Science Panels in Toxic Tort Litigation: Why We Don't Use Them,* in ICET Symposium III Immunotoxicology: From Lab to Law 115, 117 (Ithaca, N.Y.: Institute for Comparative and Environmental Toxicology, Cornell University, 1987).

12. Quoted in Fleetwood, *From the People Who Brought You the Twinkie Defense; The Rise of the Expert Witness Industry,* Washington Monthly, June 1987, p. 33.

13. Quoted in Specter, *Diagnosis or Verdict? Psychiatrists on the Witness Stand,* Washington Post, July 28, 1987, p. Z10.

14. Bredemeier, *Trial by Expert,* Washington Post Magazine, November 28, 1982, p. 19.

15. *See generally* Gerber, *Victory vs. Truth: The Adversary System and Its Ethics,* 19 Arizona State Law Journal 3, 11 (1987).

16. Quoted in Tuchman, Krizan & Korman, *The Fine Line Between Expert Witness and Hired Gun: The Whole Truth and Nothing But?* 218 Engineering News-Record 24, 25 (June 4, 1987).

17. Langbein, *The German Advantage in Civil Procedure,* 52 University of Chicago Law Review 823, 835 (1985).

18. Quoted in Fleetwood, pp. 35, 36.

19. Ibid.

20. *See* Craft, *An Expert: Preparation Is the Key; A Grab Bag of Tips,* National Law Journal, February 22, 1988, p. 15.

21. Quoted in *Expert Witnesses: Booming Business for the Specialists,* New York Times, July 5, 1987, sec. 1, p. 1.

22. Calabresi, *Concerning Cause and the Law of Torts: An Essay for Harry Kalven, Jr.,* 43 University of Chicago Law Review 69, 105–6 (1975).

23. Ibid.

24. Clark, p. 292.

Chapter 2: The Science of Things That Aren't So

1. The quote appears on p. 247 of Grosset & Dunlap's 1988 edition of the book. I must acknowledge my debt to Edward J. Burger, Jr., director of the Institute for Health Policy Analysis, Washington,

D.C., who used this most perfect introductory quote in his excellent article *Health as a Surrogate for the Environment*, Daedalus 133 (Fall 1990).

2. Klotz, *The N-Ray Affair*, 242 Scientific American 168 (May 1980). My account of the N-ray episode is drawn largely from Klotz.

3. Langmuir, *Pathological Science* (R. N. Hall, ed., General Electric Corporate Research and Development, Technical Information Series Class 1 report no. 68–C–035, April 1968). The paper was recently reprinted in 42 Physics Today 36 (October 1989).

4. Ibid., p. 4.

5. M. Gardner, Fads and Fallacies in the Name of Science 3 (1957).

6. Quoted in Terr, editorial, 79 Journal of Allergy and Clinical Immunology 423 (1987).

7. Langmuir, p. 7.

8. *See* A. R. Feinstein, Clinical Epidemiology (1985).

9. Klotz, p. 175.

10. Langmuir, p. 7.

11. Klotz, p. 174.

12. Ibid., p. 175.

13. Langmuir, p. 7.

14. Klotz, p. 169.

15. Ibid., p. 175.

16. Johnson, *The Perils of Risk Avoidance*, Regulation 15 (May/June 1980).

17. Nelkin & Gilman, *Placing Blame for Devastating Disease*, 55 Social Research 361, 378 (1988).

18. Langmuir, p. 12.

19. Quoted by Resneck, letter to the editor, Insight, August 1, 1988.

20. J. Thurber, My Life and Hard Times 25 (1933).

21. Ellis, *Clinical Ecology: Myth and Reality*, Buffalo Physician 18, 28 (February 1986), quoting *Laetrile: The Commissioner's Decision*, p. xii (H.E.W. Publication No. 77–3056, 1978).

22. Winslow, *The Radium Water Worked Fine Until His Jaw Came Off*, Wall Street Journal, August 1, 1990, p. 1.

23. Klotz, p. 170.

24. Ibid.

25. Ibid., p. 174.

Chapter 3: The Midas Touch

1. Menarde v. Philadelphia Transportation Co., 103 A.2d 681, 684 (1954).

2. Quoted in Harwood, *Dear Editor . . .* , United Press International, December 11, 1989.

3. *See* Stoll & Crissey, *Epithelioma from Single Trauma*, 62 New York State Journal of Medicine 496 (February 15, 1962).

4. Quoted in R. J. Behan, Relation of Trauma to New Growths: Medico-Legal Aspects 7 (1939).

5. *E.g.*, Wainwright, *Single Trauma, Carcinoma and Workman's Compensation*, 5 American Journal of Surgery 433 (1928).

6. Bishop, *Cancer, Trauma, and Compensation*, 32 Southern Medical Journal 302 (March 1939).

7. *See* Knox, *Trauma and Malignant Tumors*, 26 American Journal of Surgery 66, 69–70 (October 1934).

8. *See* Stoll & Crissey, p. 496.

9. Crane, *The Relationship of a Single Act of Trauma to Subsequent Malignancy, in* Trauma and Disease 147 (A. Moritz & D. Helberg, eds. 1959).

10. Jewell v. Grand Trunk Railroad, 55 N.H. 84 (1874).

11. Slack v. C.L. Percival, 199 N.W. 323, 326 (1924).

12. Santa Ana Sugar Co. v. Industrial Accident Commission, 170 P. 630 (1917).

13. Canon Reliance Coal Co. v. Industrial Commission, 211 P. 868 (1922).

14. Gaetz v. City of Melrose, 193 N.W. 691 (1923).

15. Winchester Milling Corp. v. Sencindiver, 138 S.E. 479 (1927).

16. Traders & General Insurance Co. v. Turner, 149 S.W.2d 593 (Tex. Civ. App., Ft. Worth 1941).

17. Emma v. A. D. Julliard & Co., 63 A.2d 786 (1949).

18. White v. Valley Land Co., 322 P. 707 (1958).

19. National Dairy Products Corp. v. Durham, 154 S.E.2d 752 (1967).

20. Daly v. Bergstedt, 126 N.W.2d 242 (1964).

21. Baker v. DeRosa, 196 A.2d 387 (1964).

22. Valente v. Bourne Mills, 75 A.2d 191, 194 (1950).

23. Vitale v. Duerbeck, 92 S.W.2d 691 (1936).

24. Louisville Railway v. Steubing's Administrator, 136 S.W.634 (1911).

25. Hanna v. Aetna Insurance, 259 N.E.2d 177 (1970).

26. Boyd et al. v. Young, 246 S.W.2d 10, 12 (1951).
27. National Dairy Products Corp. v. Durham, 154 S.E.2d 752 (1967).
28. Glenn v. National Supply, 129 N.E.2d 189 (1954).
29. Baker v. DeRosa, 196 A.2d 387, 392 (1964).
30. White v. Valley Land Co., 322 P.2d 707, 712 (1958) (Sadler and McGhee, JJ., dissenting).
31. Tonkovich v. Department of Labor & Industry, 195 P.2d 638, 641–42 (1948).
32. Gaetz v. City of Melrose, 193 N.W. 691, 692 (1923).
33. Ellis v. Commonwealth, 28 S.E.2d 730, 732, 735 (1944).
34. Mattfield v. Ward Baking Co., 14 A.D. 2d 942 (1961).
35. Wilson v. Doehler-Jarvis Division of National Lead Co., 91 N.W.2d 538 (1958).
36. Monkman, Orwoll & Ivins, *Trauma and Oncogenesis,* 49 Mayo Clinic Proceedings 157 (March 1974).
37. Winchester Milling Corp. v. Sencindiver, 138 S.E. 479, 481 (1927).
38. Ellis v. Commonwealth, 28 S.E.2d 730, 735 (1944).
39. Thompson v. New Orleans Railway & Light Co., 83 So. 19 (1919), as described in Small, *Gaffing at a Thing Called Cause: Medico-Legal Conflicts in the Concept of Causation,* 31 Texas Law Review 630, 640 (June 1953).
40. Winchester Milling Corp. v. Sencindiver, 138 S.E.479 (1927).
41. Hertz v. Watab, 237 N.W. 610, 611 (1931) (quoting testimony).
42. Daly v. Bergstedt, 126 N.W.2d 242, 247 (1964).
43. Valente v. Bourne Mills, 75 A.2d 191, 194 (1950).
44. Ellis v. Commonwealth, 28 S.E.2d 730, 735 (1944).
45. *See* Small, pp. 657–58.
46. Hammond v. Fidelity and Casualty Co. of N.Y., 407 So.2d 13, rev'd 419 So.2d 829, 833 (1982).
47. Daly v. Bergstedt, 126 N.W.2d 242, 246 (1964).
48. Mooney v. Copper Range R. Co., 27 N.W.2d 603, 606 (1947).
49. Winchester Milling Corp. v. Sencindiver, 138 S.E.479, 481 (1927).
50. Austin v. Red Wing Sewer Pipe Co., 204 N.W. 323, 324 (1925).
51. *See* Emma v. A. D. Julliard & Co., 63 A.2d 786, 788 (1949) (quoting trial court).
52. Valente v. Bourne Mills, 75 A.2d 191, 194 (1950).
53. White v. Valley Land Co., 322 P.2d 707, 711 (1958), cited in Comment, *Sufficiency of Proof in Traumatic Cancer Cases,* 46 Cornell Law Quarterly 581 (1961).

54. Canon Reliance Coal Co. v. Industrial Commission, 211 P. 868, 869 (1922).

55. Austin v. Red Wing Sewer Pipe Co., 204 N.W. 323, 324 (1925).

56. Koehring-Southern v. Burnette, 464 S.W.2d 820, 822 (1970).

57. *E.g.*, Ewing, *The Relation of Trauma to Malignant Tumors,* American Journal of Surgery 30, 31–34 (February 1926). *See generally* Monkman, Orwoll & Ivins, p. 157.

58. Ewing, *Modern Attitudes Toward Traumatic Cancer,* 19 Archives of Pathology 690, 692 (1935).

59. Monkman, Orwoll & Ivins, p. 160.

60. *E.g.*, Insurance Co. of North America v. Myers, 411 S.W.2d 710 (1966).

61. Dennison v. Wing, 110 N.Y.S.2d 811, 813–14 (1952).

62. Lopresti v. Community Traction Co., 117 N.E.2d 2 (1954).

63. Frankenheim v. B. Altman & Co., 177 N.Y.S.2d 302 (Sup. Ct. Bronx Cty. 1958).

64. Insurance Co. of North America v. Myers, 411 S.W.2d 710, 713 (1966).

65. Stordahl v. Rush Implement Company, 417 P.2d 95, 99 (1966).

66. Sikora v. Apex Beverage Corp., 282 A.D. 193 (1953), *aff'd,* 119 N.E.2d 601 (1954).

67. Gambrell v. Burleson, 165 S.E.2d 622, 626 (1969).

68. The "aggravation" theory had been around for much longer, of course, and appears frequently enough in the earlier decisions too. *E.g.*, Traders and General Insurance Co. v. Turner, 149 S.W.2d 593 (Tex. Civ. App., Ft. Worth 1941). In the later years, however, it displaces all others.

69. Pittman v. Pillsbury Flour Mills, 48 N.W.2d 735 (1951).

70. Koehring-Southern v. Burnette, 464 S.W.2d 820 (1970).

71. Reed v. Mullin Wood Co., 274 So.2d 845 (1972).

72. Hammond v. Fidelity & Casualty Co. of N.Y., 407 So.2d 13 (1981), *rev'd* 419 So.2d 829, 831, 832 (1982).

73. Pezzolanti v. Green Bus Lines, 494 N.Y.S.2d 168, 169 (1985).

74. Ewing, *Modern Attitudes,* p. 696.

75. Glover v. Jackson Bush Co., 267 S.E.2d 77, 80 (1980).

76. Ewing, *Modern Attitudes,* p. 696.

77. Burman, *Sarcoma of the Hand with Hemorrhage into the Palm,* 6 Bulletin of the Hospital for Joint Diseases 3, 9 (1945).

78. *See* Monkman, Orwoll & Ivins, p. 161, quoting Ewing.

79. Moritz, Pathology of Trauma 116 (2d ed., 1954).

80. Monkman, Orwoll & Ivins, p. 162, quoting other sources.
81. Stoll & Crissey, p. 499.

Chapter 4: Sudden Acceleration

1. *Out of Control*, 60 Minutes, CBS-TV, November 23, 1986.
2. Incantalupo, *Audi Cleared in Sudden-Acceleration Case*, New York Newsday, June 15, 1988, p. 61.
3. Plumb, *Ditlow's Commandos*, 24 Ward's Auto World 113 (March 1988).
4. *See* Hebert, *Ford Vehicles Added to Sudden Acceleration, Engine Surge Probes*, Associated Press, June 13, 1987; Stuart, *Inquiry on Auto Acceleration Expanded by U.S.*, New York Times, February 23, 1986, sec. 1, p. 19; Zverina, *Center for Auto Safety to Challenge Audi Payouts in Court*, United Press International, June 10, 1988.
5. Quoted in Zverina.
6. *See* Brown, *"Defect" Flap Driving Audi Buyers Away*, Los Angeles Times, December 30, 1986, sec. 4, p. 2.
7. *Groups Urge U.S. to Recall 200,000 Audis*, Los Angeles Times, March 20, 1986, p. 26.
8. Bureau of National Affairs, *NHTSA Head Urged to Review Accident Reports Alleging Audi Defect*, Daily Report for Executives, April 24, 1986, p. A-19.
9. *Consumer Group Urges Government Action on Audi 5000s*, Associated Press, May 8, 1986; Zverina, *Audi, GM Announce Recalls*, United Press International, May 29, 1986.
10. Bureau of National Affairs, *Consumer Group Seeks to Force Volkswagen Buy-Back of Audis*, Daily Report for Executives, November 26, 1986, p. A-10.
11. *Out of Control*, 60 Minutes.
12. *See* Technology Management Associates, Inc., *Review of Audi and General Motors Unwanted Acceleration Research with NHTSA/ODI and CAS Personnel*, September 22, 1986; Reinhart, *Comments Concerning Mr. Rosenbluth's Description of His Demonstration of Audi Sudden Acceleration to NHTSA*, unpublished manuscript, November 14, 1986.
13. *A Simple Solution to Runaway Cars*, Business Week, April 4, 1988, p. 128.
14. *See Volkswagen Audi Unit Wins Lawsuit*, Reuters, June 15, 1988; *Audi Wins One*, National Law Journal, July 4, 1988, p. 6.
15. *See* Fannin, *It Will Take More Than Polish to Rescue Audi's Image, a New Ad Campaign Will Try*, 24 Marketing and Media Decisions 47 (May

1989); Incantalupo, *Can Audi Turn Around?* New York Newsday, October 15, 1989, p. 58.

16. Fannin, p. 47.

17. Office of Defects Investigation Enforcement, National Highway Traffic Safety Administration, *Alleged Sudden Unwanted Acceleration, 1978 Through 1986 Audi 5000 Passenger Cars Imported by Volkswagen of America, Incorporated,* Investigative Report ODI Case No. C86–01, p. 33 (Washington, D.C.: National Highway Traffic Safety Administration, July 1989).

18. *See* Law, *Canada Blames Driver Error for Runaways,* Automotive News, February 6, 1989, p. 2; Bedard, *Driver Error,* Car and Driver, July 1989, p. 71.

19. *Class Action Lawsuit Filed Against Audi,* PR Newswire, March 3, 1987.

20. *See* Law, p. 2; Soble, *Wider Probe of Mercedes Stirs Little Reaction,* Los Angeles Times, August 4, 1988, p. 1; Bovee, *Mercedes Sudden Acceleration Probe Expanded,* Associated Press, July 26, 1988; Beamish, *Government Investigating GM Cars,* Associated Press, August 12, 1987; Asahi News Service, *Nakasone Orders Investigation of Sudden Acceleration Causes,* July 17, 1987; Hebert; Brown, *U.S. Reopens Probe of GM Cars; 2.3 Million Cars Involved in Inquiry of "Sudden Acceleration,"* Washington Post, December 31, 1986, p. E3.

21. Zverina, *Audi to Recall 250,000 Cars,* United Press International, January 15, 1987.

22. *See* Soble, *Audi Ordered to Pay Woman Injured in Crash,* Los Angeles Times, July 15, 1988, sec. 2, p. 1.

23. Quoted in Zverina, *Audi to Recall 250,000 Cars.*

24. *See* Tomerlin, *The Riddle of Unintended Acceleration: A Long Look at a Growing Problem,* Road and Track 52, 55 (February 1988).

25. *See* ibid., p. 55.

26. Bovee, *Audi 5000 Sudden Acceleration Cases Reported, Despite Recall,* Associated Press, July 30, 1987.

27. *See* Tomerlin, p. 55.

28. Ibid.

29. Norris v. Gatts, 738 P.2d 344 (Alaska 1987).

30. Baker, *Major Defense Verdicts of 1988,* American Bar Association Journal, November 1989, pp. 82, 86.

31. *Volkswagen Audi Unit Wins Lawsuit,* Reuters, June 15, 1988.

32. Baker, p. 86.

33. Quoted in Incantalupo, *Audi Cleared in Sudden-Acceleration Case,* p. 61.

34. Office of Defects Investigation Enforcement, pp. 12–13, 18.

35. Quoted in Incantalupo, *Can Audi Turn Around?* New York Newsday, October 15, 1989, p. 58.

36. Kurylko, *NHTSA Closes Audi Probe*, Automotive News, July 17, 1989, p. 6.

37. Quoted in Zverina, *Canada Closes Audi Investigation*, United Press International, February 1, 1989.

38. *See* Risen, *Audi Sales Still Weak, Despite Federal Report That Car Is Safe*, Los Angeles Times, September 14, 1989, sec. 4, p. 1.

39. Quoted in *Audi Ad: "Case Closed" on Acceleration Trouble*, Chicago Tribune, July 20, 1989, sec. C, p. 3.

40. Plaintiffs' Motion to Compel Defendants to Correct Misleading and Deceptive Advertising, In re Audi Litigation, Cook Cty. Cir. Ct., 87 CH 02076, August 14, 1989.

41. Transcript of Proceedings, In re Audi Litigation, Cook Cty. Cir. Ct. 87 CH 02706, 87 CH 02234, October 4, 1989, pp. 4, 5, 17.

42. Richissin, *Appellate Court to Decide on Nation's First Audi 5000 Case*, Associated Press, January 9, 1989.

43. *See Car Manufacturer Ordered to Pay for Faulty Pedal Location*, Associated Press, March 17, 1988; Kahn, *Punitive Damages Restored in Audi Runaway*, Automotive News, February 20, 1989, p. 24.

44. Rose v. Volkswagen of America, Inc., C 434875 (Cal. Super. Ct. L.A. Cty. 1988).

45. Soble, *Audi Ordered to Pay Woman Injured in Crash*, Los Angeles Times, July 15, 1988, sec. 2, p. 1.

46. Bedard, p. 86.

47. Kurylko, *NHTSA Blames Pedal Position for Runaways*, Automotive News, March 13, 1989, p. 3.

48. *VW's Audi U.S. Unit Says Court Settlement Reached*, Reuters, June 22, 1988.

49. Weinstein v. Volkswagen of America (E.D.N.Y., March 31, 1989).

50. Quoted in Incantalupo, *Can Audi Turn Around?* p. 58.

51. *See Audi Found Not Liable in NJ Acceleration Case*, Automotive Litigation Reporter, January 2, 1990, pp. 12,950–51; *New Jersey Jury Returns Verdict for Volkswagen*, Automotive Litigation Reporter, November 20, 1990, pp. 14,348–49.

52. Cox, *Mixed Signal Sent by Early Audi Suit Results*, National Law Journal, August 22, 1988, p. 14.

53. *Even Good News is Bad News for VW*, Automotive News, June 27, 1988, p. 10.

54. *Rejection of Settlement Brings Audi Back to Court,* Autoweek, September 19, 1988, p. 12.
55. *Audi Owners Urged to Reject Deal,* Automotive News, July 4, 1988, p. 56.
56. *See* Associated Press, *Judge Bars Settlement of Audi Flaw Charges,* New York Times, August 13, 1988, sec. 1, p. 10.
57. Incantalupo, *Can Audi Turn Around?* p. 58.
58. Warren, *Braking a Car's Accusers: Tootsies, Not Audi 5000 Accelerator, Blamed for Denting an Image,* Chicago Tribune, June 22, 1989, p. 2.
59. Quoted in ibid.
60. Bedard, p. 86.
61. Office of Defects Investigation Enforcement, p. 45.
62. Insurance Institute for Highway Safety, Status Report, November 25, 1989, pp. 1–2.
63. Data Link, Inc., Washington, D.C. (1987).
64. *Audi 100 Records Lowest Potential for Driver Head Injury in History of Federal NCAP Crash Tests,* Audi Media Information, October 3, 1989.
65. Risen, p. 1.

Chapter 5: Gadgets and Knives

1. *Couple Loses Suit After Turning Down $2.2 Million Settlement,* Associated Press, June 21, 1984.
2. *See* Nelson, *What Proportion of Cerebral Palsy is Related to Birth Asphyxia?* 112 Journal of Pediatrics 572 (April 1988); telephone interview with Dr. Leon Sternfeld, medical director of the United Cerebral Palsy Research and Education Foundation, April 26, 1990.
3. Epigraph quoted in P. Schwartz, Birth Injuries of the Newborn 100 (1961).
4. Little, *On the Influence of Abnormal Parturition, Difficult Labour, Premature Births, and Asphyxia Neonatorum on the Mental and Physical Condition of the Child, Especially in Relation to Deformities,* 3 Transactions of the Obstetrical Society of London 293 (1861); see also Paneth, *Birth and the Origins of Cerebral Palsy,* 315 New England Journal of Medicine 124 (July 10, 1986).
5. *See* Shields & Shifrin, *Perinatal Antecedents of Cerebral Palsy,* 71 Obstetrics and Gynecology 899, 902 (June 1988); Rosen, *Factors During Labor and Delivery That Influence Brain Disorders,* in Prenatal and

Perinatal Factors Associated with Brain Disorders 237 (J. M. Freeman, ed., U.S. Department of Health and Human Services, Public Health Service, National Institutes of Health, Washington, D.C., April 1985).

6. Freeman, *Intrapartum Fetal Monitoring—A Disappointing Story*, 322 New England Journal of Medicine 624, 625 (March 1, 1990).

7. Lillienfeld & Parkhurst, *A Study of the Association of Factors of Pregnancy and Parturition with the Development of Cerebral Palsy*, 53 American Journal of Hygiene 262 (January 1951).

8. *See Medical Malpractice*, Manhattan Lawyer, January 19–25, 1988, p. 131.

9. *See* Cullen, United Press International, May 28, 1982.

10. *See* Kleiman, *Malpractice Suit Gives Millions But Not Hope*, New York Times, March 11, 1985, sec. B, p. 1; La Ganga, *Traumatic-births Suit Ends in $6.8-million Settlement*, Los Angeles Times, September 20, 1985, pt. 2, p. 1; United Press International, December 17, 1987; United Press International, December 9, 1983; *$2.1 Million Awarded in Birth of Brain-Damaged Boy*, Associated Press, October 10, 1986; Associated Press, January 15, 1982.

11. Lewin, *Despite Criticism, Fetal Monitors Are Likely to Remain in Wide Use*, New York Times, March 27, 1988, sec. 1, p. 24.

12. *See* Paneth, p. 126; Committee to Study Medical Professional Liability and the Delivery of Obstetrical Care, Division of Health Promotion and Disease Prevention, Institute of Medicine, *Medical Professional Liability and the Delivery of Obstetrical Care*, vol. 1, p. 78 (1989); Quilligan & Paul, *Fetal Monitoring: Is It Worth It?* 45 Obstetrics & Gynecology 96 (1975).

13. *See* Committee to Study Medical Professional Liability and the Delivery of Obstetrical Care, pp. 77–78.

14. Freeman, p. 625.

15. *See, e.g.*, United Press International, April 9, 1987, and May 15, 1986 ($4.9 million award based in part on absence of fetal monitor); Spano, *Young Cerebral Palsy Victim Progresses; Malpractice Suit Settled in Hospital Brain Damage Case*, Los Angeles Times, June 12, 1987, pt. 2, p. 8; Opinion Research Corporation, *Professional Liability and Its Effects: Report of a 1987 Survey of ACOG's Membership*, p. 16 (prepared for the American College of Obstetricians and Gynecologists, Washington, D.C., March 1, 1988).

16. *See, e.g.*, Low v. United States 795 F.2d 466 (5th Cir. 1986); United

Press International, June 29, 1985; Garrett, *Care Bows to Costs; Insurance Rates Are Driving Obstetricians from the Delivery Room in Record Numbers,* New York Newsday, July 12, 1988.

17. *See, e.g.,* Nemmers v. United States, 612 F.Supp. 928 (C.D. Ill. 1985), 795 F.2d 628 (7th Cir. 1986); 681 F.Supp. 567 (C.D. Ill. 1988); Egner, *Judge Angered That Lawyer Compared Retarded Child to an Animal,* Associated Press, June 20, 1986; United Press International, March 16, 1984.

18. Rhoden, *The Judge in the Delivery Room: The Emergence of Court-Ordered Cesareans,* 74 California Law Review 1,951, 2,016 (1986).

19. *See* Kleiman, p. 1.

20. Ibid.

21. *$3.2 Million Negligence Award,* Associated Press, July 22, 1988; PR Newswire, December 10, 1986; *$2.1 Million Awarded in Birth of Brain-Damaged Boy,* Associated Press, October 10, 1986; United Press International, March 19, 1984; Associated Press, April 30, 1981.

22. Raab, *Former Lawyer Says He Paid Off Judges in Medical Lawsuits,* New York Times, March 7, 1985, sec. A, p. 1.

23. Statement of Schifrin, *Legal Implications of EFM,* paper presented at Conference on Medicolegal Issues in Obstetrics in New York, October 3, 1985.

24. S. Freud, Infantile Cerebral Paralysis 142 (L. A. Russin, trans., 1968).

25. Nelson & Ellenberg, *Antecedents of Cerebral Palsy: Multivariate Analysis of Risk,* 315 New England Journal of Medicine 81 (July 10, 1986).

26. Freeman & Nelson, *Intrapartum Asphyxia and Cerebral Palsy,* 82 Pediatrics 240, 241 (August 1988).

27. Meyers, *Two Patterns of Perinatal Brain Damage and Their Conditions of Occurrence,* 112 American Journal of Obstetrics & Gynecology 246 (1972); Fenichel, *Hypoxic-Ischemic Encephalopathy in the Newborn,* 40 Archives of Neurology 261 (1983); Scott, *Outcome of Very Severe Birth Asphyxia,* 51 Archives of Disease in Childhood 712 (1976); Low, Galbraith, Muir, et al., *Intrapartum Fetal Hypoxia: A Study of Long-Term Morbidity,* 145 American Journal of Obstetrics & Gynecology 129 (1983).

28. Nelson & Ellenberg, pp. 82–83.

29. Ellenberg, as quoted in Stein, *Study Casts Doubt on Suspected Causes of Cerebral Palsy,* United Press International, July 10, 1986.

30. Nelson & Ellenberg, p. 85; Kitchen, Doyle, Ford, et al., *Cerebral*

Palsy in Very Low Birthweight Infants Surviving to 2 Years With Modern Perinatal Intensive Care, 4 American Journal of Perinatology 29 (1987).

31. Illingworth, *Why Blame the Obstetrician? A Review*, 1 British Medical Journal 797 (1979); F. Stanely & E. Alberman, The Epidemiology of the Cerebral Palsies (1984); Garite, Linzey, Freeman & Dorchester, *Fetal Heart Rate Patterns and Fetal Distress in Fetuses with Congenital Anomalies*, 53 Obstetrics and Gynecology 716 (1979); Peters et al., *Delayed Onset of Regular Respiration and Subsequent Development*, 9 Early Human Development 225 (1984).

32. Towbin, *Obstetric Malpractice Litigation: The Pathologist's View*, 155 American Journal of Obstetrics and Gynecology 927 (1986).

33. Clapp et al., *Brain Damage After Intermittent Partial Cord Occlusion in the Chronically Instrumented Fetal Lamb*, 159 American Journal of Obstetrics and Gynecology 504 (August 1988).

34. Bejar et al., *Antenatal Origin of Neurologic Damage in Newborn Infants*, 159 American Journal of Obstetrics & Gynecology 357, 362 (August 1988).

35. Nelson & Ellenberg, p. 86.

36. Shields & Schifrin, p. 903.

37. Illingworth, p. 797.

38. Institute of Medicine, *Medical Professional Liability and the Delivery of Obstetrical Care*, vol. 1, p. 79 (1989).

39. Cohen, Klapholz & Thompson, *Electronic Fetal Monitoring and Clinical Practice: A Survey of Obstetric Opinion*, 2 Medical Decision Making 79, 84–91 (1982).

40. Haverkamp, Thompson, McFee & Cetrulo, *The Evaluation of Continuous Fetal Heart Rate Monitoring in High-Risk Pregnancy*, 125 American Journal of Obstetrics & Gynecology 310 (1976).

41. Thacker, *The Impact of Technology Assessment and Medical Malpractice on the Diffusion of Medical Technologies: The Case of Electronic Fetal Monitoring*, in Medical Professional Liability and the Delivery of Obstetrical Care, vol. II: An Interdisciplinary Review, p. 9 (1989).

42. Leveno et al., *A Prospective Comparison of Selective and Universal Electronic Fetal Monitoring in 34,995 Pregnancies*, 315 New England Journal of Medicine 615 (1986); Luthy et al., *A Randomized Trial of Electronic Fetal Monitoring in Preterm Labor*, 69 Obstetrics & Gynecology 687 (1987).

43. Committee to Study Medical Professional Liability and the Delivery of Obstetrical Care, pp. 81–82. Critics of the trials have main-

tained that the samples were too small to produce statistically significant results. *See* Banta & Thacker, *Assessing the Costs and Benefits of Electronic Fetal Monitoring,* 34 Obstetrics & Gynecological Survey 627, 633 (1979); R. Freeman & T. Garite, Fetal Heart Rate Monitoring 168 (1981). *See also* Haverkamp et al., *A Controlled Trial of the Differential Effects of Intrapartum Fetal Monitoring,* 134 American Journal of Obstetrics & Gynecology 399 (1979).

44. Shy et al., *Effect of Electronic Fetal-Heart-Rate Monitoring, as Compared with Periodic Auscultation, on the Neurologic Development of Premature Infants,* 322 New England Journal of Medicine 588, 592 (March 1, 1990).

45. According to the National Institutes of Health, 10 to 15 percent of the cesarean rate increase resulted from increased diagnoses of fetal distress. National Institutes of Health, U.S. Department of Health and Human Services, *Cesarean Childbirth: Report of a Consensus Development Conference* 14–17 (Pub. No. 82–2067, 1981).

46. Rhoden, *The Judge in the Delivery Room: The Emergence of Court-Ordered Cesareans,* 74 California Law Review 1,951, 1,975, 2,016 (1986).

47. Lewin, p. 24.

48. American Academy of Pediatrics, Committee on Fetus and Newborn, ACOG Committee on Obstetrics, Maternal and Fetal Medicine, March of Dimes Birth Defects Foundation, *Guidelines for Perinatal Care,* p. 67 (2nd ed., 1988).

49. Committee to Study Medical Professional Liability and the Delivery of Obstetrical Care, p. 81.

50. *See* Brody & Thompson, *The Maximin Strategy in Modern Obstetrics,* 12 Journal of Family Practice 977 (1981).

51. Claireaux, *Pathology of Perinatal Hypoxia,* Journal of Clinical Pathology 30 Suppl. (The Royal Academy of Pathology) 11, 142–48.

52. *See* Nelson & Ellenberg, p. 81 ("Despite earlier optimism that cerebral palsy was likely to disappear with the advent of improvements in obstetric and neonatal care, there has apparently been no consistent decrease in its frequency in the past decade or two."); *see also* Freeman & Nelson, p. 240 ("little change in the frequency of cerebral palsy," citing four other sources).

53. "The most recent population surveys of cerebral palsy, however, do not demonstrate consistent evidence of a decline in the prevalence since the era of the National Collaborative Perinatal Project, and some studies even show a rise. . . . Neonatal intensive care now ensures the survival of a much higher proportion of asphyxiated

infants of all weights. If these new survivors have a higher incidence of cerebral palsy than occurs in the general population, cerebral palsy might be expected to bear a stronger relation to indicators of asphyxia than was the case 20 years ago." Paneth, p. 125, citing additional sources.

54. The best epidemiological guess we have is that in the last forty years "there just hasn't been a change" in the cerebral palsy rates. (Conversation with Dr. Karin Nelson, May 15, 1990.) Nelson emphasizes that the available data are "extremely soft," in part because cerebral palsy has never been consistently defined. Over the last fifteen years, fluctuations have occurred, but epidemiologists have detected no consistent trends in either direction. *See also* Nelson & Ellenberg.

55. Poynter v. Ratcliff, 874 F.2d 219 (4th Cir. 1989).

56. Wolak v. Walczak, 335 N.W. 2d 908 (Ct. App. Mich. 1983); *see also* Lane v. Skyline Family Medical Center 363 N.W.2d 318 (Ct. App. Minn. February 26, 1985).

57. Burciaga v. St. John's Hospital, 187 Cal. App.3d 710 (1986).

58. *See* Kapsidelis, *Court Rules in Favor of Hospital,* United Press International, April 5, 1985.

59. *See* Davila v. Bodelson, 704 P.2d 1119 (1988).

60. Merewood, *Surgical Births: Are Physicians Performing Unnecessary Caesareans?* Chicago Tribune, May 7, 1989, zone C, p. 3.

61. Myers & Gleicher, *A Successful Program to Lower Cesarean-Section Rates,* 319 New England Journal of Medicine 1,511, 1,515 (December 8, 1988).

62. Quoted in Merewood, p. 3.

63. Ibid.

Chapter 6: No Immunity

1. My profile of Carnow's credentials is drawn from United Press International stories, September 4 and 5, 1984.

2. Crain's Chicago Business, August 8, 1988, p. T8.

3. T. Randolph, Human Ecology and Susceptibility to the Chemical Environment (1962).

4. Quoted in Seligmann, *"A Shadowy Area",* Newsweek, August 23, 1982, p. 45.

5. Hales, *Has Man Created a New "Allergy?"* New York Times, August 19, 1980, sec. C, p. 1.

6. Quoted in Seligmann, p. 45.

7. Quoted in Raeburn, *Tests Show No Immune System Abnormality in "Total Allergy Syndrome"*, Associated Press, March 19, 1985.
8. So described (twice) in a single undated advertising flyer for her two books, *The E. I. Syndrome* and *You Are What You Ate.*
9. Rogers, *Diagnosing the Tight Building Syndrome or Diagnosing Chemical Hypersensitivity*, 15 Environment International 75 (1989).
10. Ginsberg & Weiss, *Common Law Liability for Toxic Torts: A Phantom Remedy*, 9 Hofstra Law Review 859, 920–29 (1981); *see also* Elliott, *Toward Incentive-Based Procedure: Three Approaches for Regulating Scientific Evidence*, 69 Boston University Law Review 487 (May 1989).
11. Elliott, p. 491, n. 17.
12. Elam v. Alcolac, Inc., 765 S.W. 2d 42, 212–14 (Missouri App. 1988).
13. 765 S.W.2d at 85–86.
14. Freels v. U.S. R.R. Retirement Bd., 879 F.2d 335, 338 (8th Cir. 1989).
15. Sparks v. Metalcraft, Inc., 408 N.W.2d 347 (1987).
16. In re "Agent Orange" Prod. Liab. Litig., 597 F. Supp. 740 (E.D.N.Y. 1984), 611 F. Supp. 1223 (E.D.N.Y. 1985), *aff'd* 818 F.2d 187 (2d Cir. 1987).
17. *See* Reich, United Press International, October 17, 1984; United Press International, October 18, 1984.
18. United Press International, February 2, 1985.
19. In re Agent Orange Product Liability Litigation, 611 F. Supp. 1267 (D.C. New York 1985). The opinion records for posterity that Carnow's opening remark at a deposition was: "I have just one statement. I'd like to know who is going to take care of my fees in this case."
20. Adams v. Syntex Agribusiness, cited in *Verdict Returned for Chemical Companies in Case by Former Times Beach Residents*, 12 Chemical Regulation Reporter (BNA) 424 (June 17, 1988).
21. *Railroad Settles Claims Arising From Cleanup of Chemical Spill, Reportedly for $15 Million*, 10 Chemical Regulation Reporter (BNA) 772 (September 19, 1986).
22. Lowe v. Norfolk and Western Railway Co., 463 N.E.2d 792 (1984).
23. Stites v. Sundstrand Heat Transfer, Inc., 660 F. Supp. 1516, 1521 (D.C. W. D. Mich. 1987).
24. Monahan v. Eagle Picher Industries, Inc., 486 N.E.2d 1165 (1984).
25. Associated Press, May 1, 1985.

26. Moore v. Polish Power, Inc., 720 S.W.2d 183 (Tex. Ct. App. 1986).
27. Barth v. Firestone Tire and Rubber Co., 673 F. Supp. 1466 (N.D. Cal. 1987).
28. Menendez v. Continental Insurance Company, 515 So.2d 525 (La. App. 1987).
29. Kyles v. Workers' Compensation Appeals Board, 240 Cal. Rptr. 886 (Ct. App. 1987).
30. Grayson v. Gulf Oil Co., 357 S.E.2d 479 (Ct. App. 1987).
31. Potter v. Firestone Tire & Rubber Company, 2 Toxics Law Reporter (BNA) 862 (1988).
32. Kemner v. Monsanto, 2 Toxics Law Reporter (BNA) 612 (1987).
33. *See* Marshall, *Immune System Theories on Trial,* 234 Science 1490 (December 19, 1986).
34. Cornfeld & Schlossman, *Immunologic Laboratory Tests: A Critique of the Alcolac Decision,* Toxics Law Reporter, 381, 387 (September 6, 1989).
35. Elam v. Alcolac, Inc., 765 S.W.2d at 144.
36. Cornfeld & Schlossman, p. 387.
37. Or perhaps only eight. The exact number is uncertain because Carnow and the court of appeals were sufficiently confused about two of the tests that it's impossible to tell whether one or both were performed.
38. Cornfeld & Schlossman, p. 388.
39. Ibid., p. 389.
40. Ibid.
41. Elam v. Alcolac, Inc., 765 S.W.2d at 192.
42. Ibid., at 200 & n.79.
43. Ellis, *Evaluation of the Evidence that Environmental Toxins Cause Damage to the Immunologic System in Man,* in ICET Symposium III Immunotoxicology: From Lab to Law 37 (1987).
44. Terr, *Environmental Illness: A Clinical Review of 50 Cases,* 146 Archives of Internal Medicine 145, 148–49 (January 1986).
45. California Medical Association Scientific Board Task Force on Clinical Ecology, *Clinical Ecology—A Critical Appraisal,* 144 Western Journal of Medicine 239 (1986).
46. Executive Committee of the American Academy of Allergy and Immunology, *Position Statements, Clinical Ecology,* 78 Journal of Allergy and Clinical Immunology 269–70 (1986); American Academy of Allergy, *Position Statements—Controversial Techniques,* 67 Journal of Allergy and Clinical Immunology 333 (1981).

47. Miller, *Courtroom Science and Standards of Proof*, The Lancet, November 28, 1987, pp. 1,283–84.

48. Terr, editorial, *Clinical Ecology*, 79 Journal of Allergy and Clinical Immunology 423, 424, 425–26 (1987). *See also* American Academy of Allergy and Immunology, *Unproven Procedures for Diagnosis and Treatment of Allergic and Immunologic Diseases*, 78 Journal of Allergy and Clinical Immunology 275 (1986); Lowell, *Some Untested Diagnostic and Therapeutic Procedures in Clinical Allergy*, 56 Journal of Allergy and Clinical Immunology 168 (1975).

49. Marshall, p. 1,491.

50. Ellis, *Clinical Ecology: Myth and Reality*, Buffalo Physician 18 (February 1986); Terr, *Multiple Chemical Sensitivities: Immunologic Critique of Clinical Ecology Theories and Practice*, 2 Occupational Medicine: State of the Art Reviews 683 (October-December 1987); Executive Committee of the American Academy of Allergy and Immunology.

51. Terr, *Environmental Illness*.

52. Brodsky, *"Allergic to Everything": A Medical Subculture*, 24 Psychosomatics 731 (1983).

53. *See* Stewart & Raskin, *Psychiatric Assessment of Patients with "20th-Century Disease" ("Total Allergy Syndrome")*, 133 Canadian Medical Association Journal 1,001, 1,005 (November 15, 1985).

54. My discussion in this subsection is drawn from Terr, *Multiple Chemical Sensitivities*, and Terr, editorial, *Clinical Ecology*.

55. G. M. Bear, American Nervousness, Its Causes and Consequences (1881), *discussed in* Terr, editorial, *Clinical Ecology*.

56. Carnow & Conibear, *Medical and Toxicological Considerations in Determining Probability of Causation in Environmental Diseases* (unpublished manuscript, 1982).

57. ICET Symposium III, Immunotoxicology: From Lab to Law 131 (1987).

58. Carnow & Conibear, p. 16.

59. ICET Symposium, p. 114.

60. Terr, *Multiple Chemical Sensitivities*, p. 693.

61. Ellis, *Clinical Ecology: Myth and Reality*, p. 26.

62. *Suits, Indictments, Countersuits Spawned by Allegations of False Expert Testimony*, Toxics Law Reporter (BNA) 1,314, 1,317–18 (April 27, 1988).

Chapter 7: Nausea

1. *Experts Reveal . . . Common Drug Causing Deformed Babies*, National Enquirer, October 9, 1979, p. 20.

2. Folkenberg, *Mal de Mère: Simple Remedies Best for Morning Sickness,* 22 FDA Consumer 26 (November 1988).

3. *Experts Reveal,* p. 20.

4. Gordon, *An Interview with Bill Nicol—Author of "McBride: Behind the Myth",* 1 Australian Medicine 328 (September 18, 1989).

5. *See* Kolata, *How Safe Is Bendectin?* 210 Science 518–19 (October 31, 1980).

6. McBride, Vardy & French, *Effects of Scopolamine Hydrobromide on the Development of the Chick and Rabbit Embryo,* 35 Australian Journal of Biological Science 173–78 (1982); McBride, *The Effects of Dicyclomine Hydrocloride on the Development of the Chick Embryo,* 9 IRCS Journal of Medical Science 471 (1981); McBride, *Teratogenic Effect of Doxylamine Succinate in New Zealand Rabbits,* 12 IRCS Journal of Medical Science 536–37 (1984).

7. *See* Oxendine v. Merrell Dow Pharmaceuticals, Inc., 506 A.2d 1100, 1104–8 (D.C. App. 1986).

8. Blum et al., *Another Win for Bendectin,* National Law Journal, October 10, 1988, p. 6.

9. *See* Mekdeci v. Merrell Dow, 711 F.2d 1,510 (11th Cir. 1983).

10. *See* Mintz, *Drug for "Morning Sickness" is Suspected in Birth Defects,* Washington Post, February 11, 1980, p. A7.

11. Quoted in Lauter, *Bendectin Pact Creating Furor; Revolt in the Plaintiffs' Bar,* National Law Journal, July 30, 1984, p. 1.

12. Mekdeci v. Merrell National Laboratories, Inc., 711 F.2d 1510, 1516, 1523 (11th Cir. 1983); *see also* Lauter, *New Bendectin Studies, Ruling May Affect Cases,* National Law Journal, September 5, 1983, p. 4.

13. Mekdeci v. Merrell National Laboratories, Inc., No. 77–255 (M.D.Fla. September 26, 1980) (order denying motion to withdraw); In re Cohen and Kokus, No. 80–5839 (5th Cir. November 13, 1980); Mekdeci v. Merrell National Laboratories, Inc., 664 F.2d 295 (11th Cir. 1981); Mekdeci v. Merrell National Laboratories, Inc., 711 F.2d 1510, 1520.

14. Quoted in Lauter, *Bendectin Trial Disintegrates; Allegations of Misconduct Mar "Perfect Case",* National Law Journal, February 21, 1983, p. 20.

15. Lichtman, *Have Brief, Will Travel: Lawrence Walsh, the Ultimate Hired Gun,* New Republic, August 24, 1987, p. 14.

16. Epigraph quoted in Lauter, *Bendectin Trial Disintegrates,* p. 11.

17. *See* ibid., p. 10.

18. *See* Koller v. Richardson-Merrell, 737 F.2d 1038, 1045–46 (D.C. Cir. 1984).

19. *See* Mintz, *Lawsuits Allege Birth Defects in Children Whose Mothers Took Bendectin,* Washington Post, February 7, 1983, p. A3.

20. Graham, *Press Leaks Spark Lawyer Disqualification Battle,* Legal Times, June 27, 1983, p. 2.

21. Koller v. Richardson-Merrell Inc., Civil No. 80–1258 (D.D.C. January 6, 1984); *see also* Lauter, *Plaintiffs' Firm Removed from Bendectin Lawsuit,* National Law Journal, January 23, 1984, p. 6.

22. Kolata, pp. 518–519.

23. *See* Mintz, *Scientific Society, Science Magazine Sued for Libel,* Washington Post, September 3, 1981, p. A7.

24. *See* Perl, *$750,000 Judgment Found Against Maker of Bendectin,* Washington Post, May 28, 1983, p. A1.

25. Fanning, *Master of Disaster,* Forbes, February 22, 1988, p. 48.

26. Ibid.

27. Quoted in More, *"Master of Disaster" Builds Reputation for Mega-Settling,* Legal Times, April 1, 1985, p. 1.

28. *See* Brody, *Shadow of Doubt Wipes Out Bendectin,* New York Times, June 19, 1983, sec. 4, p. 7.

29. In re Richardson-Merrell "Bendectin" Products Litigation, 102 F.R.D. 239 (S.D. Ohio 1984).

30. *Drug Company Offers $120 Million in Settlement,* New York Times, July 15, 1984, sec. 1, p. 21.

31. Quoted in Lewin, *Proposed Drug Fund a Trade-off for 2 Sides,* New York Times, July 17, 1984, sec. D, p. 1.

32. Quoted in More, p. 1.

33. Quoted in ibid.

34. In re Bendectin Products Liability Litigation 749 F.2d 300 (6th Cir. 1984).

35. *See* In re Richardson-Merrell, Inc. "Bendectin" Products, 624 F. Supp. 1212 (S.D. Ohio 1985), *aff'd* 857 F.2d 290 (6th Cir. 1988), *cert. denied* 109 S. Ct. 788 (1989).

36. Quoted in Kaufman, *Jury Concludes Bendectin Caused No Birth Defects,* Cincinnati Enquirer, March 13, 1985, pp. A-1, A-16.

37. In re Richardson-Merrell, Inc. Bendectin Products, 624 F. Supp. 1212, 1269 (S.D. Ohio 1985).

38. *See* Kaufman, *Judge Shields Bendectin Jury from Protesters; Deformed Children Banned in Court,* National Law Journal, March 11, 1985, p. 6.

39. *See U.S. Jury Clears a Nausea Drug in Birth Defects,* New York Times, March 13, 1985, sec. A, p. 12.

40. Quoted in Kaufman, *Ohio Judge Upholds Defense Verdict in Bendectin Cases,* National Law Journal, September 30, 1985, p. 49.

41. In re Bendectin Litigation, 857 F.2d 290 (6th Cir. 1988).

42. Hoffman et al. v. Merrell Dow Pharmaceuticals, In re "Bendectin" Litigation, 109 S.Ct. 788 (1989).

43. *See* Strasser, *2d Bendectin Award Buoys Plaintiffs' Lawyers,* National Law Journal, October 13, 1986, p. 10.

44. Richardson v. Richardson-Merrell, Inc., 649 F.Supp. 799 (D.D.C. 1986); Richardson v. Richardson-Merrell, Inc., 857 F.2d 823, 826.

45. Mintz, *Deformed D.C. Boy Awarded $95 Million; Bendectin Maker Penalized,* Washington Post, July 15, 1987, p. A1.

46. Quoted in Strasser, *Judge Throws Out $1.6M Bendectin Award,* National Law Journal, January 19, 1987, p. 14.

47. Richardson v. Richardson-Merrell, Inc., 857 F.2d 823, 830–31 (D.C. Cir. 1988).

48. Quoted in Pelham, *Bendectin Ruling Tough on Plaintiffs; For Dow Lawyer, "Turning Tide" Was Long Overdue,* Legal Times, October 3, 1988, p. 1; *see also Bendectin Ruling Bad for Plaintiffs,* Legal Times, December 19, 1988, p. 17.

49. Memorandum Order, Oxendine v. Merrell Dow Pharmaceuticals, Inc., Case No. 1245–82 slip op. p. 4 (D.C. Super. Ct. February 12, 1988) (emphasis in original).

50. In Koller v. Richardson-Merrell, 737 F.2d 1038 (D.C. Cir. 1984); Lauter, *Justices to Hear Attorney Disqualification Case,* National Law Journal, October 29, 1984, p. 5; Middleton, *Lawyers Reinstated in Bendectin Controversy; "Erroneous Standard" Applied,* National Law Journal, June 11, 1984, p. 6; Richardson-Merrell, Inc. v. Koller 105 S.Ct. 2757 (1985).

51. Koller v. Richardson-Merrell, Inc., D.C. No. 80–1258 (Order June 30, 1989).

52. Ealy v. Richardson-Merrell, Inc., Nos. 87–7214 & 87–7219 (D.C. Cir. March 9, 1990).

53. Quoted in Lauter, *New Bendectin Studies,* p. 14.

54. Nace, *One Lawyer's View,* Civil Trial Manual (BNA) 435, 439 (January 1988), *but see* Austrian, *Defensive Lawyer's Perspective: Justice Prevails in Litigation,* Civil Trial Manual (BNA) 53 (January 1988).

55. Gordon; Bell, *When a Tall Poppy Is Not,* Bulletin, November 15, 1988, p. 48.

56. *See* Mintz, *Drug for "Morning Sickness"*, p. A7.

57. Bell, p. 48.

58. Shaw, *Scientist "Faked Debendox Tests",* Daily Telegraph, November 3, 1988, p. 1.

59. Skolnick, *Key Witness Against Morning Sickness Drug Faces Scientific Fraud Charge*, 263 Journal of the American Medical Association 1,468 (March 16, 1990).

60. Committee of Inquiry, Scientific Advisory Board, Foundation 41, *Report of Committee of Inquiry Concerning Dr. McBride*, 25 (November 2, 1988); Shaw, p. 1.

61. Brent, *Bendectin, Our Most Famous Tortogen-Litogen and the Best Studied Human Non-Teratogen*, 37 Teratology 447 (1988).

62. Quoted in Skolnick, p. 1,469.

63. *See* ibid.

64. *See* Swan, *Disciplinary Tribunal for McBride*, British Medical Journal 299 (December 2, 1989).

65. McBride v. Merrell Dow and Pharmaceuticals, Inc., 540 F.Supp. 1252 (D.D.C. June 8, 1982).

66. McBride v. Merrell Dow and Pharmaceuticals Inc., No. 82–1786, appeal in civil action No. 81–92639 (judgment entered September 27, 1983); *see also* Kamen, *Court Backs Libel Trial for Scientist*, Washington Post, September 28, 1983, p. A8.

67. *Riding the Circuits*, National Law Journal, November 24, 1986, p. 36.

68. Fanning, p. 48.

69. Quoted in Skolnick, p. 1,473.

70. Oxendine v. Merrell Dow Pharmaceuticals, Inc., No. 88–35, (D.C. App. August 11, 1989).

71. *See Bendectin*, 18 Product Safety & Liability Reporter (BNA) 285 (March 23, 1990).

72. Quoted in Skrzycki, *The Risky Business of Birth Control*, U.S. News & World Report, May 26, 1986, p. 42.

73. *See* Folkenberg, p. 26.

74. Quoted in Skolnick, p. 1,469.

75. Ibid., pp. 1,469, 1,473.

Chapter 8: The Paranoia Plebiscite

1. Bowley v. Duca, 120 A. 74, 75, 76 (1923).

2. *See generally* Dworkin, *Fear of Disease and Delayed Manifestation Inju-*

ries: A Solution or a Pandora's Box? 53 Fordham Law Review 527 (December 1984).

3. Watson v. Augusta Brewing Co., 52 S.E. 152, 153 (1905).

4. St. Louis, I. M. & S. Railway Co. v. Buckner, 115 S.W. 923 (1909).

5. Louisville & N. R. Co. v. Davis, 250 S.W. 978 (1923).

6. Howard v. Mt. Sinai Hosp., Inc., 217 N.W.2d 383, 385 (1974).

7. City of Baltimore v. Fairfield Imp. Co., 87 Md. 352, 359, 364, 365 (1898).

8. Everett v. Paschall, 111 P. 879, 881 (1910).

9. Everett v. Paschall, 111 P. 879, 880 (1910).

10. Stotler v. Rochelle, 109 P. 788, 790 (Kan. 1910).

11. Quoted in Z. Chafee & E. Re, Equity 717 (5th ed. 1967).

12. 3 Atk. 750, 751 (1752).

13. Matthews v. Mayor of Sheffield, 31 Solicitors' Journal 773 (1887).

14. Gowen v. O'Hara, 15 Pa. District Rep. 753, 755, 765 (1905).

15. Jardine v. City of Pasadena, 248 P. 225, 228 (1926).

16. Ferrara v. Galluchio, 152 N.E.2d 249, 251, 252 (1958).

17. Lorenc v. Chemirad Corp., 179 A.2d 401 (1962).

18. Anderson v. Welding Testing Laboratory, Inc., 294 So.2d 298, 301 *rev'd*, 304 So.2d 351, 353 (1974).

19. Dickerson v. St. Peter's Hospital, 432 P.2d 293 (1967).

20. Zeller v. American Safety Razor Corp., 443 N.E.2d 1349 (1983); *see also* Galante, *When the Mind Is Hurt; Courts Around U.S. Permitting More Payments for Psychic Pain,* National Law Journal, May 28, 1984, p. 1.

21. Murphy v. Penn. Fruit Co., 418 A.2d 480 (1980).

22. Stoleson v. United States, 708 F.2d 1217, 1220, 1222 (7th Cir. 1983).

23. Plummer v. United States, 580 F.2d 72, 76 (3d Cir. 1978).

24. Mink v. University of Chicago, 460 F. Supp. 713 (1978); *see* Reaves, *Fear Not Enough, Noncancer DES Case Fails,* 69 American Bar Association Journal 725 (1983).

25. Furrow, *Governing Science: Public Risks and Private Remedies,* 131 University of Pennsylvania Law Review 1,403, 1,466 (1983); *see also* Bell, *The Bell Tolls: Toward Full Recovery for Psychic Injury,* 36 University of Florida Law Review 333 (1984).

26. United Press International, January 6, 1988.

27. Applebome, *AIDS, Like a Roof, Is Realtors' Concern,* New York Times, March 14, 1988, p. A14.

28. *Landlords Refuse Lease for AIDS Day-Care*, United Press International, April 16, 1988.
29. Queen, *Arson Case Jury Selection Begins*, New York Newsday, June 1, 1988.
30. Jasperson v. Jessica's Nail Clinic, 265 Cal. Rptr. 301 (1989).
31. *See Justice Department Supports Discrimination Based on Fear of Contagion*, New York Times, July 15, 1986, p. A19.
32. Everett v. Paschall, 111 P. 879, 880 (1910).
33. Quoted in Boodman, *AIDS Discrimination Issue Mushrooming; Fear of Disease Puts Jobs, Housing, Child Custody, Insurance in Jeopardy*, Washington Post, November 24, 1986, p. A1.
34. School Bd. of Nassau County, Fla. v. Arline, 107 S. Ct. 1123, 1129, 1131 (1987).

Chapter 9: Harmonious Coupling

1. Berry v. Chaplin 169 P.2d 442, 452, 453 (1946).
2. Salks, *Accuracy v. Advocacy: Expert Testimony Before the Bench*, 90 Technology Review 42 (August 1987).
3. Lansing, *The Motherless Calf, Aborted Cow Theory of Cause*, Environmental Law, Northwestern School of Law of Lewis and Clark College, pp. 1, 2, 5, 6, 8, 11 (Fall 1984).
4. *See* Borgo, *Causal Paradigms in Tort Law*, 8 Journal of Legal Studies 419, 424 n. 16 (1979); Robinson, *Multiple Causation in Tort Law: Reflections on the DES Cases*, 68 Virginia Law Review 713 (1982). *See also* Jacob, *Of Causation in Science and Law: Consequences of the Erosion of Safeguards*, 40 Business Lawyer 1229 (1985).
5. *See* Associated Press, January 3, 1979.
6. Quoted in Margolick, *Antismoking Climate Inspires Suits by the Dying*, New York Times, March 15, 1985, sec. 2, p. 1.
7. *See* Mintz, *Defense Raises Doubts; Destruction of Documents Alleged*, Washington Post, April 11, 1985, p. A1.
8. *See* P. Brodeur, Outrageous Misconduct 234–35 (1985).
9. See 16 Product Safety & Liability Reporter (BNA) 565 (June 17, 1988).
10. O. Nash, The Tortoise, *in* Ogden Nash's Zoo 26 (1987).
11. Mossman et al., *Asbestos: Scientific Developments and Implications for Public Policy*, 247 Science 294 (1990). *See also* Block & Marantz, *Recent Scientific Evidence Questions Perception of Asbestos Exposure Risks*, New York Law Journal, March 14, 1990, p. 39.

12. Quoted in Graham v. Wyeth Laboratories, 906 F.2d 1399, 1415 (1990).
13. *See, e.g.,* Product Safety & Liability Reporter (BNA), March 23, 1990, p. 282.
14. Lansing, pp. 24–25.
15. Bedard, *Driver Error,* Car and Driver, July 1989, p. 71.
16. U.S. Surgeon General, *Health Consequences of Smoking: Cancer and Chronic Lung Disease in the Workplace,* DHHS Pub. No. 85–50207, U.S. Dept. of Health and Human Services, Washington, D.C., 1985.
17. *See* Saracci, *The Interactions of Tobacco Smoking and Other Agents in Cancer Etiology,* 9 Epidemiologic Reviews 175, 181–83 (1987).
18. Ernzen v. Board of Trustees, Etc., 421 N.E.2d 1065 (1981).
19. McAllister v. Workmen's Compensation Appeals Board, 445 P.2d 313 (1968).
20. *See* ICET Symposium III Immunotoxicology: From Lab to Law, p. 130 (1987).
21. Sterling v. Velsicol Chemical Corp., 647 F. Supp. 303, 502–3, 1 TXLR 559 (W.D. Tenn. 86), *aff'd in part, rev'd in part,* 855 F.2d 1188 (6th Cir. 1988) (Tr. of Testimony of Dr. Alan S. Levin).
22. Berry v. Chaplin 169 P.2d at 453.

Chapter 10: The Cargo Cult

1. M. Harris, Cows, Pigs, Wars, and Witches: The Riddles of Culture 133, 134 (1989).
2. R. Feynman, Surely You're Joking, Mr. Feynman! 310, 311 (1986).
3. Selikoff, Churg & Hammond, *Asbestos Exposure and Neoplasia,* 188 Journal of the American Medical Association 22–26 (1964).
4. Borel v. Fibreboard Paper Products Corp., 493 F.2d 1076 (5th Cir. 1973), *cert. denied,* 419 U.S. 869 (1974).
5. *See* Grimshaw v. Ford Motor Co., 119 Cal. App. 3d 757, 174 Cal. Rptr. 348 (1981).
6. Mills, *Ford Recall,* Associated Press, June 9, 1978.
7. *See* Kahn, *When Bad Management Becomes Criminal,* Inc., March 1987, p. 46.
8. Grimshaw v. Ford Motor Co., 119 Cal. App. 3d 757; 174 Cal. Rptr. 348 (1981).
9. Herbst, Ulfelder & Poskanzer, *Adenocarcinoma of the Vagina: Association of Maternal Stilbestrol Therapy with Tumor Appearance in Young Women,* 284 New England Journal of Medicine 878 (1971).

10. Sindell v. Abbott Laboratories, 26 Cal. 3d 588, 163 Cal. Rptr. 132, 607 P.2d 924, *cert. denied,* 449 U.S. 912 (1980).

11. *See* In re Swine Flu Immunization Prods. Liab. Litig., 533 F. Supp. 567, 571 (D. Colo. 1980).

12. Schonberger et al., *Gullian-Barre Syndrome Following Vaccination in the National Influenza Immunization Program, United States, 1976–1977,* 110 American Journal of Epidemiology 105, 112–13 (1979).

13. *See.* Kehm v. Procter & Gamble Mfg. Co., 724 F.2d 613, 616–20 (8th Cir. 1983).

14. Todd et al., *Toxic-Shock Syndrome Associated with Phage Group-I Staphylococci,* The Lancet 1,116–18 (November 25, 1978).

15. Centers for Disease Control, *Follow-up on Toxic Schock Syndrome,* 23 Morbidity and Mortality Weekly Report 441 (September 19, 1980).

16. Lampshire v. Procter & Gamble, 94 F.R.D. 58 (1982).

17. Wells v. Ortho Pharmaceutical Corp., 615 F. Supp. 262 (N.D. Ga. 1985), *aff'd,* Wells v. Ortho Pharmaceutical Corp., 788 F.2d 741 (11th Cir.), *reh'g denied en banc,* 795 F.2d 89 (11th Cir.), *cert. denied,* 107 S. Ct. 437 (1986).

18. Watkins, letter, *Vaginal Spermicides and Congenital Disorders: The Validity of a Study,* 256 Journal of the American Medical Association 3095 (1986); Holmes, in reply, *Vaginal Spermicides and Congenital Disorders: The Validity of a Study,* 256 Journal of the American Medical Association 3096 (1986).

19. Mills & Alexander, *Occasional Notes: Teratogens and "Litogens",* 315 New England Journal of Medicine 1,234, 1,235 (1986).

20. *See* Hinmon & Koplan, *Pertussis and Pertussis Vaccine: Reanalysis of Benefits, Risks, and Costs,* 251 Journal of the American Medical Association 3,109 (1984).

21. *See* H. Coulter & B. Fisher, DPT: A Shot in the Dark (1984); Engelberg, *Vaccine: Assessing Risks and Benefits,* New York Times, December 19, 1984, sec. 3, p. 1.

22. *See* Russell, *Firm Ceases Making Vaccine,* Washington Post, June 19, 1984, p. A1; *The Cost of Ignoring Vaccine Victims,* New York Times, October 15, 1984, sec. 1, p. 18; Boffey, *Vaccine Liability Threatens Supplies,* New York Times, June 26, 1984, sec. 3, p. 1; Engelberg, *Vaccine,* p. 21; Engelberg, *Official Explains Gaffe on Vaccine Shortage,* New York Times, December 15, 1984, sec. 1, p. 10.

23. *E.g.* MacRae, *Epidemiology, Encephalopthy, and Pertussis Vaccine,* in FEMS-Symposium Pertussis: Proceedings of the Conference Or-

ganized by the Society of Microbiology and Epidemiology of the GDR, April 20–22, 1988, Berlin; Stephenson, *Pertussis Vaccine on Trial; Science vs. the Law (High Court of London)* in ibid.; Walker et al., *Neurologic Events Following Diphtheria-Tetanus-Pertussis Immunization,* 81 Pediatrics 345–49 (1988); Shields et al., *Relationship of Pertussis Immunization to the Onset of Neurologic Disorders,* 113 Journal of Pediatrics 801–5 (1988).

24. Griffin et al., *Risk of Seizures and Encephalopathy After Immunization with the Diptheria-Tetanus-Pertussis Vaccine,* 263 Journal of the American Medical Association 1,641–45 (March 23–30, 1990); *see also* Kolata, *Whooping Cough Vaccine Found Not to Be Linked to Brain Damage,* New York Times, March 23, sec. 1, p. 19.

25. Cherry, *"Pertussis Vaccine Encephalopathy": It Is Time to Recognize It as the Myth That It Is,* 263 Journal of the American Medical Association 1679–80 (March 23–30, 1990).

26. W. Keeton, D. Dobbs, R. Keeton, & D. Owen, Prosser and Keeton on Torts 187 (5th ed., 1984).

27. *See, e.g.,* Toliver v. General Motors Corp., 482 So.2d 213 (Miss. 1985).

28. The T.J. Hooper, 60 F.2d 737, 740 (2d Cir.), *cert. denied,* 287 U.S. 662 (1932).

29. *E.g.* Johnson v. Hannibal Mower Corp., 679 S.W.2d 884 (Mo. App. 1984).

30. Harris, p. 236.

31. Clark, p. 290.

32. Grady, *Why Are People Negligent? Technology, Nondurable Precautions, and the Medical Malpractice Explosion,* 82 Northwestern University Law Review 293 (Winter 1988).

33. Brodsky, *"Allergic to Everything": A Medical Subculture,* 24 Psychosomatics 731, 742 (August 1983).

34. Marshall, *Immune System Theories on Trial,* 234 Science 1490 (Dec. 19, 1986); Djerassi, *The Bitter Pill,* 245 Science 356 (July 28, 1989).

35. Jacobson v. Massachusetts 197 U.S. 11, 17–18 (1905).

36. Calabresi, *Concerning Cause and the Law of Torts: An Essay for Harry Kalven, Jr.,* 43 University of Chicago Law Review 69, 105–6 (1975).

37. Priest, *The New Legal Structure of Risk Control,* 119 Daedalus 207 (Fall 1990); Priest, *The Continuing Crisis in Liability,* 1 Product Liability Law Journal 243 (October 1989); Priest, *The Current Insurance Crisis and Modern Tort Law,* 96 Yale Law Journal 1521 (1987).

38. *See* Chambers, *Experts Need To Put Their House in Order,* National Law Journal, April 18, 1988, p. 13; Blum, *Larger Robins Probe Under Way? Indicted Expert Denies Charges,* National Law Journal, March 21, 1988, p. 10.
39. Harris, p. 215.
40. Klotz, p. 175.
41. Calabresi, p. 105.

Chapter 11: Stopping Points

1. *See* Raytheon Co. v. California Fair Employment & Housing Commission, 261 Cal. Rptr. 197 (Cal. App. 1989); Ray v. School District of DeSoto County, 666 F. Supp. 1524, 1535 (M.D. Fla. 1987); District 27 Comm. School v. Board of Educ., 502 N.Y.S.2d 325, 335 (Sup. 1986); Thomas v. Atascadero Unified School District, 662 F. Supp. 376 (C.D. Cal. 1987); Chalk v. United States Distict Court Central District of California, 840 F.2d 701 (9th Cir. 1988).
2. *See* Seitzman v. Hudson River Associates, 513 N.Y.S.2d. 148 (1987) and cases cited above.
3. Chalk v. United States Distict Court Central District of California, 840 F.2d 701 (9th Cir. 1988).
4. Roisman, *Law And Science: Partners Or Protagonists? in* ICET Symposium III Immunotoxicology: From Lab to Law, pp. 105, 132 (1987).
5. Levin, *Environmental Illness a Scientific Reality, a Legal Boondoggle, a Potential American Tragedy, in* ICET Symposium III Immunotoxicology: From Lab to Law, p. 88 (1987).
6. My discussion here and later, on the evolution of medical science, draws from J. Burke, The Day the Universe Changed 195–237 (1985). Epigraph quoted in Burke, p. 226; *see also* J. Eyler, Victorian Social Medicine: The Ideas and Methods of William Farr 9 (1979).
7. Burke, p. 213.
8. *See* T. E. Allibone, The Royal Society and Its Dining Clubs 1 (1976).
9. M. Gardner, Fads and Fallacies in the Name of Science 10 (1957).
10. J. R. Ravetz, Scientific Knowledge and Its Social Problems (1971).
11. Ibid., p. 427.
12. M. Twain, Pudd'nhead Wilson (1894).
13. Black, *A Unified Theory Of Scientific Evidence,* 56 Fordham Law Review 595 (1988).

14. *Cf.* Smith, *Scientific Proof in Relations of Law and Medicine,* 23 Boston University Law Review 143 (1943).

15. In re Air Crash Disaster at New Orleans, 795 F.2d 1230, 1234 (5th Cir. 1986).

16. *E.g.* Richardson v. Richardson-Merrell, Inc., 857 F. 2d 823 (D.C. Cir. 1988); Will v. Richardson-Merrell, 647 F. Supp. 544 (S.D.Ga. 1986); Brock v. Merrell Dow Pharmaceuticals, Inc., 874 F.2d 307, 316 (5th Cir. 1989), *pet. for reh'g denied,* 884 F.2d 166, *reh'g en banc denied,* 884 F.2d 167 (5th Cir. 1989), *cert. denied*—U.S.—(March 19, 1990); Lynch v. Merrell-National Laboratories, 830 F.2d 1190, 1195 (1st Cir. 1987).

17. *See* Note, *Of Reliable Science: Scientific Peer Review, Federal Regulatory Agencies, and the Courts,* 7 Virginia Journal of Natural Resources Law 27, 30–31 (1987); Cole, Rubin & Cole, *Peer Review and the Support of Science,* 237 Scientific American 34 (October 1977); Merton & Zuckerman, *Institutionalized Patterns of Evaluation in Science,* in The Sociology of Science 460 (W. Storer, ed., 1973); Lynch v. Merrell-National Labs., Inc., 830 F.2d 1190 (1st Cir. 1987); Johnston v. United States, 597 F. Supp. 374 (D. Kan. 1984); Perry v. United States, 755 F.2d 888 (11th Cir. 1985).

18. *See* Black & Lilienfeld, *Epidemiologic Proof In Toxic Tort Litigation,* 52 Fordham Law Review 732 (April 1984); In re "Agent Orange" Prod. Liab. Litig., 611 F. Supp. 1223 (E.D. N.Y. 1985); Brock v. Merrell Dow Pharmaceuticals, Inc., 874 F.2d 307 (5th Cir. 1989).

19. *E.g.* Kubs v. United States, 537 F. Supp. 560 (E.D. Wis. 1982).

20. Will v. Richardson-Merrell, Inc., 647 F. Supp. 544 (S.D. Ga. 1986).

21. Trower v. Jones 121 Ill.2d 211 (1988).

22. Viterbo v. Dow Chemical Co., 646 F. Supp. 1420 (E.D. Tex. 1986), 826 F.2d 420 (5th Cir. 1987).

23. Polo v. Gotchel, 225 N.J. Super. 429 (1987).

24. *See* Holthaus, *States Judge Expert Witnesses Before They Testify,* 62 Hospitals 60 (March 5, 1988).

25. 1987 Act of June 11, 1987 No. 87–189, sec. 9 (E), 1987 Ala. Laws.

26. West's C.R.S.A. sec. 13–64–401.

27. *See Engineers Draft Witness Code,* Engineering News-Record, October 23, 1986, p. 40.

28. *See* Lee, *Court-Appointed Experts and Judicial Reluctance: A Proposal to Amend Rule 706 of the Federal Rules of Evidence,* 6 Yale Law & Policy Review 480 (1988).

29. *See* In re Swine Flu Immunization Products Liability Litigation,

495 F. Supp. 1185 (1980), *aff'd* 707 F.2d 1141; *Science in Court* 243 Science 1658 (March 31, 1989); Louis Harris & Assoc., *Judges' Opinions on Procedural Issues*, p. 45, table 6.1 (Study No. 874017) (October-December 1987), cited in Elliot, *Issues of Science and Technology Facing the Federal Courts*, p. 11 (draft of April 4, 1988).

30. American Medical Association, Current Opinion 9.07 (1986 Edition), quoted in AMA Report of the Board of Trustees, Medical Expert Witness Qualifications (Resolution 22, I-88), Report SS (A-89) p. 2.

31. Quoted in Richards, *Doctors Seek Crackdown on Colleagues Paid for Testimony in Malpractice Suits*, Wall Street Journal, January 7, 1988, sec. 2, p. 1.

32. R. Feynman, Surely You're Joking, Mr. Feynman! 311, 312 (1986).

33. Ibid., p. 314.

34. K. Popper, Conjectures and Refutations (1963).

35. W. C. Clark, *Witches, Floods, and Wonder Drugs: Historical Perspectives on Risk Management*, p. 291 (RR-81-3) (Laxenburg, Austria: International Institute for Applied Systems Analysis, March 1981).

36. *See* Everett v. Paschall, 111 P. 879 (1910); *see also* Stratton v. Conway, 301 S.W.2d 331 (1957).

Chapter 12: Science and Certitude

1. R. P. Feynman, What Do You Care What Other People Think? 245 (1986).

2. M. Gardner, Science: Good, Bad and Bogus xiii (1989).

3. R. Herman, *Allowing Jurors to Decide: Evidence Review*, National Law Journal, July 30, 1990, pp. 15, 18.

4. *See* Mitchell, *Legal Standards of Causation in Chemical Exposure Litigation*, 7 Regulatory Toxicology and Pharmacology 206, 207 (1987).

5. L. H. Silberman, *The American Bar Association and Judicial Nominations*, speech delivered to the D.C. Lawyers Chapter, The Federalist Society for Law and Public Policy Studies, Washington, D.C., March 23, 1990.

6. Mashaw, *A Comment on Causation, Law Reform, and Guerrilla Warfare*, 73 Georgetown Law Journal 1393, 1396 (1985) [citing Calabresi, *Concerning Cause: An Essay for Harry Kalven*, 43 University of Chicago Law Review 69 (1975)].

7. J. Mortimer, Rumpole à La Carte, p. 1 (1990).

8. McLean v. Arkansas Bd. of Ed., 529 F. Supp. 1255, 1268 (E.D. Ark. 1982).

9. Edwards v. Aguillard, 107 S. Ct. 2573 (1987).

10. Barefoot v. Estelle, 463 U.S. 880, 901 n. 7 (1983).

11. *See, e.g.,* Belkin, *Expert Witness Unfazed by 'Dr. Death' Label,* New York Times, June 10, 1988, p. B9.

12. *See* United Press International, *Placard-Wielding Crowds Cheer Twin Injections,* October 30, 1984.

13. Jehovah's Witnesses in State of Washington v. King County Hospital, 278 F. Supp. 488, 503 (W.D. Wash. 1967), *aff'd without opinion,* 390 U.S. 598 (1968).

14. *See* Goodrich, *Twitchell Attorneys To Seek New Trial,* Christian Science Monitor, August 13, 1990, p. 7.

15. Walker v. Superior Court (People), 763 P.2d 852 (1988).

16. *See Double Injustice in Child's Death,* Chicago Tribune, July 8, 1990, p. 2.

17. *Does Ideology Stop at the Laboratory Door? A Debate on Science and the Real World,* New York Times, October 22, 1989, p. E24.

18. Feynman, p. 312.

19. M. Lewis, *Liar's Poker* 211 (1989).

20. Harris, p. 235.

21. T. Kuhn, The Structure of Scientific Revolutions (2d ed., 1970).

22. *Cf.* Christenson, *Uncertainty In Law And Its Negation: Reflections,* 54 University of Cincinnati Law Review 347 (1985).

23. Harris, pp. 235, 251.

24. W. C. Clark, *Witches, Floods, and Wonder Drugs: Historical Perspectives on Risk Management* (RR-81–3) (Laxenburg, Austria: International Institute for Applied Systems Analysis, March 1981), p. 308.

25. Quoted in Schlesinger, *The Opening of the American Mind,* New York Times, July 23, 1989, sec. 7, p. 1.

ACKNOWLEDGMENTS

This book was written under the auspices of the Civil Justice Program of the Manhattan Institute for Policy Research. I am deeply grateful to the Institute's president, Bill Hammett, for his patient, unstinting support and encouragement.

My good friend and colleague Walter Olson provided editorial help and criticism too extensive and valuable to be adequately acknowledged here. Suffice it to say that readers who have come this far in my book will certainly want to rush out and buy Olson's own book, *The Litigation Explosion,* which provides a broad-ranging and highly entertaining account of "what happened when America unleashed the lawsuit." Tom Clayton, Emily Haller, Michael Hoenig, Janey Huber, Peter Kaplan, Bob Nichols, and Michael Ross also read and commented on parts of the manuscript, and I am grateful for their help too. Tammy Giles and David Bernstein provided meticulous research assistance. Adam Pinchuk checked the citations. Linda Carbone and Jen Fleissner edited the manuscript with skill and persistence. Martin Kessler has been a calm source of advice and encouragement throughout.

Parts of the book were first presented as papers or lectures at the University of Chicago Law School, the Valparaiso University Law School, and the Yale Law School, and in *Daedalus*. The Alfred P. Sloan Foundation's funding of a related project at the Manhattan Institute stimulated much of the thinking behind this book.

INDEX